Early praise for *Test-Driving JavaScript Applications*

Not only does this book provide step-by-step instructions for how to test JavaScript, Venkat also presents a simplified, well-rounded approach to driving out good design. Venkat writes with a compelling and humorous voice that makes the content educational and entertaining.

➤ **Kimberly D. Barnes**
Senior software engineer, GoSpotCheck

Venkat has, in his usual inimitable style, taken the swamp of JavaScript testing and drained it into a clear pool. He has taken a welcome pragmatic approach to the subject of testing this sometimes tricky platform, providing frameworks, tools, and valuable tips and insights along the way. Highly recommended.

➤ **Neal Ford**
Director/software architect/meme wrangler, Thoughtworks, Inc.

If you are a seasoned TDD practitioner in another language, this book answers all the questions to test-drive JavaScript applications. If you are a JavaScript programmer who hasn't yet embraced TDD, Venkat takes you through several real-world examples to get you started with confidence.

➤ **Naresha K.**
Chief technologist, Channel Bridge Software Labs

Test-Driving JavaScript Applications has shown me how to use TDD for the front end. This book was exactly what I was looking for. It has practical examples and lots of useful information. I've learned good practices, and I've stopped writing legacy code.

➤ **Astefanoaie Nicolae Stelian**
Senior programmer, PRISA

Test-Driving JavaScript Applications

Rapid, Confident, Maintainable Code

Venkat Subramaniam

The Pragmatic Bookshelf
Raleigh, North Carolina

Our Pragmatic books, screencasts, and audio books can help you and your team create better software and have more fun. Visit us at *https://pragprog.com.*

The team that produced this book includes:

Jacquelyn Carter (editor)
Potomac Indexing, LLC (index)
Liz Welch (copyedit)
Gilson Graphics (layout)
Janet Furlow (producer)

For sales, volume licensing, and support, please contact *support@pragprog.com.*

For international rights, please contact *rights@pragprog.com.*

Printed in the United States of America.
ISBN-13: 978-1-68050-174-2
Printed on acid-free paper.
Book version: P1.0—October 2016

In loving memory of professor and uncle PSK,
for lighting my passion for programming.

Contents

Acknowledgments

I spent several weekends and nights away from my family to write this book. This book would not be possible without the incredible support of my family. So, I'd like to first thank my wife Kavitha and sons Karthik and Krupakar.

My sincere thanks to the technical reviewers who shared their invaluable time, knowledge, and wisdom to make this a better book. Many thanks to Kim Barnes (@kimberlydbarnes), Nick Capito, Neal Ford (@neal4d), Rod Hilton (@rodhilton), Brian Hogan (@bphogan), Charles Johnson (@charbajo), Pelle Lauritsen (@pellelauritsen), Daivid Morgan (@daividm), Kieran Murphy, Ted Neward (@tedneward), Maricris Nonato (@maricris_sn), Al Scherer (@al_scherer), Jason Schindler (@Volti_Subito), and Nate Schutta (@ntschutta). Each one of them helped improve this book. Any errors that remain are solely mine.

I'd like to thank the early readers of this book for providing valuable feedback on the forum[1] of the book and reporting errors on the errata page.[2] Thank you, Robert Guico, Naresha K, Dillon Kearns, Chip Pate, Astefanoaie Nicolae Stelian, and Bruce Trask. Special thanks to Tim Wright for his eagle-like eyes and for meticulously trying out each example.

I was truly fortunate to have Jackie Carter edit another of my books. Every interaction with her reminded me of the reasons I requested her to edit this book. I learned a great deal from her, about writing, patience, and so much more. Thank you, Jackie, for all your help, guidance, encouragement, and conversations.

The inspiration to write this book came from developers with whom I interacted at different conferences. I want to thank each one of them for the interesting questions and for engaging in deep conversations that helped solidify the concepts in my mind. Also, thanks to the conference organizers for giving me a platform to speak and interact with the excellent developers.

1. https://pragprog.com/book/vsjavas#forums
2. https://pragprog.com/titles/vsjavas/errata

Many thanks to the wonderful folks at the Pragmatic Bookshelf for accepting this book and working with me to turn the idea of writing this book into a reality. Thanks to Janet Furlow, Andy Hunt, Susannah Pfalzer, Dave Thomas, and many others whose support made this book possible.

Introduction

The passion to code was seeded in me early. Decades later, though I'm still addicted to coding, the economics of software development equally intrigues me. The cost of change and the speed at which we can respond to change matters a lot. We work in an industry that's still developing and maturing. We get paid to write code, and if we do a poor job, we get paid to go back and fix the mess. That can become a vicious cycle. As professionals we have to raise that bar—a lot higher.

JavaScript is truly a black swan[1]—who would've thought it would grow into one of the most ubiquitous languages? It's powerful, highly flexible, and quite dangerous, all at the same time. I actually like JavaScript—quite a lot—for the power and flexibility it offers.

Shunning powerful and flexible solutions, just because they are risky, will set us back. Instead we have to embrace them with better engineering practices. Using automated testing and continuous integration are part of better engineering practices. We can rely on automated testing and short feedback loops to alleviate the pain that comes from the dangerous side of JavaScript.

There's been explosive growth in the JavaScript ecosystem in recent years. There's also been tremendous development of automated testing tools. Thanks to these tools, as well as short feedback loops, continuous integration, and so on, good engineering discipline is not a theory—it's what every programmer using JavaScript can apply today. I've written this book to motivate and inspire you, and guide you along so you can do your share to raise that bar, to elevate our field to higher standards. Thank you for reading this book.

1. https://en.wikipedia.org/wiki/Black_swan_theory

What's in This Book?

This book focuses on automated testing and related practices necessary to sustain a rigorous development pace. From this book, you'll learn to apply tools and techniques to automatically verify both client-side (including jQuery and Angluar) and server-side (Node.js and Express) JavaScript applications.

You'll learn to effectively use the following tools in this book:

- Karma
- Mocha
- Chai
- Istanbul
- Sinon
- Protractor

While exploring these tools, you'll also learn and use quite a few software design principles that lead to lightweight design and maintainable code. If you're already using other tools, like Jasmine or Nodeunit, for example, you can readily use the testing techniques presented in this book with those tools.

The book is organized into two parts. Part I covers the fundamentals of automated testing. Here, you'll learn how to write tests, both for synchronous and asynchronous functions. You'll also learn how to approach automated testing when the code involves intricate dependencies. In Part II you'll apply what you learned in Part I to write automated tests for both client side and server side, by test-driving a practical example.

The chapters are organized as follows:

Chapter 1, *Automation Shall Set You Free*, on page 1 brings out the reasons why automated verification is critical for sustainable development.

Chapter 2, *Test-Drive Your Design*, on page 11 walks you through the steps to create automated tests for both server-side code and client-side code with a small example. You'll learn to create a test list and develop code incrementally, implementing the minimum code for one test at a time.

Some asynchronous functions take in callbacks while some may return a Promise. Chapter 3, *Test Asynchrony*, on page 45 presents the challenges asynchronous functions pose and different ways to test them.

Dependencies are pervasive in both client side and server side. They can make testing really hard, brittle, nondeterministic, and slow. Chapter 4, *Tactfully Tackle Dependencies*, on page 61 demonstrates how to remove dependencies where possible. For intricate dependencies, it shows how to decouple and replace dependencies with test doubles to facilitate testing.

Chapter 5, *Test-Drive Node.js Apps*, on page 91 walks you through test-driving a fully functional server-side application. It illustrates how to start with a high-level strategic design and to evolve the design using tests. You'll measure the code coverage to get a feel for how much the automated tests verified as the code evolved.

With Express you can breeze through writing web applications. Chapter 6, *Test-Drive Express Apps*, on page 121 will teach you how to sustain that pace with automated tests to create maintainable code. You'll start with the design of automated tests for database connections; then you'll learn about the model functions, all the way through to the routes functions.

Chapter 7, *Working with the DOM and jQuery*, on page 161 focuses on creating automated tests for the client side of the application developed in the previous chapter. It shows how to write tests for code that directly manipulates the DOM and also code that relies on the jQuery library.

AngularJS is declarative, reactive, and highly fluent. Besides making it easy to write client-side code, the framework also provides a powerful set of tools to write automated tests. In Chapter 8, *Using AngularJS*, on page 195 you'll learn the techniques to test AngularJS 1.x applications by creating another version of the client side for the Express application.

To say that AngularJS has gone through a makeover is an understatement. Angular 2 is different from AngularJS 1.x in many ways—components instead of controllers, pipes instead of filters, more explicit dependency injection, annotation-based wiring—and it's written using TypeScript instead of JavaScript. In Chapter 9, *Test-Drive Angular 2*, on page 229 you'll re-create the client side from the previous chapter, from the ground up, test first, using Angular 2 and good old JavaScript.

End-to-end, or UI-level, testing is essential but has to be minimal. It should focus and cover parts that aren't covered through the other tests. In Chapter 10, *Integrate and Test End-to-End*, on page 285 you'll learn what areas to focus on, what's critical to test, and what should be avoided. The chapter also shows how to create fully automated integration tests, from the database layer, through the model functions, the routes, and all the way to the UI.

Chapter 11, *Test-Drive Your Apps*, on page 315 brings the details from the rest of the book together. It discusses how we approached automated testing through the examples, the levels of testing, the size of tests, and the benefits reaped. It concludes the book with a discussion of how to take this forward for your own projects.

Who Is This Book For?

If you program in JavaScript, this book is for you. Programmers, hands-on architects, team leads, technical project managers, and anyone who wants to create maintainable JavaScript applications at a sustainable pace will benefit from this book.

The book assumes programmers are familiar with JavaScript—it does not teach any of the language features. Different parts of the book also assume familiarity with technologies used to create examples in that part. For example, Chapter 8, *Using AngularJS*, on page 195 and parts of Chapter 10, *Integrate and Test End-to-End*, on page 285 assume that the readers know AngularJS 1.x, but the rest of the book does not depend on that knowledge.

Every page in this book has something for programmers to directly apply on their projects, be it unit testing, integration testing, code coverage, or simply learning about reasons to practice the techniques. Architects and technical leads can use this book to guide their teams toward better technical practices that have an impact on a sustainable pace of development. Technical project managers can learn the reasons to test-drive JavaScript applications, understand the levels and size of testing, and decide how their team can approach automated testing. They can also use the book to motivate their teams to create applications with rapid feedback loops.

If you're already familiar with these techniques, you could use this book to influence and train other developers.

This book is written for software practitioners who extensively use JavaScript and care about their craft.

Online Resources

You can download all the example source code for the book from the Pragmatic Bookshelf website for this book.[2] You can also provide feedback by submitting errata entries or posting your comments and questions in the forum.

If you're reading the book in PDF form, you can click on the link above a code listing to view or download the specific examples.

2. http://www.pragprog.com/titles/vsjavas

A number of web resources referenced throughout the book are collected for your convenience in Appendix 1, *Web Resources*, on page 329.

Your Own Workspace

As you read along you'll want to practice the code examples. This requires installing various tools and creating directories and files for each code example. These steps can quickly get mundane and tedious. You can alleviate most of that pain by using the pre-created workspace provided as part of this book.

The workspace mainly contains package.json files that describe the dependencies and tools that are needed to code each programming example. It also includes the appropriate directory structures needed, along with files that you can readily open and start editing. When you start coding an example, you do not have to manually and repeatedly type in the installation commands for all the needed tools. Instead, once you change directory to an example project, a single npm install command will download everything you need to your system. Once the installation is done, you can conveniently start playing with the example by keying in the tests and the necessary code.

At this time, take a minute to download the workspace from the Pragmatic Bookshelf Media link[3] for this book. On Windows systems, download the file tdjsa.zip to the c:\ directory. On other systems, download it to your home directory. Once the download is complete, unzip the file using the command

```
unzip tdjsa.zip
```

Now you should see a directory named tdjsa with different subdirectories. Each chapter will direct you to the appropriate subdirectories for you to practice along as you make your way through the examples.

A word of caution: In general, copying and pasting code from a PDF reader into editors or IDEs does not work well. The outcome depends on both the source PDF reader and the destination editor/IDE. Depending on the tools used, after copying and pasting, you may have to reformat the code or it may not work. Your mileage may vary. Instead of copying and pasting from the PDF reader, you may download the code from the book's website as described in *Online Resources*, on page xvi.

Venkat Subramaniam

October 2016

3. https://media.pragprog.com/titles/vsjavas/code/tdjsa.zip

CHAPTER 1

Automation Shall Set You Free

Everyone benefits a great deal when the applications we create actually work. Failure in production is expensive, and we should do our best to minimize that. With today's technology, reach, and visibility, when applications fail the entire world can take notice. With automated tests, we can fail fast and safely, and in the process create resilient applications that work well in production.

Automated testing also has a deep impact on the design of the code. It naturally forces the code to be modular, cohesive, and loosely coupled. That, in turn, makes the code easier to change, and that has a positive impact on the cost of change.

You're probably eager to start coding, but learning a bit about whys and the possible impediments of automated testing will get you ready for the deeply technical things that follow this chapter. Let's quickly discuss the benefits and challenges of automated testing and how you can prepare and make use of the fast feedback loops.

The Challenges of Change

Code gets modified several times in its lifetime. If programmers tells you their code has not changed since the initial writing, they're implying that their project got canceled. For an application to stay relevant, it has to evolve. We make enhancements, add features, and often fix bugs. With each change comes a few challenges:

- The change should be affordable and cost effective.
- The change should have the right effect.

Let's discuss each of these challenges.

The Cost of Change

A good design is flexible, easier to extend, and less expensive to maintain. But how can we tell? We can't wait to see the aftermath of the design to learn about its quality—that may be too late.

Test-driven design can help to address that concern. In this approach, we first create an initial, big picture, strategic design. Then, through small tactical steps, and by applying some fundamental design principles (see *Agile Software Development, Principles, Patterns, and Practices [Mar02]*), we refine the design further. The tests, among other things, provide continuous feedback to ensure that the design being implemented in code meets the requirements. Tests promote good design principles—high cohesion, low coupling, more modular code, a single level of abstraction—traits that make change affordable.

The Effect of Change

"Does it work?" is a dreaded question we often hear when we change code. "I hope" is the usual response we developers give. There's nothing wrong in having hope that our efforts have the right effect, but we can strive for better.

Software is a nonlinear system—a change here can break something over there. For example, one small incorrect change to a data format can adversely affect different parts of a system. If disparate parts of a system begin to fail after a change is deployed, the result is frustration and pain. It's also embarrassing—our customers think of us as amateurs rather than as professionals.

When we make a change, we should quickly know if the code that worked before continues to work now. We *need* rapid, short, *automated* feedback loops.

Testing vs. Verification

Using automated feedback loops doesn't mean no manual testing.

It is not about automated instead of manual—we need the right combination of both. Let's define two different terms that need to stand apart—testing and verification.

Testing is an act of gaining insights. Is the application usable? Is it intuitive, and what's the user experience like? Does the workflow make sense? Are there steps that can be removed? Testing should raise these kinds of questions and provide insight into the key capabilities and limitations of an application.

Verification, on the other hand, is an act of confirmation. Does the code do what it's supposed to do? Are the calculations right? Is the program working as expected after a code or configuration change? Did the update of a third-party library/module break the application? These are largely the concerns of verifying an application's behavior.

Manual testing is quite valuable. On a recent project, after hours of coding-and-automated verification cycle, I manually exercised the application. As soon as the page popped up in the browser I wanted to change quite a few things—that's the *observer effect*. We need to manually exercise and test applications often. However, keep in mind the intent: to gain insights, not to verify.

In the same application, I changed the database within weeks before production. A quick run of the automated tests immediately resulted in verification failures. Within minutes I was able to rectify and reverify, without even bringing up the web server. Automated verification saved my day.

Do Both Testing and Verification

Do manual testing to gain insights and automated verification to influence the design and to confirm the code continues to meet the expectations.

Adopting Automated Verification

The efforts toward automated verification, or what we'll loosely call *automated testing*, varies widely across the industry; broadly there are three different adoption efforts:

- No automation, only manual verification. These are largely done by teams in denial. They struggle to validate their applications after each change and suffer from the consequences.
- Automation mostly at the user interface (UI) level. Quite a few teams have realized the need for automation verification, but have focused most of their efforts at the UI level. This leads to pathway-to-hell automation—we'll shortly discuss why.
- Automation at the right levels. This is done by mature teams that have gone beyond the first step of realizing the need for automation. They've invested in short feedback loops at various levels of their application, with more tests at lower levels.

Extreme focus on UI-level test automation results in the ice-cream cone antipattern.[1]

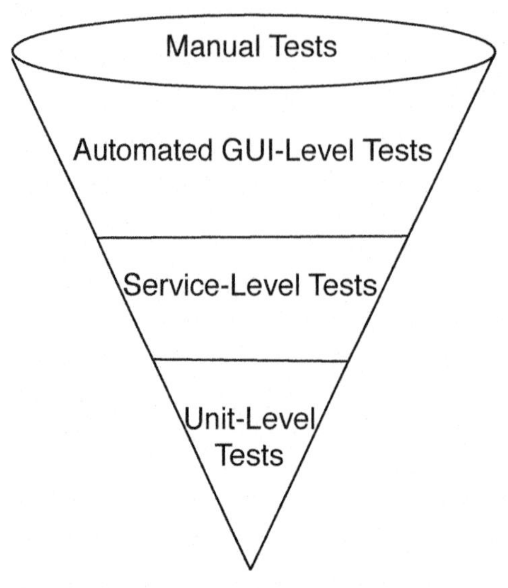

One reason why teams end up with this antipattern is the lack of alignment between different members of the teams. Eager to automate, the teams hire automation engineers tasked with creating automated test suites. Unfortunately, the programmers are often not on board and do not provide test hooks at different layers in the application—that's not something they had to do before. As a result, the automation engineers are limited to writing tests at the level they can get their arms around. This often is the GUI and any external-facing APIs.

Testing mostly at the UI level has many drawbacks:[2]

- It's brittle. UI-level tests break often. UI is one of the most fluid parts of an application. It changes when the code it depends on changes. It also changes when customers or testers walk by, giving their feedback on how the UI should look and feel. Keeping tests in sync with changes in the UI is quite arduous, much more than at lower levels.
- It has too many moving parts. UI-level tests often need tools like Selenium and require different browsers to be up and running. Keeping these dependencies up and running takes effort.

1. http://watirmelon.com/2012/01/31/
2. http://martinfowler.com/bliki/TestPyramid.html

- It's slow. These tests need the entire application to be up and running: the client side, the server side, the database, and connections to any external services that may be needed. Running thousands of tests through full integration is often much slower than running isolated tests.
- It's hard to write. One of my clients struggled for well over six months to write a UI-level test for a simple interaction. We eventually discovered the problem was due to the timing of the tests compared to the running of the client-side JavaScripts that produced the results.
- It does not isolate the problem area. When a UI-level test fails, we only know something is amiss—can't tell readily where or at what level.
- It does not prevent logic in the UI. We all know putting logic in UI is bad, yet we've all seen it permeate and duplicate at this level. UI-level tests do nothing to mitigate this.
- It does not influence a better design. UI-level tests don't discourage the so-called "big ball of mud"—the opposite of modular code.

Mike Cohn suggests in *Succeeding with Agile: Software Development Using Scrum [Coh09]* the idea of a test pyramid—more tests at the lower levels and fewer end-to-end tests at the higher levels.

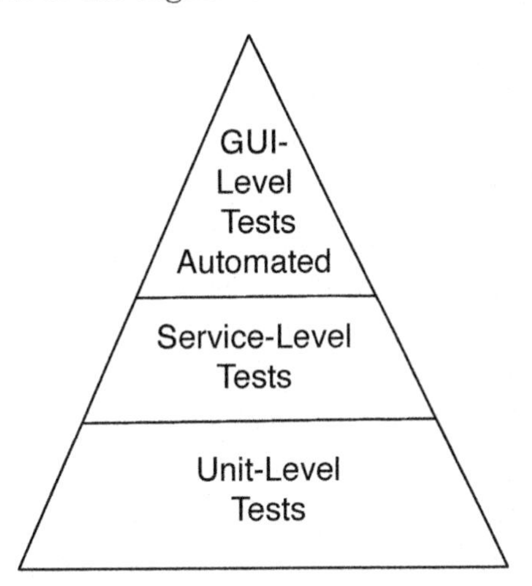

We should follow the test pyramid rather than falling into the traps of the ice-cream cone antipattern. Writing more tests at the lower levels has many benefits. The tests at the lower level run faster, they're easier to write, and they provide shorter feedback loops. They also lead to better modular design, and as a result, it gets easier to isolate and identify problems when they happen.

We'll follow that spirit in this book, to write tests at the right levels—more unit tests, then functional tests, and a few end-to-end UI-level tests.

Automated Verification Is Not Optional

Developing any nontrivial application without automated tests at the right level is an economic disaster.

If automation at the right level is so critical, then why don't more developers do it? Let's discuss some reasons next.

Why Is It Hard to Verify?

It's easier to say the code should be testable than to actually make it testable. Programmers often find it really hard to automate the test because of one or both of the following:

- The code is poorly designed.
- The programmer has no clue how the code works.

Those words may seem harsh, but they're not intended to offend anyone. Instead, my hope is for you to understand the core reasons and find ways to remove the impediments.

It's incredibly hard to write automated tests on legacy code. Legacy code often is not very modular, lacks cohesion, and has high coupling—telltale signs of poor design. Even though we have the best intentions, writing tests after the fact rarely seems to work.

For code to be testable, it has to be highly cohesive and loosely coupled. If the code does a lot of things—that is, it has low cohesion—it would need a lot more tests, to the extent it would be practically impossible to write. Also, if the code is directly wired to a service—that is, it has tight coupling—it is tough to write deterministic automated tests. Automated testability _is a design issue_.

Furthermore, if we really don't have a clue how a piece of code works, it's hard to write automated tests for it. We often start with tutorials that show us how to use a library or a framework. We quickly get some code up and running, but we may not have taken the time to really understand how different parts come together. While it's easy to write more code to produce results, programmers often are baffled when asked to write automated tests for that code. The lack of knowledge, especially one level below the level of abstraction they depend on, is often the culprit.

Sometimes, we may be tempted to assume that it's impossible to write automated tests. Let's not confuse our lack of knowledge or skill with impossibility. Impossibility is dire, but lack of knowledge or skill is curable. We may not know now how to do something, but we can learn from others and collaborate to achieve the goals. Automated testing is a skill; it's easier to learn and implement when we're motivated.

How to Approach Automated Testing

Programmers rarely have trouble writing code, but they find it extremely hard to write tests before writing code.

One reason for that is programming is really a series of small experiments carried in sequence, every single day—it's an act of continuous discoveries. We write some code, see it fail, read up a bit, give it another shot, try out a few different paths, and through small trials and errors we get the code to work—that's natural, that's how we write code.

When we don't have a clear picture of the code, how can we write tests first? It seems counterintuitive, but there are ways to work that in.

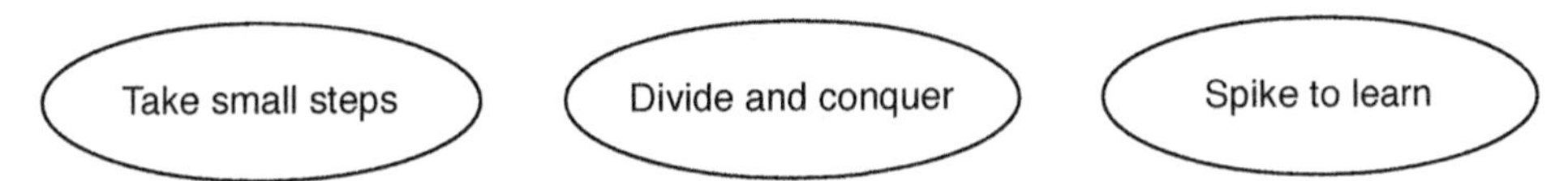

First, *take small steps*. If a test appears too hard to implement, the chances are we're taking on way more than we should. In order to implement a function using test-first coding, we'd have to work through a series of tests: three, five, or maybe fifteen tests. Think of each test as a step in a stairway—each one is small, is spaced comfortably, and moves us up with each step we take.

Second, *divide and conquer*. If a test is hard to write for a function, maybe that function we're designing is not as cohesive as it should be or it may have more coupling than desirable. It's a sign that we may have to break the function we have in mind into smaller functions and drive each one of them through tests.

Third, *spike to learn*. If the function you're designing is similar to what you've done several times before, then write one test at a time and the minimum code to make each test pass. On the other hand, if you are pretty new to the implementation of a function—it's complex, asynchronous, or very elusive—don't try to write a test for it right away. Instead, create active isolated spikes to learn. Let's explore how to spike a bit further.

Leaving the current project in place, scoot over to a small spike project and wildly experiment. Don't care about code quality or tests at this moment. Get something to work, to produce the result you're looking for. Once you have that little piece of code working, summon your courage and have the discipline to discard it. Switch back to your active project, start with the test first, and drive the design of the code. You will notice that it's not as intimidating to write tests first as it appeared. Also, you will notice that the design of the code that evolves is often quite different from what you cranked out during spiking.

Wrapping Up

There's value in both manual testing and automated verification. Testing can give us a great deal of insight. Without automated verification, it's impossible to sustain the pace of development. Any nontrivial application requires automated tests at the right level. It takes time, effort, and discipline to automate tests, but it's a skill that we should invest in. Write tests before writing code. If that proves to be difficult, learn from active spiking.

As you've seen in this chapter, automated testing is very crucial. In the next part we'll dive into some fundamental techniques for automated testing of both client-side and server-side code.

Part I

Creating Automated Tests

The nature and complexity of code widely affects the ability to write and run automated tests. One piece of code may focus on business logic or computations. Another piece may use an asynchronous API, and yet another may mostly rely on interactions with external services. Since these concerns result in code that widely differs, the tests for them differ widely as well.

In this part, you'll learn to write automated tests and measure code coverage. You'll also explore ways to write tests for code that's asynchronous and code with intricate dependencies.

CHAPTER 2

Test-Drive Your Design

It's incredibly hard to write effective tests after coding is done—the code often is not in a form for tests to easily fall in place after the fact. It's better to start early with tests.

Writing tests before creating a piece of code naturally makes the code testable. Good tests shape the code, making it modular, more cohesive, and loosely coupled. This, in turn, can make the design lightweight, easier to change, and less expensive to maintain. In addition, the quick feedback we get from the tests improves our confidence that things will continue to work when we change the code.

But creating tests before writing a piece of code can also be challenging.

In this chapter you'll learn how to write tests just-in-time and influence the design of code using these tests. You'll see how the first few tests nudge us to focus on the interface of a function while the remaining tests that follow lead us through the guts of the function.

You'll create tests for both server-side and client-side JavaScript. For the server side we'll run the code within Node.js. The client-side code will run within different browsers. Regardless of where the code runs, we'll write automated tests for it. You can exercise these tests quickly to get feedback that the code is working as expected, through each step of the design of the code.

In addition to the techniques to write the tests, you'll learn to use a few tools: Karma, Mocha, Chai, and Istanbul. By the end of this chapter you'll be ready to apply the techniques and tools to create better-quality design that will make change easier and less expensive.

Let's Get Started

You should get comfortable writing and running tests before we dive into designing with tests. That's what we'll do first: get a project set up and get a few tests running.

We'll use a very simple function that converts Fahrenheit to Celsius as a vehicle to learn about the test writing fundamentals. As a first step we'll check the installation of Node.js and npm on your system. Then we'll get an example project set up and install the tools necessary for writing the tests. Next, we'll warm up and confirm that everything got installed by writing an introductory test. Along the way you'll learn about test suites and the organization of test and source code files. Finally, we'll write a test to verify the behavior of the example code under test.

Check npm and Node.js Installations

We need Node.js for two reasons. First, we need it for running the server-side code and tests. Second, it comes bundled with npm, the JavaScript package manager, which has become the go-to tool for installing JavaScript modules. We'll use npm to install tools for both the server-side and the client-side testing.

If you don't already have the latest version of Node.js[1] on your system, get that installed and verify it's on the system path by running the following command:

```
node --version
```

Also ensure that npm is on your system path by running this command:

```
npm --version
```

Using npm is a convenient way to download the different modules we'll need. Now that you've confirmed that these two tools are installed and updated on your system, let's get started with writing some tests and running them.

Set Up a Sample Project

We'll start with a simple problem—writing tests for a function that converts from Fahrenheit to Celsius. We'll keep this example extremely rudimentary so you can get comfortable with the project setup process and writing tests.

---

1. https://nodejs.org

Let's start by getting the project set up. You'll use npm init to create a project and npm install to get a few tools in place.

In this section, you'll learn—or refresh if you know already—the steps to create a project. This will help when you create your own projects in the future. In the examples that follow this section, however, we'll skip the initialization step and start with a pre-created project to save some time and effort.

If you haven't downloaded the workspace mentioned in *Your Own Workspace*, on page xvii, do so at this time. Then cd to the tdjsa/tdd/sample directory on your system. Once in that directory, type the command

```
npm init
```

to create a project. All that this command does is create a package.json file that will hold details of the dependencies or the tools we'll need and the commands to exercise them.

The command npm init will ask you to enter a few details. Take the default for all the questions, except for test command: enter mocha—that's the testing tool we'll use.

Here's the package.json file created by running the npm init command:

```
{
  "name": "sample",
  "version": "1.0.0",
  "description": "",
  "main": "index.js",
  "directories": {
    "test": "test"
  },
  "scripts": {
    "test": "mocha"
  },
  "author": "",
  "license": "ISC"
}
```

The nice thing about this file is once you set it up, installing dependencies becomes straightforward. You don't have to go through the setup manually again, say, on a build machine or on a colleague's computer.

We'll need two tools, Mocha and Chai, to facilitate automated testing. Let's get those two installed now:

```
npm install mocha chai --save-dev
```

This command installs the tools locally under the node_modules directory within the current sample directory. In addition, npm updates the package.json file with a devDependencies section to convey the development dependencies of the project. Take a peek into the package.json file to confirm that the command created the devDependencies section similar to the following:

```
"devDependencies": {
  "chai": "^3.5.0",
  "mocha": "^2.4.5"
}
```

The tools we need are ready. We'll place the test in the test directory and the code being tested in the src directory. In general you'd have to create these directories and the files in it. However, for your convenience, these directories are already included in your workspace. Empty files are provided in those directory as well to save you some effort—you can start editing them as you follow along the example.

We're all set to write our first test. We'll write tests to verify the behavior of an f2c function that will convert a given input from Fahrenheit to Celsius. We'll walk step by step, through organizing the tests to implementing the code to make the tests pass, and we'll see the tests in action, verifying the code's behavior.

Create a Test Suite and a Canary Test

Before we start writing any real tests, we want to make sure the tools were installed properly and that we're able to write and exercise tests. It will be frustrating if, after writing test and code, tests fail to run because of a setup issue. To avoid such annoyance, we'll start with a *canary* test. A canary test is the silliest test one could write. True to its origin, *canary in a coal mine*, it's a sacrificial test that provides a quick way to verify that things are in place to run tests.

Open the file util_test.js that's already included under the test directory for your convenience and enter the following code for the canary test:

```
var expect = require('chai').expect;

describe('util tests', function() {
  it('should pass this canary test', function() {
    expect(true).to.eql(true);
  });
});
```

That's a Mocha[2] test file. Mocha is a test engine that identifies and executes tests in JavaScript files. By default, Mocha looks for tests in the test directory.

In the test file, the call to require loads up the chai assertion library and brings in a reference to the expect assertion function. The library file will be loaded from the node_modules directory under our sample project directory.

Our test file contains one test suite. A test suite is a cohesive collection of tests that verify the behavior of either one function or a small group of closely related functions. describe is a keyword used by Mocha to define a test suite. The describe function takes two arguments: the test suite name and a function that houses tests in that suite. We named our example test suite util tests.

Each test is defined with a call to the it function. This, in turn, has two arguments—the name for the test and the actual body of the test. The name should clearly and concisely express the intention of the test and convey what's expected of the code being tested.

Let's exercise the test to verify that Mocha and Chai work together as expected. To run the test, type

```
npm test
```

This instructs npm to run the test command we provided during the initialization of the package.json file—in short, it runs Mocha. Let's take a look at the result of running Mocha on this canary test:

```
...
> mocha
  util tests
    ✓ should pass this canary test

  1 passing (6ms)
```

Mocha reports the canary test as passing. That confirms that both Mocha and Chai are installed properly and working in tandem.

Let's go ahead and change the true that's passed as an argument to the expect function to false and save the test file. Then run npm test and observe how Mocha complains about the failure. Once done with your little experiment, let's put back the test argument, ensure the test is passing, and then move on.

In the test we used expect for assertion. Mocha does not include an assertion library; it only takes on the single responsibility to identify and run tests. That assertion function comes from Chai,[3] a popular assertion library. Chai

2. https://mochajs.org
3. http://chaijs.com

> **Joe asks:**
> ### Is There Value to Keeping the Canary Test?
>
> The canary test has little value other than getting us started, but it's good to leave this test in place. If you upgrade your automated testing tools, move to another machine, or change your environment settings, the canary test can help to quickly verify that the most basic test works, confirming again that the test environment is OK.

supports three styles of assertions: *assert*, *expect*, and *should*. Which style to use is purely a matter of personal choice. The *expect* style is quite fluent, expressive, and pleasant to read, so that's the style we'll use in this book.

Verifying a Function's Behavior

The first test gave us quick feedback about the setup and got us moving. Let's continue that momentum by writing the second test. In this warm-up exercise, we're writing tests to verify the behavior of an f2c function that converts input from one unit of measure to another. In the next test, let's verify that the function properly converts 32 degree Fahrenheit to 0 degree Celsius.

In the test suite file, we first need to load the src/util.js file, which will contain the code to be tested. This is an empty file already provided for your convenience in your workspace. Let's change the test/util_test.js file to load that file.

```
var expect = require('chai').expect;
var Util = require('../src/util');
```

The newly added call to require brings in the source code file util.js file from the src directory. The path starting with .. is relative to the test directory. The uppercase Util, based on JavaScript convention, says that the loaded file will return a class or constructor function. We need to create an instance for this class in our test. However, as we continue writing more tests, multiple tests in the test suite may need an instance. Rather than duplicating the code for that in each test, a good place to tuck away the instance creation is in a beforeEach function. Let's create that function within the test suite, right after the canary test.

```
describe('util tests', function() {
  //...canary test not shown...

  var util;

  beforeEach(function() {
    util = new Util();
  });
});
```

The beforeEach function, if present in a test suite, is automatically run by Mocha before each test in that suite is executed. Likewise, if we add an afterEach function to perform any optional cleanup operations, then that function will be executed after each of the tests in the suite. beforeEach and afterEach are sandwich functions—they're executed around each of the tests in the suite.

In the beforeEach function we assign to the variable util an instance of the Util class. As an effect of this, each test will get a fresh instance of Util created just in time before its run.

Let's write the test to verify the aforementioned behavior of the f2c function—this test will go right below the beforeEach function in the test/util_test.js file:

```
it('should pass if f2c returns 0C for 32F', function() {
  var fahrenheit = 32;

  var celsius = util.f2c(fahrenheit);

  expect(celsius).to.eql(0);
});
```

When compared to the canary test, this test has a few more lines. In general, tests follow an *Arrange-Act-Assert* (3-As) pattern.[4] It's a good practice to separate the three parts with a blank line for clarity. The arrange part sets up what's needed for the code under test. The act part exercises the code under test. The assert part finally verifies that the code fulfills the expectations.

Even though there are three parts in each test, remember to keep tests really short. If tests run on to several lines, it's a sign of poor design of the tests and the ensuing code.

Use the 3-As Pattern

Except in very simple cases, structure tests to follow the Arrange-Act-Assert pattern, with each part clearly separated by a blank line.

In the test, we arranged the fahrenheit variable to have a value of 32. Then we performed an action of calling the function under test. Finally, we asserted that the result of the action is the expected value.

Let's run the test and see it fail—red, green, refactor is a mantra in TDD. We write a failing test; then we write the minimum code to make it pass; then we refactor the code to make it better.

4. http://c2.com/cgi/wiki?ArrangeActAssert

First make sure the test fails and confirm that it fails for the right reasons. Occasionally, a test may pass as soon as we write it, without any code change, because the existing code may already satisfy the expectations. In such a case, scrutinize the code to make sure it passes for the right reasons.

As the next step, we'll create the minimum code to make this test pass. Open the source code file util.js that's in the src directory and enter the following code:

```
module.exports = function() {
  this.f2c = function() {
    return 0;
  };
};
```

exports is the actual object within module that's returned to the caller of the require function that loads a file. In the util.js file we create a function—a constructor function, to be specific—that represents a JavaScript class. The f2c function belongs to this class and when called merely returns 0. That result is quite adequate to make the test we wrote to pass.

Let's exercise the test and verify that the f2c function, the code under test, is working as expected. Proceed to make a quick call to the npm test command and take a look at the feedback it provides:

```
...
> mocha
  util tests

    ✓ should pass this canary test

    ✓ should pass if f2c returns 0C for 32F

  2 passing (7ms)
```

The two tests we have so far passed. We're warming up to this pretty quickly. Let's write one more test.

Verify Behavior for Another Data Point

The previous test verified that the function worked properly for an input value of 32 Fahrenheit. There are literally an infinite number of values that could be passed as input to this function. We can't be testing the function for each one of those possible values, for obvious reasons. A good automated verification should pick a relatively small but good set of values as test candidates. Let's pick the value 50 to verify the result of the function. Let's add a third test to the test suite in util_test.js.

```
it('should pass if f2c returns 10C for 50F', function() {
  var fahrenheit = 50;

  var celsius = util.f2c(fahrenheit);

  expect(celsius).to.eql(10);
});
```

This test is akin to the previous one except for the input and the expected result. Let's run this test and watch it fail—the implementation currently in place in the f2c function is not adequate to meet the expectations set by the new test.

```
...
> mocha
  util tests

    ✓ should pass this canary test

    ✓ should pass if f2c returns 0C for 32F

    1) should pass if f2c returns 10C for 50F

  2 passing (13ms)
  1 failing

  1) Util test should pass if f2c returns 10C for 50F:

      AssertionError: expected 0 to deeply equal 10
      + expected - actual

      -0
      +10

      at Context.<anonymous> (test/util_test.js:29:24)

npm ERR! Test failed.  See above for more details.
```

Making the test fail helped us to see that when a test fails, Mocha provides a fairly good amount of information about what went wrong. This rich detail is highly essential; we can use it to fix and recover from any failure or regression that we run into as we evolve the code. In this example, it clearly tells us which test is failing and that a value of 10 was expected but instead a value of 0 was received. Let's modify the function f2c in util.js to make this test pass:

```
module.exports = function() {
  this.f2c = function(fahrenheit) {
    return (fahrenheit - 32) * 5 / 9;
  };
};
```

We introduced a parameter to the function and modified the body of the function as well. After saving this change, run the test and verify that it passes.

That test prompted us to move from the fake implementation to the real formula. That also raises a few question. Does the function work properly for negative temperatures? The results that we verified so far are integer values, but what if the result were a decimal number? If you like, take a few minutes to try out a few tests and experiment with a few values that intrigue you.

In the first test suite we created, there are a total of three tests, including the canary test. Writing tests is not a mechanical process. It requires some serious thinking and analysis. Let's discuss a few things we should keep in mind when writing tests:

- We should consider these guiding principles when writing tests: both tests and tests suites should have a single responsibility. If a group of functions work closely together, then keep their tests in one suite. Otherwise, separate their tests to different suites. Also, we should give test quality the same care that we give to the quality of functions and classes we write.

- Tests should be relevant and verify the correct behavior of the code. The tests we write describe, express, and document the behavior of code, but the onus is on us to ensure that such behavior is correct and relevant. In order to know what the correct behavior is, programmers will have to get input and feedback from business analysts, domain experts, testers, product owners, and other members of the team. For a test to be relevant to the application, developers have to communicate and collaborate with other members of the team.

We evolved the test and the code incrementally. Let's step back and take a look at the entire test file we created:

tdd/sample/test/util_test.js

```
var expect = require('chai').expect;
var Util = require('../src/util');

describe('util tests', function() {
  it('should pass this canary test', function() {
    expect(true).to.be.true;
  });

  var util;

  beforeEach(function() {
    util = new Util();
  });
```

```
  it('should pass if f2c returns 0C for 32F', function() {
    var fahrenheit = 32;

    var celsius = util.f2c(fahrenheit);

    expect(celsius).to.eql(0);
  });

  it('should pass if f2c returns 10C for 50F', function() {
    var fahrenheit = 50;

    var celsius = util.f2c(fahrenheit);

    expect(celsius).to.eql(10);
  });
});
```

And, let's also take a look at the code that makes those tests pass:

tdd/sample/src/util.js

```
module.exports = function() {
  this.f2c = function(fahrenheit) {
    return (fahrenheit - 32) * 5 / 9;
  };
};
```

We got a feel for setting up a project, the necessary tools, writing tests, and running them. We also saw how the feedback—both successes and failures—from running the tests looks. Let's turn our attention from writing tests to driving the design using tests.

Design with Positive, Negative, and Exception Tests

Writing tests before writing code is a skill. It may appear hard at first, but it gets better with practice. The result of that effort is a more modular, cohesive, and loosely coupled design.

By writing tests first, we put ourselves in the shoes of the person who will be using our code before we write it. Thus, from the very first step, we can approach the design of code from the point of view of someone using the code. In this approach each function we design will be shaped by a series of tests. The first few tests will help to shape the interface of the function—that is, its skin. The tests that follow will then help shape the implementation or the guts of the function.

Let's discuss where to begin and the type of tests we should create when test-driving the design of code.

Whether you're creating server-side or client-side code, it's usually hard to decide where to start. Break the inertia; once you get moving it becomes easier to write the tests. Start with a fairly simple test; don't worry about making it perfect just yet. However, instead of identifying trivial functions that get or set state, focus on an interesting behavior to start with. Think of a function, a unit of code, that is useful, interesting, but not too complex to start with—make that your first function to write tests for.

Focus on Behavior Rather than State

Avoid the common antipattern of writing tests for getting and setting state. Instead, start by testing interesting and useful behavior. Let any necessary state fall in place along the way.

When you start the design of a function, visualize the types of tests you'd write to verify the behavior of the function. A good way to incrementally develop code is through a series of positive, negative, and exception tests. Let's discuss these three types of tests:

- *Positive tests* exercise and verify that the code does what's expected when its preconditions are met.
- *Negative tests* verify that the code gracefully behaves when things don't go as expected—that is, when its preconditions or input are not valid.
- *Exception tests* verify that if code is supposed to throw an exception, it does in fact.

We'll explore each one of these throughout the book. When thinking of tests, think of keeping them FAIR: *fast*, *automated*, *isolated*, and *repeatable*.

- Fast tests mean fast feedback loops. If tests are slow, you'll be tempted to run them less often.
- A major benefit of tests is verification—we've discussed why these should be automated and not be manual.
- Isolated tests can be run in any order, and you can also run a select few of them as you desire or all of them. No test should require that any other test be run before it—such tests are brittle and turn into time sinks.
- Finally, tests should be repeatable; you should be able to run them any number of times without needing manual or time-consuming setup or cleanup operations.

As we evolve the design using tests, we should keep everything working at all times, so that we're never more than one step away from functioning code.

Evolve Applications Using Tests

Each test should take us from a delta of working code to the next delta of working code with a small additional capability.

With some practice you'll soon find a comfortable test-code rhythm—create a good test and write or change the minimum code to make it and other existing tests pass.

Now that you have an idea of the types of tests to write, let's practice test-driving the design of a server-side code.

Design Server-Side Code

To practice the concepts of test-driving the design, we'll test-drive the design of server-side code that checks if a given string is a palindrome. That's a fairly simple problem, but keeping it simple now will help you ease into test-driven design without getting dragged too quickly into complexities. Once you get comfortable with the basics, you'll be well prepared to handle gruesome complexities in later chapters.

JavaScript on the server side has gained prominence in recent years and Node.js has become the de facto runtime environment. It's not only a great platform to deploy, but it's also charming from the testability point of view. Let's explore testing JavaScript running in Node.js with an example.

We'll design a function to check if a given input is a palindrome. That's a simple problem that most programmers know how to code right away, but as an exercise, let's create it test first.

Start with a Test List

Before touching the keyboard, scribble on a piece of paper short phrases for some positive, negative, and exception tests that come to mind. This *test list* will evolve quite a bit as you begin to write code—new tests will come to mind while you're in the middle of coding, and this list is a perfect place to quickly jot them down.

Take a few minutes to jot down short phrases for some tests. Don't try to think about the tests for too long—avoid any analysis paralysis. The list doesn't have to be perfect. Once we break the inertia and get moving, things will fall into place.

Joe asks:
Why Keep the Test List on a Piece of Paper?

We live in the digital age, so shouldn't we be keeping the list of tests in electronic tools, on smartphones, on wikis...

Paper still offers some key benefits. Spontaneity. Several edge cases and scenarios will come to mind while writing code and implementing tests. Capturing those details spontaneously is critical—nothing's as fast as pencil and paper for scribbling down ideas. Also, you don't risk losing focus by switching windows or tools. Striking obsolete tests and checking completed ones is effortless. Watching new tests being added to the list and seeing them marked as completed with a quick glance is also quite motivating during strenuous coding sessions.

Here are some initial tests, jotted on a piece of paper, for the problem at hand:

- `mom` is a palindrome
- `dad` is a palindrome
- `dude` is not a palindrome

That's a good starting point. These are empirical tests that use sample data for function arguments. We can add more tests as they come to mind—tests often spring up naturally once we get into the rhythm of the test-code cycle.

Switch to the Palindrome Project

For the palindrome exercise, we need to set up a project. Instead of running `npm init` and going through the setup sequence from scratch, you can save some time and effort by starting with a pre-created `package.json` file.

Change the directory to the `tdd/server/palindrome` directory under your workspace. In this project we'll use the tools Mocha, Chai, and Istanbul.

Let's take a look at the `package.json` file that's already present in this directory:

tdd/server/palindrome/package.json

```
{
  "name": "palindrome",
  "version": "1.0.0",
  "description": "",
  "main": "index.js",
  "directories": {
    "test": "test"
  },
  "scripts": {
    "test": "istanbul cover node_modules/mocha/bin/_mocha"
  },
```

```
  "author": "",
  "license": "ISC",
  "devDependencies": {
    "chai": "^3.5.0",
    "istanbul": "^0.4.4",
    "mocha": "^3.0.1"
  }
}
```

Let's ask npm to install the necessary packages for this project to your local machine, using the command

```
npm install
```

That command will read the package.json file and automatically download the packages mentioned in the devDependencies section. It will install Mocha and Chai, the tools that we've seen already. In addition, it will install Istanbul, a tool we'll use soon for code coverage.

You may wonder why we have to install Mocha and Chai again. These are development tools specific to the project at hand and are located under the node_modules directory that's local to the project. When you switch to a different project, you'll have to install the tools needed for that project. Thankfully, the npm init command reduces the burden and it will skip installation if it finds the files are already installed in the current project. Avoid any temptation to copy the node_modules directory from one project to another—that often does not go well and may end in errors later when the tools are used, resulting in wasted time. We can avoid those troubles by installing the tools on a per-project basis.

Also notice that for the test command, instead of calling mocha we're calling istanbul. As part of measuring the code coverage, this tool will run the automated tests. However, instead of directing Istanbul to run the command mocha, we've asked it to run the tool _mocha. This is necessary due to the intricacies of how Mocha forks processes.[5] The good news is those commands that appear complicated are nicely tucked away in that package file and all we have to remember is to run npm test to run the tests.

Now that the new project is ready for our use, as a first step we should verify that things are in place. For that, you guessed right, we'll need to write a canary test. The project already contains the necessary directory structure and empty source and test files ready for your use. Open the file named palindrome-test.js under the tdd/server/palindrome/test directory and enter the following code:

5. https://github.com/gotwarlost/istanbul/issues/44#issuecomment-16093330

tdd/server/palindrome/test/palindrome-test.js

```
var expect = require('chai').expect;

describe('palindrome-test', function() {
  it('should pass this canary test', function() {
    expect(true).to.be.true;
  });
});
```

We named the test suite palindrome-test and placed the canary test in it. Run the command npm test to verify that the test passes.

It's time to write our first test for the palindrome function.

Create Positive Tests

Let's implement the first test, from our test list, for the palindrome function. Add the test right below the singing canary in the palindrome-test.js file:

```
var expect = require('chai').expect;
var isPalindrome = require('../src/palindrome');

describe('palindrome-test', function() {
  it('should pass this canary test', function() {
    expect(true).to.be.true;
  });

  it('should return true for argument mom', function() {
    expect(isPalindrome('mom')).to.be.true;
  });
});
```

At the top of the file we added a call to require, to load the currently empty source file palindrome.js from the src directory. The newly added test *should return true for argument mom* will tease out the interface of the function we've set out to design. Furthermore, it will verify that the function, once implemented, continues to return the expected result every single time the test is run. To this end, the test invokes the isPalindrome() function, passes the sample test string 'mom' to it, and asserts the result is true.

This test has only a single line, but it does three things. To get a feel for the structure of a test, let's break the single line into multiple lines:

```
var aWord = 'mom';

var result = isPalindrome(aWord);

expect(result).to.be.true;
```

This reveals the three parts of a test—the Arrange, Act, Assert, or 3-As pattern—we discussed earlier. For simple cases, having a single line is perfectly OK. However, if a function under test takes a few parameters and/or the results have more details to verify, then we should not attempt to compress all that into one line. Readability of tests is quite important; it's better to be a bit more verbose than terse.

The first positive test is ready, but don't rush to implement the code. Use the initial tests to shape the function's interface, to make the code expressive and readable. Play with some options, or change the method name to see if it can be more intuitive—should the return value be something different? Once you've settled on the interface you like, write a minimum implementation for the function.

Here's the first stab at the code. Open the file src/palindrome.js that's already in your workspace and enter this code:

```
module.exports = function(word) {
  return true;
};
```

That implementation is quite minimal—in fact, trivial. That's good. If you keep the implementation minimal at this time, you can focus on the function's interface—its name, its parameter names, the type to return, and so on—instead of worrying too soon about the implementation.

The parameter to the function is named word, but while writing this minimal implementation we could ask if the input could be something other than a word—maybe multiple words, a sentence? The answer to such questions generally depends on the domain and the application. We'd have to discuss it with our colleagues, fellow programmers, testers, and business analysts to get the answer.

Test-driven development is not a series of mundane mechanical steps. Tests should greatly influence the design of code, through a series of questions. Tests should help us gradually uncover the details about the problem at hand and lead us to discover the interface and implementation of code to meet the requirements.

Let Tests Drive the Design

Tests should raise many questions in our minds, help us uncover hidden details, and along the way, tease out the interface of the code.

Suppose the business analyst confirmed that the input may have multiple words. Let's not let that decision slip through the cracks; add a couple more tests to the list you're keeping on paper:

- ✓ mom is a palindrome
- dad is a palindrome
- dude is not a palindrome
- ⇒mom mom is a palindrome
- ⇒mom dad is not a palindrome

We should then change the parameter name from word to phrase. Once you make that change, run the tests and make sure both the canary test and the new test pass.

We can now move on to write the next test. With the test "mom is a palindrome" passing, you may wonder if we need to test for "dad" being a palindrome. It's a good idea to verify that the code behaves correctly for a handful of values and not just one. That can give us a greater confidence in the long run that the code behaves as intended for at least a few select values among all the possible values.

Back in the palindrome-test.js file, add another positive test:

```
it('should return true for argument dad', function() {
  expect(isPalindrome('dad')).to.be.true;
});
```

Instead of writing this new test, you may be tempted to add another assert to the previous test—but don't. When we modify the code we want to get a quick feedback of the impact of change. If we group multiple *independent* asserts in one test, the failure of one assert will prevent the evaluation of asserts that follow. This blocks visibility of the impact of change. Only after we fix the failing assert will we know about the state of the next assert in that test. This is like having a compiler that stops on the first failure; it will be a very long and frustrating journey to fix all the hidden errors.

Avoid Placing Multiple Independent Asserts in One Test

Each test should have the fewest number of asserts possible. Avoid grouping independent asserts together into one test.

This is not to say that a test should never have multiple asserts. For example, if the effect of a function is to change the first and last name of a person, then by all means check to make sure both the first name and the last name are correct, with two asserts. In this case, the two asserts are closely related; they're not independent. On the other hand, asserting that the name change function worked for two sets of names would not be a good idea, because the first two sets of asserts would be independent of the other two sets.

The new test we added should pass since the minimal—in fact trivial—implementation we have in the function is still adequate. Go ahead and run the tests to make sure all three tests are passing.

Now let's write the next test in the palindrome-test.js file, the one from our test list for the argument dude.

```
it('should return false for argument dude', function() {
  expect(isPalindrome('dude')).to.be.false;
});
```

This test asserts that the function returns false if a non-palindrome is passed as an argument. Run the test and you'll see this one fail—the error message clearly tells us which test failed:

```
  palindrome-test
    ✓ should pass this canary test
    ✓ should return true for argument mom
    ✓ should return true for argument dad
    1) should return false for argument dude

  3 passing (6ms)
  1 failing

  1) palindrome-test should return false for argument dude:
     AssertionError: expected true to be false
      at Context.<anonymous> (test/palindrome-test.js:20:39)
...coverage details not shown...
```

It's time to replace the trivial implementation with a more realistic code to make this test pass. Let's modify the palindrome function in the file palindrome.js:

```
module.exports = function(phrase) {
  return phrase.split('').reverse().join('') === phrase;
};
```

After this change to the code, run the tests and make sure all four tests pass. Continue to write the other two tests we added to the test list, but one at a time, keeping to the test-code-run cycle:

```
it('should return true for argument mom mom', function() {
  expect(isPalindrome('mom mom')).to.be.true;
});

it('should return false for argument mom dad', function() {
  expect(isPalindrome('mom dad')).to.be.false;
});
```

Let's see the result of running all six tests:

```
  palindrome-test
    ✓ should pass this canary test
    ✓ should return true for argument mom
    ✓ should return true for argument dad
    ✓ should return false for argument dude
    ✓ should return true for argument mom mom
    ✓ should return false for argument mom dad

  6 passing (6ms)
...coverage details not shown...
```

The tests we wrote so far verify that the code works well under normal conditions. Next let's think about a few negative cases.

Create Negative Tests

While writing code and tests, we often think of edge cases, invalid inputs, and various things that could go wrong. Instead of jumping to write code for those immediately, we should write those thoughts down in the test list.

While coding the palindrome function, you may wonder what happens if the phrase is an empty string or if it's blank. Let's jot those cases down:

- ...
- ✓ `mom dad` is not a palindrome
- An empty phrase is not a palindrome
- A phrase with two spaces only is not a palindrome

Should blanks and empty strings be treated as palindromes or not? The specific answer to this and similar questions may vary depending on the application and other factors; whatever the answer, the tests serve to document your decisions and verify that the code holds up to those expectations throughout its lifetime.

Tests Are a Form of Documentation

Tests are a form of documentation. Unlike traditional documentation or specifications, they are live and active documentation that verify code's behavior with each change.

If in the future we want to change how to handle an edge case, we'll have to change the related tests. That's a small price compared to the long-term benefits we get out of these tests.

Let's write one of the new tests—a negative test—in the palindrome-test.js file.

```
it('should return false when argument is an empty string', function() {
  expect(isPalindrome('')).to.be.false;
});
```

Run the tests and notice the new test fails. The implementation of isPalindrome needs to change to meet these new expectations. Let's edit the function in the palindrome.js file:

```
module.exports = function(phrase) {
  return phrase.length > 0 &&
    phrase.split('').reverse().join('') === phrase;
};
```

The newly added check for the length to be greater than 0 should make the negative test pass. However, as we'll see it may not be enough to satisfy the second negative test. Let's add this test to the palindrome-test.js file:

```
it('should return false for argument with only two spaces', function() {
  expect(isPalindrome('  ')).to.be.false;
});
```

Run the tests and notice the failure. The implementation of isPalindrome needs to change yet again to meet these new expectations. Let's edit the function in the palindrome.js file:

```
module.exports = function(phrase) {
  return phrase.trim().length > 0 &&
    phrase.split('').reverse().join('') === phrase;
};
```

Now instead of checking for the length of the given argument, we perform a trim operation and then check. That should help to make all the current tests pass.

Think of other edge cases and variations in the input—for example, multiple blanks, mixed case string, punctuations... What is the right behavior for each of the cases? Express those as tests and alter the implementation to make those tests pass.

Now that we have a few tests to verify the code's behavior, modify the implementation that currently uses the reverse() function to other implementations you can think of. Try your different ideas and run the tests to check if those alternative implementations satisfy the behavior expected of the function.

Besides thinking about positive and negative tests, we also have to verify that the code throws any exceptions as expected. Let's explore exception tests next.

Create Exception Tests

JavaScript is dynamic and flexible, which means more power to us, but it's also error prone. For instance, what if the isPalindrome function is called without any arguments? Would the code handle that? Will JavaScript quietly misbehave, or simply blow up? We have to think through scenarios like this and program defensively to get the most of the language.

If the parameter is absent we could return false, throw an exception, play sad music... Whatever you decide, express that behavior as a test. If you'd like to design the code to throw an exception, then express your intention using an exception test.

An exception test should pass if and only if the code fails in the way expected; otherwise the test should fail. For the palindrome problem, let's decide to throw an invalid argument exception if no argument is passed. Let's write the test first, again in the palindrome-test.js file.

```
it('should throw an exception if argument is missing', function() {
  var call = function() { isPalindrome(); };
  expect(call).to.throw(Error, 'Invalid argument');
});
```

We wrapped the call to isPalindrome within a function assigned to the call variable. In the previous tests we called the code under test directly and verified the result. We can't do that here since the test would blow up due to the exception being thrown by the code under test. Thankfully the expect function is not limited to receiving only values; you may also pass a function as an argument. If a value is passed, expect checks to see if the value matches the expectations specified. On the other hand, if a function is provided, then expect defensively calls that function and examines any exception that may be thrown. If the function throws the exception specified in the throw clause that follows, expect quietly moves on; otherwise it reports a failure.

In the test we assert that the function under test is throwing an Error with the message 'Invalid argument'—the first argument to throw is the exception type and the optional second argument is a string or a regular expression for the expected message. Use a string, if you like, to match that the exact string is contained in the error message. Use a regular expression, if you like, to look for patterns of text in the error message.

For the exception test to pass, the isPalindrome function has to change. Let's edit the palindrome.js file:

```
module.exports = function(phrase) {
  if(phrase === undefined)
    throw new Error('Invalid argument');

  return phrase.trim().length > 0 &&
    phrase.split('').reverse().join('') === phrase;
};
```

The code does a preemptive strike to check if the parameter is undefined and, if so, throws an Error with the desired failure message.

Let's run the tests to be sure all of them now pass after the previous change.

```
  palindrome-test

    ✓ should pass this canary test

    ✓ should return true for argument mom

    ✓ should return true for argument dad

    ✓ should return false for argument dude

    ✓ should return true for argument mom mom

    ✓ should return false for argument mom dad

    ✓ should return false when argument is an empty string

    ✓ should return false for argument with only two spaces

    ✓ should throw an exception if argument is missing

  9 passing (11ms)
...coverage details not shown...
```

All of the positive, negative, and exception tests are passing. With the aid of these tests, we incrementally created the minimal code to meet the expectations set in those tests. As we evolved the code, the new tests helped uncover design details, while the old tests ensured that the code continued to meet the expectations expressed thus far. Such feedback can give a reasonable confidence that the code continues to work with each change. Furthermore, any suggestion to improve the implementation can be quickly tried out—the tests will tell us whether or not those suggestions are keepers.

Measure Server-Side Code Coverage

Code coverage reports can be quite valuable. A code coverage report quickly indicates lines of code not touched by any tests. Istanbul is a pretty good JavaScript tool to create coverage reports. It instruments code, and keeps track of whether each line of code is called and how many times. It gives both line coverage and branch coverage.

The actual code coverage numbers, like 80 percent or 90 percent, are not that important. These numbers are like the cholesterol numbers used to monitor health—a poor value is a cause for concern, but a good value doesn't receive any celebrations. More than the number, a peek at the lines not covered by the tests is more valuable. Also, ensure that the coverage numbers never decrease while the application evolves.

We'll use Istanbul to measure the code coverage of the isPalindrome function we designed. The package.json file in your workspace already references the Istanbul package that was installed when you ran npm install. With each test run, the coverage report was generated and it's been patiently waiting for us to view.

When you run the npm test command, you should see output much like this—the test results and the coverage details:

```
palindrome-test

  ✓ should pass this canary test
               ...
  ✓ should throw an exception if argument is missing

9 passing (10ms)

============================== Coverage summary ==============================
Statements   : 100% ( 4/4 )
Branches     : 100% ( 4/4 )
Functions    : 100% ( 1/1 )
Lines        : 100% ( 4/4 )
==============================================================================
```

The top part of the report is from Mocha. The bottom part shows the coverage details. To look at an elaborate report, open the index.html file under the coverage/lcov-report directory.

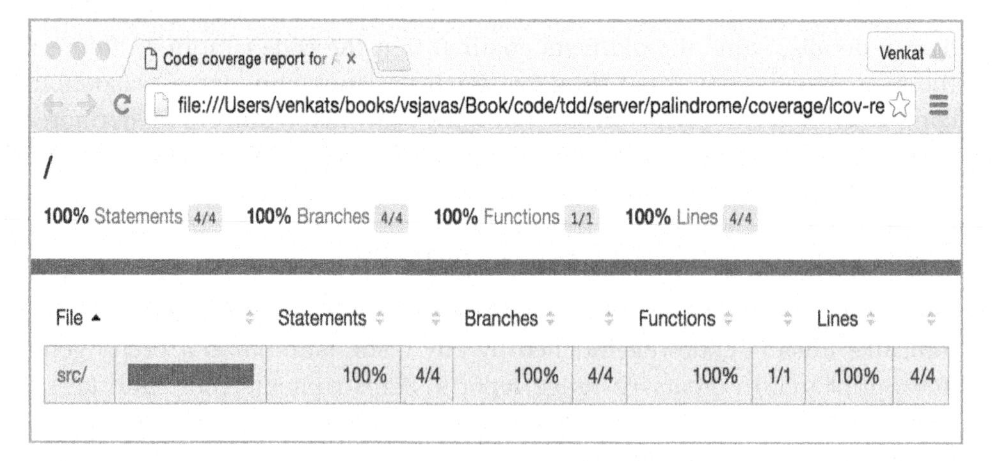

The top-level view shows we have good coverage. Click on the src link and drill down to the source file–level coverage to see the line-by-line coverage report.

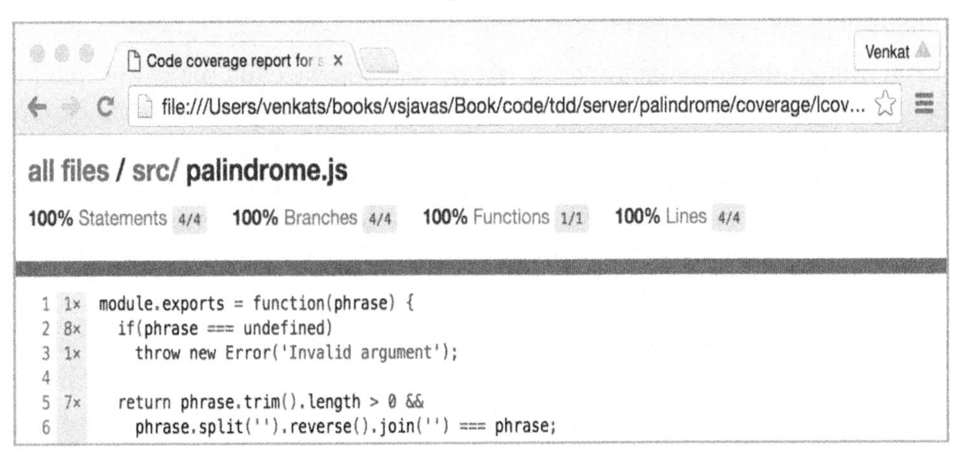

The count next to the line shows the number of times that line was exercised. If one or more lines of code were not covered by any tests, then the entire line will be highlighted red, instead of the count being highlighted in green. Since we only had one exception test, the line with the throw clause shows 1.

Suppose, instead of first writing the exception test, we sneaked in the code to throw the exception. Then the coverage report will expose that, like so:

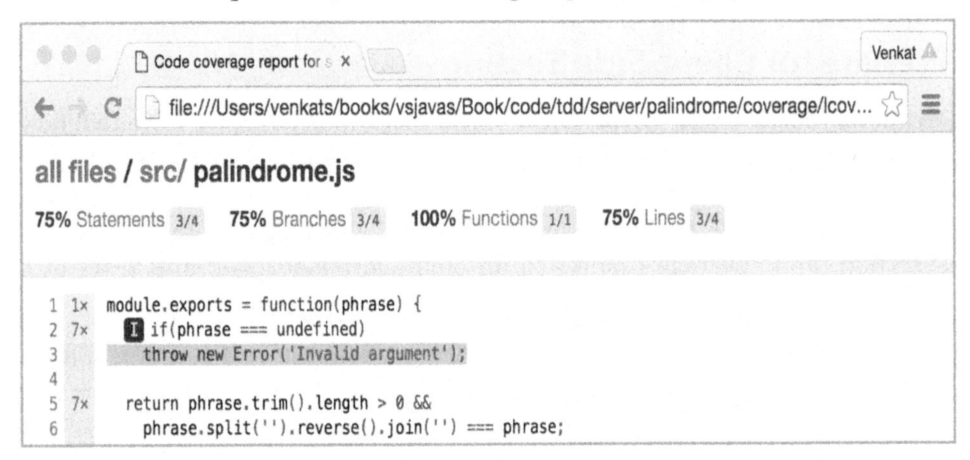

While we all want to believe that we'd never sneak in code without tests, there's a significant imperfect part of us called *human*. We can rely on the code coverage tools to keep an eye out for code that sneaks in without tests.

While a coverage report is useful, don't rely on it too much. A red highlighted line in the report clearly calls out missing tests, but green doesn't mean the code is well tested. For example, remove the negative tests and run the coverage. The report will still show all green, albeit with lower coverage counts, because the positive test exercises both conditions in the code and the coverage report does not show the lack of tests.

Even though the coverage report is not perfect and we can't make any claims about the health of the application based on the report, I use it quite extensively. In my experience, anytime I've noticed uncovered code, it also pointed to either poor-quality code or a design flaw that needed refactoring. As far as the coverage report not catching missing tests, good code reviews compensate for that. In my projects, we not only review code, we also review tests—this has helped create better-quality code and tests.

We've written automated tests for code that runs in Node.js, but we've barely scratched the surface. Later in the book, you will learn about testing more server-side code—asynchronous code, code with dependencies, and code running in Express.

We've seen how to set up the tools and write tests for server-side code. Let's shift gears and talk about testing client-side code. The structure and the syntax of the tests are going to look a lot similar to what we've seen on the server side. However, the environment to run the tests in and the tools that will help us achieve that are going to be a lot different. Let's explore the client-side test automation next.

Prepare for Client-Side Testing

To automatically verify the behavior of the client-side code, we have to follow a few steps: load the code and the tests into different browsers, execute the tests, assert expectations, and generate a report of the run. The three tools we already looked at, Mocha, Chai, and Istanbul, can help with test execution, assertion, and coverage report. To automatically load code and tests into browser—that's where Karma comes in.

Karma is a lightweight server that manages the loading and running of tests in different browsers. You can tell Karma what browsers you'd like to use and also what testing tools to employ, and Karma takes care of the rest.

Karma can run in auto watch mode, which means that anytime any code under the current directory hierarchy changes, Karma can automatically rerun tests. This is a great feature to use; during the short test-code cycle, you don't have to take the extra effort to run the tests. Simply save the file you're working on and Karma will notice the change and rerun the tests.

We'll re-create the tests for the palindrome function, this time to run on the client-side browsers instead of within Node.js. Karma will take care of loading the tests and the code within the browser for testing. Before using Karma, we first have to set up a project for the client-side example—that's the next step.

Switch to the Client-Side Project

For the server-side project we used only three tools. For the client side, we need a lot more. Instead of manually installing each one of them, we'll employ another pre-created package.json file.

In your workspace, change to the tdd/client/palindrome directory and take a look at the package.json file in that directory:

tdd/client/palindrome/package.json

```
{
  "name": "palindrome2",
  "version": "1.0.0",
  "description": "",
  "main": "index.js",
  "scripts": {
    "test": "karma start --reporters clear-screen,dots,coverage"
  },
  "author": "",
  "license": "ISC",
  "devDependencies": {
    "chai": "^3.5.0",
    "istanbul": "^0.4.4",
    "karma": "^1.1.2",
    "karma-chai": "^0.1.0",
    "karma-chrome-launcher": "^1.0.1",
    "karma-clear-screen-reporter": "^1.0.0",
    "karma-cli": "^1.0.1",
    "karma-coverage": "^1.1.1",
    "karma-mocha": "^1.1.1",
    "mocha": "^3.0.1"
  }
}
```

That's a boatload of dependencies, but we can install all of them in a snap onto your system using this command:

```
npm install
```

The dependencies include Mocha, Chai, and Istanbul, but there are also plugins for Karma to interact with these tools. The Chrome launcher plugin is necessary to run the tests within the Google Chrome browser. If you like to use other browsers, like Firefox, then include the appropriate plugins.

You may wonder about the purpose for the karma-clear-screen-reporter package in the list of dependencies. If you're a fan of keeping the console clean, this plugin will make you happy. When Karma reruns the tests, upon seeing the code or test change, it displays the output on the terminal right below the output from the previous runs. A quick glance at the test run can be frustrating. You'll have to discern the output of the latest run from the previous runs. The karma-clear-screen-reporter solves that issue. It will clear out the console before Karma kicks in to run the tests—this helps to keep your eyes focused on the current test run results.

Now that we have the tools installed, we're almost set to write our first test, but there's one final step. We need to configure Karma to tell it what to use and where the files are. Let's do that next—again in this section you'll do it manually to learn the steps, but in later examples we'll use a pre-created file to save time and effort.

Configure Karma

To successfully run and do its job, Karma needs to know a few things. It needs details on the automated testing tool you like to use, where your test files are located, where to look for the source files, and what other tools, like the coverage tool, you would like it to run. Karma expects you to provide these details through a configuration file.

If no filename is provided, Karma reads a configuration file named karma.conf.js. We'll create this file under your current workspace directory tdd/client/palindrome. Instead of hand-creating this file, we can use the following interactive command to create it with the details we desire:

```
node node_modules/karma/bin/karma init
```

When you run this command, it will interactively ask you about the testing framework and the browsers you like to use. Enter the following details for each of the questions it asks:

- Testing Framework: It offers Jasmine by default; tab until you see Mocha and then hit enter.
- Want to use Require.js: Take the default 'no'.
- Browser to capture: Select Chrome and then hit enter twice.
- Hit enter to take the default for all other questions.

After running the previous command and providing the inputs, you'll see a file named karma.conf.js in the current directory. Edit that file to include chai and the location of the source files, like so:

tdd/client/palindrome/karma.conf.js

```
//...
// frameworks to use
// available frameworks: https://npmjs.org/browse/keyword/karma-adapter
frameworks: ['mocha', 'chai'],

// list of files / patterns to load in the browser
files: [
  './test/**/*.js',
  './src/**/*.js'
],
//...
```

While you have the config file open, take a look at the browsers: setting:

tdd/client/palindrome/karma.conf.js

```
// start these browsers
// available browser launchers:
//   https://npmjs.org/browse/keyword/karma-launcher
browsers: ['Chrome'],
```

Even though we only asked Karma to run Chrome, you can list any number of browsers and Karma will run the tests in each one of them. Make sure to include your target browsers in this list to verify that the code works well in each one of them.

Now we're all set to write our tests and run them using Karma.

Start with a Canary Test

We already used Mocha and Chai to create tests for the server side. Since we're using the same tools for the client-side testing, syntax-wise the tests for the client side will look the same as the server-side tests. The main difference will be how we *require* files and run the tests. Let's start with a canary test to get comfortable with those steps.

Open the file named palindrome-test.js in the tdd/client/palindrome/test directory and enter the following code:

tdd/client/palindrome/test/palindrome-test.js

```
describe('palindrome-test', function() {
  it('should pass this canary test', function() {
    expect(true).to.be.true;
  });
});
```

Let's get this client-side canary singing—run npm test to run Karma.

With just a few keystrokes, you asked Karma to do multiple things: start a server, internally generate an HTML file to launch in the browsers, load up the JavaScript files you mentioned in the configuration file, start the browsers you asked for in the configuration file, run the tests, and report the results. I'm almost breathless listing the things Karma does, but it gets through them in a breeze. Right after that it faithfully waits for you to make changes to files so it can rerun the tests upon seeing the change.

When you run the command npm test, you'll see Chrome pop up and execute the test. Then Karma sits there waiting for you to make a code or test change. If you want to run the tests just once, and shut down the browser(s) automatically at the end, change the test command in the package.json file to add the --single-run option, like so:

```
"scripts": {
  "test": "karma start --reporters clear-screen,dots,coverage --single-run"
},
```

Regardless of which options you chose to run Karma, it will report the result of running the tests. The dots reporter will display a dot for each test as it runs. This can be useful feedback when there are large number of tests to run and if you're impatient like me to know that things are progressing and not blocked. Here's our canary singing at the issue of the previous command:

```
.
Chrome 48.0.2564 (Mac OS X 10.10.5):
  Executed 1 of 1 SUCCESS (0.009 secs / 0.001 secs)
```

Now that we have the canary test working, let's proceed to the real tests for the palindrome function on the client side.

Design Client-Side Code

JavaScript that runs within browsers poses some additional challenges. You'll want to check that the code

- Works well in all target browsers
- Interacts properly with the server
- Correctly acts on user commands

That's a lot of stuff to take care of and we have the rest of the book to walk through these concerns. Right now, we'll take the first step toward that goal—using a small example, you'll learn how to load code into a browser and run multiple automated tests.

We've already implemented the isPalindrome function, with tests, to run on the server side within Node.js. We're all set to implement the same function for the client side to run within a browser.

Open the file tdd/client/palindrome/test/palindrome-test.js in your workspace and add the following test below the canary test:

tdd/client/palindrome/test/palindrome-test.js
```
it('should return true for argument mom', function() {
  expect(isPalindrome('mom')).to.be.true;
});
```

That test is pretty much what we wrote on the server side—the only difference is there is no require at the top of the file to bring in the isPalindrome function into scope. Karma and the browser will collaborate to take care of bringing that on board. Open the file tdd/client/palindrome/src/palindrome.js and add the minimum code to make this test pass:

```
var isPalindrome = function(phrase) {
  return true;
};
```

That's also kind of what we wrote as minimum code to make the first test pass on the server side except for one difference—instead of modules.exports = we have var isPalindrome =, a regular function instead of an exported function.

Typically we include JavaScript files within HTML pages using the <script> tag. Karma will do that for us without any effort on our part. Run npm test and watch Karma load the test and source file into the browser, and run the tests.

Continue along one test at a time to design the isPalindrome function for the client side. The tests you write will pretty much follow the same steps we took for the server-side tests. The isPalindrome function, likewise, will evolve incrementally to meet the expectations of the tests. Even though the code is going to look similar to the code we wrote for the server side, this is a good exercise to practice the concepts and the use of the client-side tools.

When done, compare the content of the tdd/client/palindrome/test/palindrome-test.js file that you evolved in your workspace to the code listed here:

tdd/client/palindrome/test/palindrome-test.js
```
describe('palindrome-test', function() {
  it('should pass this canary test', function() {
    expect(true).to.be.true;
  });

  it('should return true for argument mom', function() {
    expect(isPalindrome('mom')).to.be.true;
  });

  it('should return true for argument dad', function() {
    expect(isPalindrome('dad')).to.be.true;
  });
```

```
  it('should return false for argument dude', function() {
    expect(isPalindrome('dude')).to.be.false;
  });

  it('should return true for argument mom mom', function() {
    expect(isPalindrome('mom mom')).to.be.true;
  });

  it('should return false for argument mom dad', function() {
    expect(isPalindrome('mom dad')).to.be.false;
  });

  it('should return false when argument is an empty string', function() {
    expect(isPalindrome('')).to.be.false;
  });

  it('should return false for argument with only two spaces', function() {
    expect(isPalindrome('  ')).to.be.false;
  });

  it('should throw an exception if argument is missing', function() {
    var call = function() { isPalindrome(); };
    expect(call).to.throw(Error, 'Invalid argument');
  });
});
```

Also, compare the file tdd/client/palindrome/src/palindrome.js that you changed in your workspace with the listing here:

tdd/client/palindrome/src/palindrome.js

```
var isPalindrome = function(phrase) {
  if(phrase === undefined)
    throw new Error('Invalid argument');

  return phrase.trim().length > 0 &&
    phrase.split('').reverse().join('') === phrase;
};
```

Run npm test to run the tests and observe the tests passing:

```
.........
Chrome 48.0.2564 (Mac OS X 10.10.5):
  Executed 9 of 9 SUCCESS (0.017 secs / 0.003 secs)
```

Mocha reports all the tests as passing from within the Chrome browser. If you wrote that code incrementally and got it working, give yourself a high-five. Go ahead, no one's watching.

Karma makes life easy, but a word of caution. When creating the files, be sure the path of the directory where the JavaScript files are located doesn't have a whitespace in it. For example, a path named c:\my projects\palindrome\..., where there's a space between the words my and projects, is bad Karma—the tool chokes up on some operating systems and does not produce any useful error message.

We wrote and exercised tests for the client side. Next, study the coverage report.

Measure Client-Side Code Coverage

We used Istanbul to measure the coverage of server-side code. The same tool can be used for client side as well. The package.json file we used for the client-side project in the workspace already had the necessary tools listed, Istanbul and the necessary Karma plugin. Also, the test command already specified that the coverage report be generated with each test run. All we have to do is take a peek at the coverage report file—well, almost. We need a small tweak to the karma.conf.js file in the tdd/client/palindrome directory:

tdd/client/palindrome/karma.conf.js

```
// preprocess matching files before serving them to the browser
// available preprocessors:
//   https://npmjs.org/browse/keyword/karma-preprocessor
preprocessors: {
  '**/src/*.js': 'coverage'
},

// test results reporter to use
// possible values: 'dots', 'progress'
// available reporters: https://npmjs.org/browse/keyword/karma-reporter
reporters: ['progress', 'coverage'],
```

We added the location of the source files that need to be instrumented for coverage to the preprocessors property. We also asked Karma to use the coverage report by changing the reporters property.

Save the changes to the karma.conf.js file and run npm test. When Karma is run, Istanbul will now instrument the source code, measure the code coverage, and generate a report. Take a look at the coverage directory that is created. Drill down into the subdirectory named for the browser you're using to run the tests—Chrome in our case—and open the index.html file using your favorite browser.

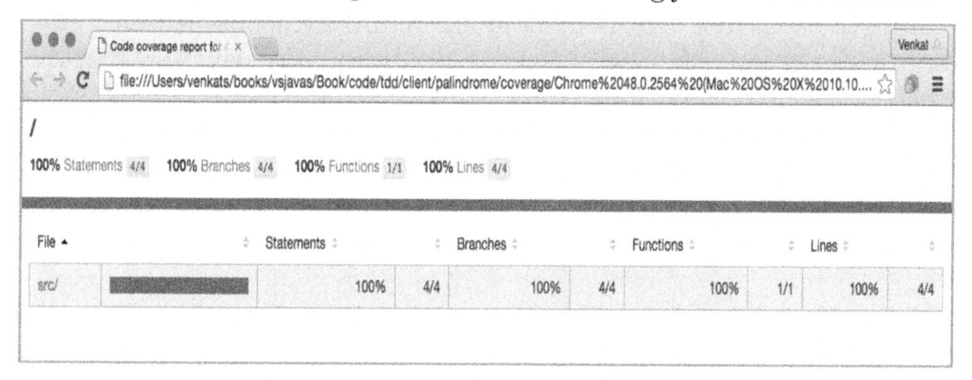

The top-level view shows we have good coverage. Click on the src link and navigate to the source file–level coverage to see the line-by-line coverage report, just like we did for the server-side code.

Getting the coverage report took little effort overall. There's nothing to stand in the way of your team keeping an eye on the code coverage as the code is evolved with tests.

Wrapping Up

Automated tests give us the benefit of regression. Writing those tests alongside writing the code, instead of after, has an added benefit—it can help shape the design. For a piece of code to be verified automatically, it has to be modular, cohesive, and decoupled.

In this chapter we dipped our toes into test-driven design. You learned to use Mocha, Chai, Karma, and Istanbul to write tests, run them, and keep an eye on the coverage. We used the same set of tools to write tests for both server- and client-side code. The tests were not really different—the main difference was in how we brought in the functions being tested. That will change when we start doing server-side and client-side specific coding.

Testing methods that take in an input and return a response is rather easy, but that's not the only kind of code we deal with every day. Now that this chapter has given us the foundation, we'll tackle those gnarly asynchronous functions in the next chapter.

CHAPTER 3

Test Asynchrony

JavaScript libraries are filled with async functions. For example, to read a file, give the filename to the *fs* library and it'll get back later with data or an error. Likewise, talking to services involves async functions—we can't escape asynchrony. Let's embrace asynchrony with automated tests.

Writing and executing automated tests for asynchronous functions poses some challenges. A call to a synchronous function blocks and waits for the result. However, a call to an asynchronous function is nonblocking and the result or error will arrive later through callbacks or promises. To write automated verifications for async functions, you need to go beyond the techniques you learned in the previous chapter.

Let's focus now on testing asynchronous functions and temporarily set aside our desires for test-first design. Doing so will help us to more easily explore the nitty-gritty details of writing tests for asynchronous functions. We will write tests that run within Node.js and tests that run within browsers. To meet this goal, we'll start with pre-created asynchronous functions. The techniques you learn here will help you in the later chapters when we take on the test-first approach.

To verify async functions, you have to deal with two issues. Since results may not arrive immediately after you make the calls, you'll have to make the tests wait for the results to show up in the callbacks or through promises. Also, you have to decide how long to wait for the results—the timeout. Set the timeout too low, tests fail prematurely. Set it too long, and you'll wait longer than necessary if a function were to become nonresponsive. These efforts may seem overwhelming, but tools and techniques are available to effectively deal with these challenges.

We'll first explore testing functions that use callbacks; then we'll dig into promises. Let's get started.

Server-Side Callbacks

A caller of a synchronous function blocks until it gets the result or the intended action is completed. But calls to asynchronous functions are nonblocking. A caller of such functions typically sends one or more callback functions as extra parameters and moves on. Asynchronous functions that use callbacks eventually invoke one or more callbacks when the processing is completed. It's through these callbacks that they indirectly send a response back to the caller. The difference in the nature of the functions poses some challenges from the point of view of testing.

Due to the nature of the call, a test for a synchronous function automatically waits for the result to arrive. The test for an asynchronous function needs to induce a wait since the call is nonblocking. Introducing a sleep or delay in execution will not suffice. For one, it will make tests run slower. Furthermore, there is no guarantee the asynchronous function has responded within the duration of delay. Rather, we need a reliable mechanism to test these functions. Let's explore this with an example.

The function we'll test reads a given file and returns the number of lines in it. It currently has no tests—we'll write the tests for it together.

We'll first write a test naively for the asynchronous function, like we did for the synchronous functions. You'll learn from that experience the reasons why asynchronous testing needs to be different. Then we'll write a proper asynchronous test and make it pass. Finally we'll write a negative test for the asynchronous function as well. Let's get started.

A Naive Attempt to Test

Let's first approach testing an asynchronous function like we approached tests of synchronous functions. This exercise will get you familiar with the code to be tested and also help you see why a different testing approach is necessary.

Switch to a new `files` project by changing to the `tdjsa/async/files` directory in your workspace. The tools we'll use in this project are Mocha and Chai. Let's get them installed right away by running the `npm install` command in the current project directory—this will be our routine each time we step into a project directory and see a `package.json` file in the directory.

Take a look at the code in the src/files.js file. You'll see a function that takes a filename and eventually returns, through callbacks, either the number of lines in the file or an error.

async/files/src/files.js

```
var fs = require('fs');

var linesCount = function(fileName, callback, onError) {
  var processFile = function(err, data) {
    if(err) {
      onError('unable to open file ' + fileName);
    } else {
      callback(data.toString().split('\n').length);
    }
  };

  fs.readFile(fileName, processFile);
};

module.exports = linesCount;
```

Let's write a test for this function, using the approach we've used for synchronous functions so far. Open the empty file test/files-test.js in the current files project in the workspace and enter the following code:

```
var expect = require('chai').expect;
var linesCount = require('../src/files');

describe('test server-side callback', function() {
  it('should return correct lines count for a valid file', function() {
  //Good try, but this will not actually work
    var callback = function(count) {
      expect(count).to.be.eql(-2319);
    };

    linesCount('src/files.js', callback);
  });
});
```

We want to verify that the linesCount function correctly returns the number of lines in a given file. But for that, we need to pass a filename as a parameter. It's hard to predict what files are available on different systems. But we both know that the source code file exists on our system, so we will use that filename as a parameter to the linesCount function.

At the top of files-test.js, the file containing the code under test is loaded and the function within that file is assigned to the variable named linesCount. The test calls the linesCount function, sends it the name of the source file as the filename, and registers a callback function. Within the callback the test asserts that the count received as the parameter is -2319. We know that the count of number of lines can't be negative—clearly the test is broken. If all went well this test should report a failure, but we'll see what happens.

Let's run the test with the command npm test. When run, the test passes instead of failing, as we see in the output:

```
test server-side callback

  ✓ should return correct lines count for a valid file

1 passing (5ms)
```

From the automation point of view, there's nothing worse than tests that lie. Tests should be highly deterministic and should pass only for the right reasons. This test called the linesCount function, passed a filename and a callback, and immediately exited. There is nothing in the test that tells Mocha to wait for the callback to be executed. So, the test did not actually wait to exercise the assert that's within the callback when it's eventually called. It would be nice if tests failed when there are no asserts in their execution path, but that's not the case, as we saw.

We need to tell Mocha not to assume that the test is complete when it exits out of the test function. We need the tool to wait for the execution of the callback function, and the assert within that, before it can declare the test to have passed or failed.

This example serves as a good reminder to make each test fail first and then, with minimum code, make it pass. Let's make the test fail first.

Writing an Asynchronous Test

Tests written using Mocha can include a parameter that can be used to signal the actual completion of tests. When a test exits, Mocha will wait for the signal that the test is actually completed. If an assertion fails before this signal is received or if the signal is not received within a reasonable time, it will declare the test as failure.

Let's edit the test so that exiting the test does not imply completion of the test:

```
it('should return correct lines count for a valid file', function(done) {
  var callback = function(count) {
    expect(count).to.be.eql(-2319);
  };

  linesCount('src/files.js', callback);
});
```

Unlike the previous tests, this test takes on a parameter—it can be named anything you like, but done is quite logical. It's a way to signal to Mocha when a test is really complete. In other words, if a parameter is present, Mocha does not assume a test is done when it completes the test function. Instead, it waits for a signal through that parameter to declare that the test is done. Whether the function being tested is synchronous or asynchronous, this technique may be used to verify results in callbacks.

Let's run the test now and see it go up in flames, like it should:

```
test server-side callback

  1) should return correct lines count for a valid file

0 passing (9ms)
1 failing

1) test server-side callback
  should return correct lines count for a valid file:

    Uncaught AssertionError: expected 15 to deeply equal -2319
    + expected - actual

    -15
    +-2319

    at callback (test/files-test.js:8:27)
    at processFile (src/files.js:8:7)
    at FSReqWrap.readFileAfterClose [as oncomplete] (fs.js:404:3)
```

To make the test pass, let's change -2319 to 15 in the body of the callback. As an astute reader you may protest, "Wait, won't this test break if the file is changed?" Yes it will, but let's keep our eyes on asynchrony at this time; we'll focus on other concerns later in the book. Here's the change to the callback with the correct expected value:

```
it('should return correct lines count for a valid file', function(done) {
  var callback = function(count) {
    expect(count).to.be.eql(15);
  };

  linesCount('src/files.js', callback);
});
```

The callback verifies the value passed, but when npm test is run again, Mocha reports

```
test server-side callback

  1) should return correct lines count for a valid file

0 passing (2s)
1 failing
```

```
1) test server-side callback
  should return correct lines count for a valid file:
   Error: timeout of 2000ms exceeded.
     Ensure the done() callback is being called in this test.
```

Even though the assert in the callback passed, the test failed after a 2 second wait—the default timeout. That's because the test never signaled its completion. To fix that, we'll add a call to `done()` at the end of the callback function. You'll soon see how to change the default timeout. Here's the modified test:

```
it('should return correct lines count for a valid file', function(done) {
  var callback = function(count) {
    expect(count).to.be.eql(15);
    done();
  };

  linesCount('src/files.js', callback);
});
```

Let's now run `npm test` and see the test passing, but this time for the right reasons:

```
test server-side callback

  ✓ should return correct lines count for a valid file

1 passing (7ms)
```

Let's write another asynchronous test to gain practice, but this time we'll make it a negative test.

A Negative Asynchronous Test

The test we wrote covers only the happy path of the function. The behavior of the function when an invalid file is given needs to be verified as well. Let's write a test for that, again in the test/files-test.js file.

```
it('should report error for an invalid file name', function(done) {
  var onError = function(error) {
    expect(error).to.be.eql('unable to open file src/flies.js');
    done();
  };
  linesCount('src/flies.js', undefined, onError);
});
```

The second test sends an invalid filename—flies instead of files—to the function under test. The test assumes such a misnamed file doesn't exist. Such tests are troublesome—they're brittle and may fail if the dependency changes. Again, we'll address that concern later on.

The second argument to the function is `undefined` since it will not be used during this call. The new third argument is a callback that verifies the error details. Once again, this test takes in the `done` parameter and the callback signals the completion of the test through that. Let's run the test and Mocha should report great success:

```
test server-side callback
  ✓ should return correct lines count for a valid file
  ✓ should report error for an invalid file name
2 passing (8ms)
```

Joe asks:
Does the 3-As Pattern Apply to Async Tests?

Good tests follow the 3-As pattern mentioned in *Create Positive Tests*, on page 26. Asynchronous tests are no exception. The arrange part is followed by the act part, but the assert part is embedded within the callbacks. Even though it may not be apparent, the execution flow of the tests follows the sequence of arrange, act, and assert.

Mocha relies on the parameter of its test functions to know when a test on an asynchronous function is completed. Now that you know how to test asynchronous functions running on the server side, let's explore doing the same for the client side. Along the way, you'll pick up a few more tricks.

Client-Side Callbacks

Like the server side, a number of libraries used on the client side also rely on callbacks. Even if an asynchronous function runs within browsers, verifying its behavior isn't much different. You can use the techniques you learned for server-side code for client-side code as well.

We'll practice testing client-side asynchronous functions using an example that gets the current location of the user, using the *geolocation* API. The project for this example is located under the `tdjsa/async/geolocation` directory in your workspace. This project will make use of Mocha, Chai, Karma, and the plugins that Karma needs to integrate with these tools and with the browser. For a complete list of tools, take a look at the `package.json` file in the current project directory. Also, let's take a minute to install these tools by running the `npm install` command in the current project directory.

The code to test is in the file `src/fetch.js`. Let's take a quick look at it:

async/geolocation/src/fetch.js

```
var fetchLocation = function(onSuccess, onError) {
  var returnLocation = function(position) {
    var location = {
      lat: position.coords.latitude, lon: position.coords.longitude };

    onSuccess(location);
  };

  navigator.geolocation.getCurrentPosition(returnLocation, onError);
};
```

The geolocation API is asynchronous, since getting the location from cell towers or GPS satellites is not an instantaneous operation. If all goes well, the fetchLocation function retrieves the latitude and the longitude values of the current location.

First, the function merely passes the onError argument to the getCurrentPosition function. Second, it registers its own callback for the success scenario, processes the response to get the desired values, and sends it to the onSuccess callback.

The test for the happy path of this function will be much like the test we wrote for the linesCount function. However, we need to increase the timeout from the default 2 seconds. Chances are, more time will be needed to get the location; if left to the default value the test may fail before the response arrives. We'll set a timeout value of 10 seconds or 10000 ms. Let's enter the following code in the test/fetch-test.js file in the current project:

async/geolocation/test/fetch-test.js

```
describe('fetch location test', function() {
  it('should get lat and lon from fetchLocation', function(done) {
    var onSuccess = function(location) {
      expect(location).to.have.property('lat');
      expect(location).to.have.property('lon');
      done();
    };

    var onError = function(err) {
      throw 'not expected';
    };

    this.timeout(10000);

    fetchLocation(onSuccess, onError);
  });
});
```

Before calling the fetchLocation function, the test sets the timeout to a reasonably higher value than the default. Then within the onSuccess callback it verifies that the response received has some expected values and calls the done function to signal test completion. If the onError callback was called, instead of the expected onSuccess, then the test will report a failure.

To run the test we need to fire up Karma. The necessary karma.conf.js file is already provided for your convenience in this project directory. Run npm test to exercise Karma, which will load the whole shebang of tools into the browser and run the test.

Karma will launch Chrome, which in turn will ask your permission to get your current location.

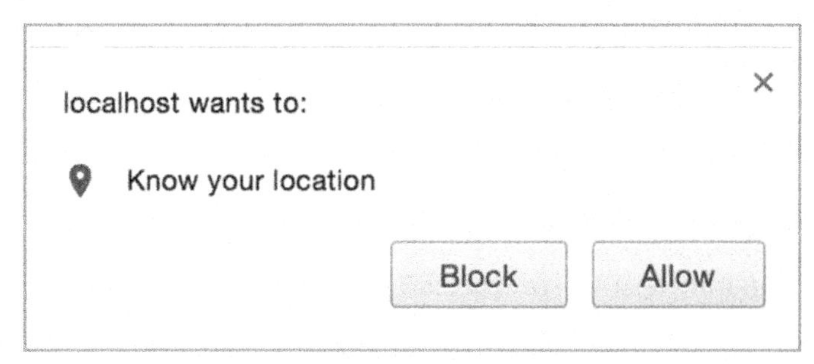

Swiftly click the Allow button. Karma will close the browser and report the test passing—hopefully—as long as you gave permission within 10 seconds and the API was able to get the location.

```
.
Chrome 48.0.2564 (Mac OS X 10.10.5):
  Executed 1 of 1 SUCCESS (6.017 secs / 6.011 secs)
```

This test has some lessons to teach us, both good and bad.

On the good side, it showed how to set up and run tests for asynchronous functions on the client side. Also, it illustrated why and how to set the timeout. It demonstrated how Karma launches and closes down an interactive browser like Chrome when we run in the single-run mode—that's what we asked in the npm test command in the package.json file.

On the bad side, this and the earlier tests in this chapter showed us the difficulties that dependencies create for test automation. The test for fetchLocation is actually manual since it requires intervention to permit the location API to fetch the user's location. Furthermore, if the permission is denied or not given in a reasonable time, the test will fail. The test will also bomb if the API could not get the location. Finally, the test execution was slow compared to the other tests we've run so far. In other words, without any change to code, a test that's passing may end up failing for so many reasons—that's preposterous. Automated tests that fail once in a while are a sign of pretty poorly designed tests.

These examples have helped you learn how to write tests for asynchronous functions. Realistically, however, the code has to be structured differently to get the most out of automated testing. You'll learn how to do that and appropriately deal with dependencies in the next chapter.

Asynchronous functions have traditionally used callbacks, but promises are gaining traction in JavaScript. Let's look at writing tests for them next.

Test Your Promises

Now let's explore testing for promises in code running within Node.js. The same techniques work for client-side code that use promises as well. We'll start with a short introduction to promises and then dive into testing code that uses promises.

A Short Introduction to Promises

Before digging into testing promises, let's review how promises works—I promise to keep it short.

Traditionally asynchronous functions have used callbacks. But callbacks have a few drawbacks. Callbacks have to be registered before the asynchronous functions generate any response. For example, when using an instance of XMLHttpRequest, calling the send function before registering a callback with the onreadystatechange property may result in some events being missed. Also, it's hard to compose callbacks—the code become overly verbose and cumbersome when a callback in turn has to invoke other asynchronous functions and register other callbacks.

Promises don't have those issues and that's one of the reasons they're gaining in popularity. Functions that use promises immediately return a Promise object in response to calls. They then respond to the caller through the Promise object.

Promises more clearly express the intent of asynchrony than callbacks do. Here's a figure that shows the propagation of promises through a series of function calls.

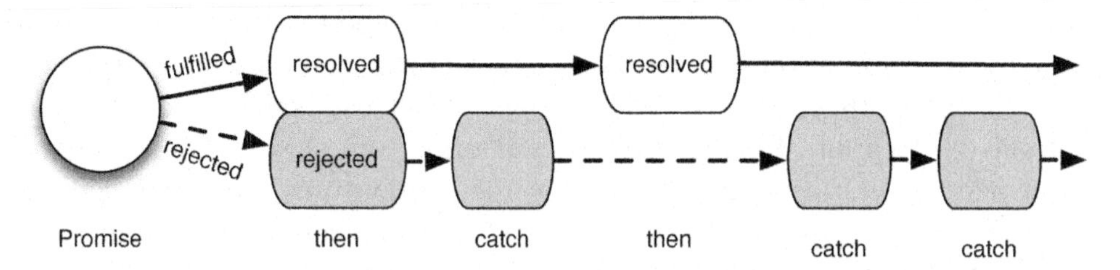

Code that uses promises may form a chain of then and catch calls. Either the top path or the bottom path in the chain is taken, depending on whether a promise is resolved or rejected. If the Promise is resolved, then the *resolved* part of the then function will transform the resolved value and pass it on, as a Promise, to the next receiver in the chain. On the other hand, if the Promise is rejected, then a series of catch functions transform the rejected reason through the call chain. This chain may also optionally include the *rejected* part of the then function.

Types of Asynchronous Tests for Promises

Let's turn our attention to testing functions that return promises. Even though a function returns a Promise, the intended task of the function may not have completed yet—well, it's *asynchronous*. A test on that function will have to wait for the promise to either be *resolved* or *rejected*.

Some tools like Mocha provide special testing capabilities for testing functions that return promises. Mocha's asynchronous tests come in two flavors:

1. The tests may take a done parameter, which can be used to signal test completion.
2. The tests themselves may return a Promise to signal the eventual test completion.

The first flavor may be used for functions with callbacks and functions with promises. The second option, obviously, is intended for functions with promises.

Promises in Functions vs. Promises in Tests

We're focused on testing functions with promises. Any JavaScript testing tool can be used to test such functions. However, some tools also provide the capability to return promises from tests.

Let's explore, with an example, the different ways to write tests for promises and discuss the pros and cons of each.

A Promise Returning Function

We'll practice testing with promises using a modified version of the linesCount function we saw earlier. Let's switch to a new promises project by changing to the tdjsa/async/promises directory in your workspace. In this project, we'll use the now familiar Mocha and Chai along with a new package, chai-as-promised, which we'll discuss shortly. Let's take a minute to install these packages by running the npm install command.

A function that returns Promise is already provided in the project. Take a look at the content of the file src/files.js. The function counts the number of lines in a file, much like the earlier version of this function did, but uses promises instead of callbacks.

async/promises/src/files.js
```
var fs = require('fs-promise');

module.exports = function(fileName) {
  var onSuccess = function(data) {
    return Promise.resolve(data.toString().split('\n').length);
  };

  var onError = function(err) {
    return Promise.reject(new Error('unable to open file ' + fileName));
  };

  return fs.readFile(fileName)
           .then(onSuccess)
           .catch(onError);
};
```

The function needs the fs-promise module, but, no worries, it's already included in the dependencies section of the package.json file in the current project. During the run of npm install that module got installed for you along with the other dependencies needed to work with this project.

The good old fs module's functions take callbacks. While the fs-promise module's functions perform the same tasks as functions in the fs modules, they return Promises instead of taking callbacks. Let's take a look at how we use the fs-promise modules in the previous code.

Let's read the function in the file promises/src/files.js from the bottom up. Toward the end of the function, we pass the given filename to the readFile function of fs-promise. The function immediately returns a Promise object upon call. When the readFile function eventually reads the file, it will send the file content to the function registered as parameter to the then call—the onSuccess function. If there was an error reading the file, then it will invoke the function registered with the catch call—the onError function. The onSuccess function figures out the number of lines in the content of the file and returns that data, wrapped in another Promise object. The onError function returns the error details, if any, wrapped in a Promise.

Tests with done()

We can use the same techniques we used to test functions with callbacks to test functions that return promises. Let's start with a test for the happy path through the promise returning the linesCount function. We'll use the done parameter in the test.

Edit the test/files-test.js in the current project and enter the following code for the first test for promises:

async/promises/test/files-test.js

```
var expect = require('chai').expect;
var linesCount = require('../src/files');

describe('test promises', function() {
  it('should return correct lines count for a valid file', function(done) {
    var checkCount = function(count) {
      expect(count).to.be.eql(15);
      done();
    };

    linesCount('src/files.js')
      .then(checkCount);
  });
});
```

The test creates a checkCount verifier function that asserts that the given count is correct and signals that the test is done. Then, the test calls the function under test and registers checkCount as the function to call if the promise returned by linesCount is resolved.

Run npm test on the command prompt from the promises directory. The test will pass when the Promise created within the linesCount function is resolved and the response arrives into the checkCount function. If the Promise were instead rejected within the linesCount function, the test would fail.

It's better for functions to return promises than return callbacks for the reasons discussed earlier. So, we may expect tests for functions that use promises to be better than tests for functions that use callbacks. But the previous test does not have anything special when compared to the tests for functions with callbacks—thankfully, it can be improved. Next, we'll see how to make the test for functions with promises more expressive.

Tests Returning Promises

We can make the test more concise and expressive by returning a Promise from the test. If a test returns a Promise, then Mocha will wait—at most for the duration of timeout—for the Promise to be resolved or rejected before declaring a test done. Let's get a feel for a test that returns a Promise by adding another test to the test/files-test.js file:

async/promises/test/files-test.js

```
it('should return correct lines count - using return', function() {
  var callback = function(count) {
    expect(count).to.be.eql(15);
  };

  return linesCount('src/files.js')
           .then(callback);
});
```

That's a notch better. No done parameter and the function that verifies the result is a bit more concise. It's cool that we can return a Promise and Mocha knows what to do with that. But we can make this more concise with the help of another library.

Using chai-as-promised

Instead of returning the Promise object returned by the function under test, the test can assert that the function under test *eventually* completes with the expected response. To achieve this we will use the chai-as-promised library that was created exclusively for testing promises.

The library chai-as-promised extends the fluent API of Chai with functions to verify promises' responses. To use this module, we first need to add the following line to the test file test/files-test.js:

async/promises/test/files-test.js

```
require('chai').use(require('chai-as-promised'));
```

The use function extends the Chai functions with an eventually property. Finally, instead of the expect...to.be.eql you've seen so far, we'll use the chai-as-promised syntax expect...to.eventually.eql. Let's add a new test to see the eventually feature in action:

async/promises/test/files-test.js

```
it('should return correct lines count - using eventually', function() {
  return expect(linesCount('src/files.js')).to.eventually.eql(15);
});
```

The eventually property tactfully makes the test concise and more expressive. The eventually bundles a Promise that will be resolved if the expression in the expect satisfies the value in the eql. Otherwise, the Promise will be rejected, resulting in the failure of the test.

Mixing eventually and done()

Returning a Promise from a test is a good approach, but not all testing tools offer that capability. If you're using a testing tool that's unaware of promises or if you simply prefer not to return a Promise, you may combine eventually and the done parameter to test functions that return promises. To see how that looks, let's add yet another test:

async/promises/test/files-test.js
```
it('should return correct lines count - using no return', function(done) {
  expect(linesCount('src/files.js')).to.eventually.eql(15).notify(done);
});
```

Both the previous tests are so much more concise than the first test we started out with.

Writing Negative Tests for Promises

Thus far the tests verified the fulfillment or successful resolution of the promise returned by linesCount. Of course, a Promise may be rejected under some execution context and we need to test for that behavior as well.

If an invalid filename were passed to the linesCount function, then the function will respond with a Promise reject. Let's verify that behavior by sending a bad filename as an argument to the function, in a new test.

async/promises/test/files-test.js
```
it('should report error for an invalid file name', function(done) {
  expect(linesCount('src/flies.js')).to.be.rejected.notify(done);
});
```

The rejected property waits for a Promise rejection. If the promise resolves instead or fails to reject in a timely fashion, then the test will fail. If it follows through the expectation, then notify signals the completion of the test.

Just like we did for the eventually call, we may return the Promise instead of using notify for the rejected check. Pick the version you like the most.

The previous test only confirmed that the Promise was rejected, but it's important to verify that proper error was passed upon failure. For that, we can replace rejected with rejectedWith, like in the next test:

async/promises/test/files-test.js
```
it('should report error for an invalid file name - using with',
  function(done) {
  expect(linesCount('src/flies.js'))
    .to.be.rejectedWith('unable to open file src/flies.js').notify(done);
});
```

With Mocha combined with the chai-as-promised library, the tests for both the resolution and rejection of promises are highly concise and expressive.

Let's run npm test and ensure all the different flavors of tests we wrote for promises work. Here's the output from the run:

```
test promises
  ✓ should return correct lines count for a valid file
  ✓ should return correct lines count - using return
  ✓ should return correct lines count - using eventually
  ✓ should return correct lines count - using no return
  ✓ should report error for an invalid file name
  ✓ should report error for an invalid file name - using with

6 passing (12ms)
```

The tests worked like a charm, but what if you're dealing with slow functions? Mocha's default timeout is 2 seconds. If a Promise does not complete within that time, the test will fail. If you want to give a function a bit more time to complete, then use the timeout function, like you did earlier in this chapter.

Wrapping Up

We've made good progress in this chapter. You learned how to write automated verification for asynchronous functions, both on the server side and the client side. The tools make it relatively easy to wait on the asynchronous functions to invoke the callback or respond through a Promise. The tests, unfortunately, are hard to automate due to the dependencies—you'll learn how to fix such issues in the next chapter.

CHAPTER 4

Tactfully Tackle Dependencies

Dependencies arise almost everywhere: when code talks to remote services, read from or write to a file, update the DOM, get the user's location...the list goes on. Dependencies are like taxes—they provide value but can turn into a burden. Keep them to a minimum. From the automated testing point of view, dependencies are irksome. They can make tests nondeterministic, brittle, slow, and cumbersome—we saw the tip of that iceberg in the previous chapter.

Good design is critical to tackling dependencies. You can use some nice tricks and techniques to decouple and replace the dependencies so that the tests are automated and deterministic, and run fast. In this chapter, you'll first learn how to remove dependencies when possible. Then, in cases where the dependencies are intrinsic, you'll explore ways to replace them with test doubles like fakes, stubs, mocks, or spies.

Although test doubles are helpful, use them sparingly. If you're not careful, it's easy to get into a mocking hell. With those cautionary words in mind, let's explore some decoupling techniques. Let's dive in to writing automated tests for a problem with intricate dependencies.

A Problem and Spiking to Learn

First we'll take on a small problem with significant dependencies in it. We'll create an HTML page with a "Locate Me" button. When the user clicks that button, a JavaScript function will invoke the geolocation API to get the user's location. If it succeeds, then the program will display the location on Google Maps. If the request fails, an error message will be displayed on the HTML page.

That's not a hard problem, but thinking through automated tests for this program may not be easy. Setting the mind on writing tests may lead to many confusing questions: where to start, what to test, what do we actually code... When the path is not clear, rely on spiking.

Let's create a quick spike to gain insight into one possible solution to the problem. Once we have something working and a better understanding of how to approach coding for this problem, we can start over, test first.

Switch Over to the Spike Project

To create a spike, we'll use the spike project in your workspace, so change to the tdjsa/tackle/spike directory. To save some typing, make use of the file named index.html, already provided in the workspace, with the following content:

tackle/spike/index.html

```
<!DOCTYPE html>
<html>
  <head>
    <title>Locate Me</title>
  </head>
  <body>
    <button onclick="locate();">Locate Me</button>
    <div id="error"></div>
    <script src="src/locateme.js"></script>
  </body>
</html>
```

The HTML file has a button with an onclick event registered to call a locate function. It also has div element with the id named error. Finally the file refers to a locateme.js file under the src directory.

For this spiking exercise, your mission, should you choose to accept it, involves implementing the locate function in the src/locateme.js file. An empty function is provided in that file for you to fill in. Call the navigator.geolocation.getCurrentPosition function, get the latitude and longitude values from the position, create a URL for Google maps, and set window.location to that URL. If the call to get the geolocation fails, set an error message in the error DOM element.

Don't write any tests at this time. Focus only on the spiking effort. Take a few minutes to spike.

When done, take a look at the package.json file in the current project directory. The dependencies section refers to the http-server package. We'll use this lightweight web server to serve files in the current directory. The command to start the server is given in the package.json file, under the scripts section. The server is asked to use port 8080. Change that to some other port number, like 8082, if there's a port conflict on your system. Run the command npm start to start the server, open your favorite browser, and view http://localhost:8080. Click the "Locate Me" button and ensure that the code created during your spiking effort works. Take the time to fix any errors you may run into—we almost always run into errors.

Gain Insights from Spiking

Once you're done, you may compare the code you created in your spiking session with the following code:

```
//This is a brute-force sample created during a spiking session
var locate = function() {
  navigator.geolocation.getCurrentPosition(
    function(position) {
      var latitude = position.coords.latitude;
      var longitude = position.coords.longitude;

      var url = 'http://maps.google.com/?q=' + latitude + ',' + longitude;
      window.location = url;
    },
    function() {
      document.getElementById('error').innerHTML =
        'unable to get your location';
    });
};
```

The spiking session gives us some helpful insights:

- getCurrentPosition is an asynchronous function. We need to register two event handlers with it—one for success and one for failure.
- When an error is received, we have to navigate the DOM to get the div element to set the error details.
- Given a position we need to extract the latitude and longitude values from it to create the URL for Google maps.
- Setting the location property, which is an implicit variable in the ubiquitous window object, causes the browser to change location.
- That code is one bowl of spaghetti—we need to create a modular design for automated testing.

Remember, testability is a design issue—poorly designed code is hard to test. The first step to tackle dependency in a piece of code should be to remove it, if at all possible. If a dependency in a function is intrinsic, then loosely couple the code to what it relies on, by passing in or injecting the dependency. Then, instead of using a real object or function, you can replace it with test doubles and test for interactions. We'll use the example at hand to learn and apply these design techniques.

Visualize a Modular Design

The locate function that we created during spiking does everything. That's perfect for its intended purpose—to gain insight into the problem at hand. However, the production code we write should not resemble the spike. A function that does a lot generally fails the single responsibility principle,[1] lacks cohesion, and has high coupling. Such code is often expensive and difficult to maintain; also, its behavior is hard to verify quickly.

There are multiple little functions waiting to spring out of that spike to make the design modular and code testable. Let's visualize those little functions, each with a single responsibility and minimum dependencies.

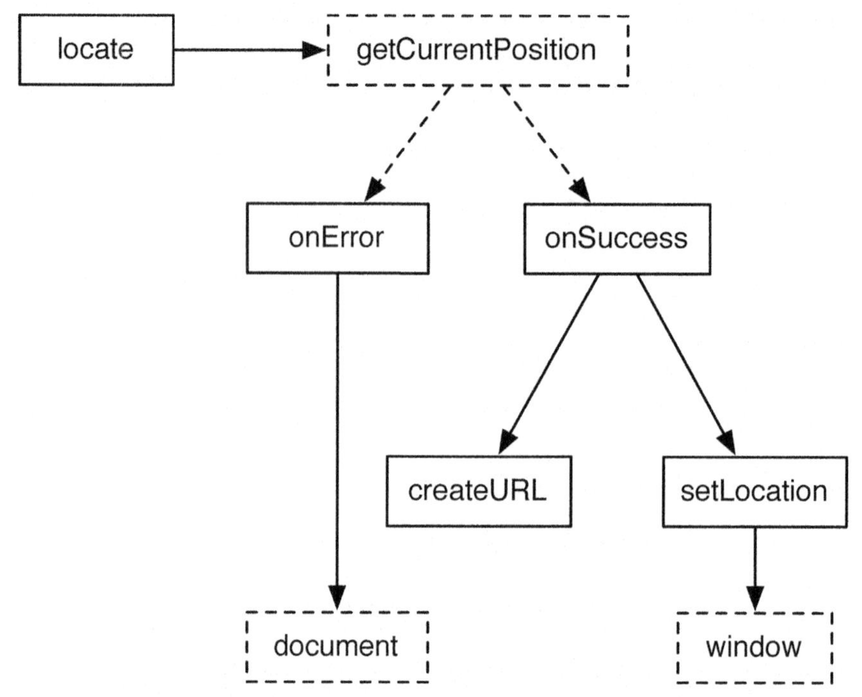

The dotted boxes are the external dependencies and the solid boxes are the code we'd write for the problem at hand. A solid line represents a direct call to a function and a dotted line indicates an asynchronous call. Viewing the design from the bottom of the diagram, the createURL function takes the single responsibility to create the URL, given the values for latitude and longitude. The setLocation function sets the given URL into the location property that is part of the browser-provided window object. The onError function updates the DOM

1. https://en.wikipedia.org/wiki/Single_responsibility_principle

to indicate an error. The onSuccess function extracts the latitude and longitude from a given position and delegates further actions to the functions it depends on. Finally, the only responsibility of the locate function is to register onSuccess and onError with the geolocation's getCurrentPosition function.

Let's automate the tests for each of these functions to verify their behavior. At the end of the series of the following steps, you will know how to deal with dependencies. At the same time, we will have arrived at a fully automated tested version of code to implement the problem at hand.

Separate Dependencies Where Possible

Dependencies play a major part in the overall problem at hand. Looking at the spike, automated testing efforts may appear bleak. But the modular design we visualized is encouraging. The first step toward writing automated tests should be to identify one or more functions with no intrinsic dependencies. Those functions should be the starting point of automated tests.

Looking at the spike, the URL is created right in the middle, after extracting the latitude and longitude from position and before setting the URL into the location. From the testing point of view, in addition to verifying that the URL is created correctly, we must also check that any errors are handled appropriately. But such testing is very hard because the code to create the URL is mixed among dependencies and code that does other things. In reality, though, to create the URL we don't really care where the required values come from or where the created URL goes to. If these values are given to us, we can easily create the URL and return it. That's the single responsibility of the createURL function—separated from the surrounding dependencies.

It's relatively easy to test a piece of code that has no dependencies. Simply call the function under test with sample arguments, and assert that the result is as you'd expect. Let's design the createURL function with tests.

Remove Dependencies Where Possible

As a first step, try to remove dependencies from code being tested as much as possible. Extract the function and pass to it the minimally needed data as parameters.

End Spiking, Prepare for Test Automation

Leave the spike project behind and switch over to the locateme project, under the tdjsa/tackle/locateme directory in your workspace. We want to keep the spiking efforts separate and away from code whose design is being driven using tests. The locateme project contains the following files/directories:

```
index.html
karma.conf.js
package.json
src/
test/
```

index.html is a copy of the file we saw in the spike project. The karma.conf.js file has been initialized to load all the necessary plugins for Karma to run. The package.json file contains mostly the dependencies you're already familiar with: Mocha, Chai, Karma-plugins. There are, however, four new packages related to Sinon. Pretend for now that these do not exist; we'll discuss their purpose later in this chapter.

The src directory has an empty locateme.js file ready for you to edit. The test directory contains a handful of empty test files, also ready for you to edit as you practice along as the example evolves.

Run npm install to get all the dependencies for this project downloaded to your system. Once that's complete, let's step forward to write our first test.

Testing createURL

The sole responsibility of the createURL function is to take the latitude and longitude values as parameters and return a URL for Google maps. That code's like a well-fed baby—you should have no trouble taking care of it. As a first test, let's send two valid arguments and verify that the URL return is a good one.

Let's open the test/create-url-test.js file under the current project, create a test suite, and write the first test, like so:

tackle/locateme/test/create-url-test.js

```
describe('create-url test', function() {
  it('should return proper url given lat and lon', function() {
    var latitude = -33.857;
    var longitude = 151.215;

    var url = createURL(latitude, longitude);

    expect(url).to.be.eql('http://maps.google.com?q=-33.857,151.215');
  });
});
```

The name of the test suite tells us that our focus will be only on the createURL function in the tests in this suite. The test calls the function under test with valid latitude and longitude values and verifies that URL returned is what Google maps would be happy to accept.

Let's write, in the file src/locateme.js, minimum code to make this test pass:

tackle/locateme/src/locateme.js
```
var createURL = function(latitude, longitude) {
  return 'http://maps.google.com?q=' + latitude + ',' + longitude;
}
```

The newly created createURL function merely returns a formatted string with the given arguments in the appropriate position.

Run the command npm test to fire up Karma and exercise this test. Ensure the test is passing. Leave Karma running in the background—it will eagerly wait for us to write the next test.

We can't gain confidence about a piece of code just because one test passes. Let's write another positive test. Again open the test/create-url-test.js file and add the second test below the first one:

tackle/locateme/test/create-url-test.js
```
it('should return proper url given another lat and lon', function() {
  var latitude = 37.826;
  var longitude = -122.423;

  var url = createURL(latitude, longitude);

  expect(url).to.be.eql('http://maps.google.com?q=37.826,-122.423');
});
```

This test merely sends a different set of values to the code under test and verifies the response is as expected. This test will pass with no change to code. Let's move on to a negative test.

Our effort to isolate the code to create the URL from the rest of the code has already paid off—it's now easy to create tests for various what-if scenarios. For example, what if the value of latitude or the longitude is not provided? Let's write a test for the first scenario, but before that we should figure out what the appropriate response should be.

If the latitude is not provided, we could throw an exception, call another function, blame the government, simply return an empty string... Consider different possibilities on how to deal with the situation. On a real project we could consult the domain experts, business analysts, testers, colleagues, fortune tellers... For this project, pick the one that makes most sense to you. Returning an empty string may not a bad idea. It's rare that the values will be missing, and if they end up so, the browser won't move to another URL if the location is set to an empty string. Let's add a test for undefined latitude value:

tackle/locateme/test/create-url-test.js

```
it('should return empty string if latitude is undefined', function() {
  var latitude = undefined;
  var longitude = 188.123;

  var url = createURL(latitude, longitude);

  expect(url).to.be.eql('');
});
```

To make this test pass, in the createURL function we need to check the latitude value and, if it's undefined, return an empty string. Give that a shot and then move on to the next test, to check for the longitude value:

tackle/locateme/test/create-url-test.js

```
it('should return empty string if longitude is undefined', function() {
  var latitude = -40.234;
  var longitude = undefined;

  var url = createURL(latitude, longitude);

  expect(url).to.be.eql('');
});
```

Let's change the createURL function, once more, to make this new test pass:

tackle/locateme/src/locateme.js

```
var createURL = function(latitude, longitude) {
  if (latitude && longitude)
    return 'http://maps.google.com?q=' + latitude + ',' + longitude;
  return '';
};
```

We've driven the design of a small piece of code using automated tests and managed to keep dependencies at bay so far. Take a glance at the command window to ensure Karma is reporting all the four tests written so far as passing. The createURL function was set free from the bondage of dependencies, but the rest of functions need our help. It's time to move on to the next function and deal with the dependencies waiting to crash in on us.

Looking at the design diagram we created in *Visualize a Modular Design*, on page 64, all the prospective functions yet to be implemented have dependencies. Let's take that on next: the testing and design of the setLocation function.

Employ Test Doubles

Test doubles are objects that replace real dependencies to enable automated testing. Test doubles are the automated testing equivalent of movie stunt people —they take the place of the original since having the real one is expensive or impractical. You will learn the role of test doubles using the setLocation function as an example.

The setLocation function is a simple one. It takes a URL for Google Maps and sets that into the location property of the window object, thus instructing the browser to display the map with the user's current location. It's easy to write but may appear hard to test.

We don't want to load an HTML page in a browser, then call the setLocation function to see if the browser navigates to the page at the given URL—that would be manual, not automated. We could write a UI-level test, way up at the top of the test pyramid. But we discussed that if a test can be written at a lower level then we should.

The issue here is that we're setting the location property of the window object that's provided by the browser, and when set, it will respond by making a request to that page. How we test for that, automated and at a lower level, is the real concern.

It turns out we don't have to really test for that. Our goal is not to test if the browser responds to a set of the location. We need to verify that the setLocation function properly sets the location property of a window object—that's right, "a" window and not "the" window. Let's discuss further what that means. We can break the testing for the overall behavior of page navigation into three parts:

1. If window.location is set, the browser will navigate to the set URL. We can separately write tests to confirm this if we're doubtful—say for a new browser or a new version of a browser.

2. If a window object is given to setLocation we can test that the function set a location property on the given window object. JavaScript does not care what object you give it—it's happy to set whatever properties you ask to be set. So, this can be tested without needing the real window object.

3. We can separately test that "the" correct window object is passed to the setLocation function from where it's called.

We'll skip test 1; we can trust the browsers have been well tested. We'll write test 2 shortly and address test 3 later when designing the onSuccess function.

To write the test for setLocation we need a window object, but it does not have to be the real window object—in fact, it shouldn't be. The location property of the window object is implemented in such a special way that it's practically impossible to write non-UI-level automated tests. To avoid that issue, we'll use a test double.

Different names are thrown around for test doubles that replace dependencies during testing: fakes, stubs, mocks, spies. Let's take a few minutes to learn about these and how they differ from each other.

All four types of test doubles stand in for dependencies, and the code being tested will interact with one of them, during testing, instead of talking to their actual dependency.

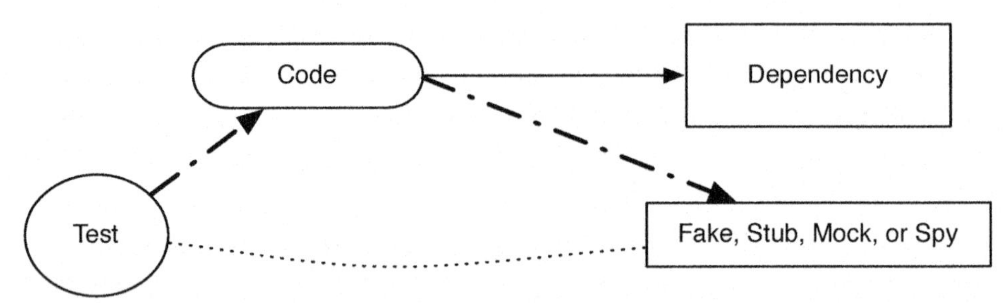

Each of these test doubles has a fairly clear purpose as discussed by Martin Fowler in the blog[2] titled "Mocks Aren't Stubs":

- *Fakes*: These are implementations suitable for testing, but not for production. For example, interacting with a real production credit card service is not practical during testing—no one wants to incur charges each time tests are run. By replacing the production service with a fake during testing, you can get quick feedback that the code handles successes and failures of interacting with the service properly. Credit card processing services offer two services, one for production use and a fake for use during testing.

- *Stubs*: These are not real implementations but may readily return canned response when called. These are useful to verify code's behavior in response to (pre-set) results from its (stub) dependency. Stubs are also useful to verify that the code being tested updates the state of their dependencies properly. It's not a good idea to create one big stub for a dependency. Instead create small stubs in each test, where needed, tailored specifically to help make that test pass.

- *Mocks*: These are like stubs in that they may return canned values. However, these keep track of interactions, like how many times and in what order calls were made. Mocks tattletale about interactions and help verify communication between the code being tested and its dependencies.

2. http://martinfowler.com/articles/mocksArentStubs.html

- *Spies*: Unlike the other three, spies stand as proxies in front of the actual dependency. They may interact with the real service while stubbing or mocking out some select parts. These are useful when interaction with the actual service during testing is not an issue but we still want to verify the interactions or mock out select parts.

Depending on the particular dependency you run into, you'll reach for one of these test doubles. You'd use stubs to verify state while you'd use mocks to verify behavior. In other words, if you're interested in checking if the code under test sets an appropriate state into its dependency, you'd use a stub. On the other hand, if your interest is to verify that the code under test calls the right methods on its dependency, in the right order, then you'd use a mock.

In the rest of this book, you'll see stubs, mocks, and occasionally spies come to the rescue when tackling dependencies. Now that we know what test doubles are and how they can help, let's put them to use to write the automated tests for the setLocation function.

Inject the Dependencies

Dependency injection is a popular and common technique to replace a dependency with a test double. Rather than the code under test asking for its dependency, the dependency is injected—our industry likes fancy words—that is, passed in as an argument at the time of call. Let's learn about this technique using the setLocation function as an example.

We discussed that the setLocation function should set the location property on a window object. What would otherwise be a very complex test to write turns out to be a simple test if we pass—ahem, *inject*—a stub for the window object. Let's write the test for setLocation.

Let's open the test/setlocation-test.js file in the locateme project in your workspace. To this file, we'll add a new test suite named setLocation test to emphasize our focus on the setLocation function. Within that new test suite, we'll write our next test:

tackle/locateme/test/setlocation-test.js

```
describe('setLocation test', function() {
  it('should set the URL into location of window', function() {
    var windowStub = {};
    var url = 'http://example.com';
    setLocation(windowStub, url);

    expect(windowStub.location).to.be.eql(url);
  });
});
```

The test first creates an empty JSON object and assigns it to the windowStub variable. Then it calls the setLocation function, the code under test, with the stub as the first argument and a sample URL as the second argument. Finally, it asserts that the location property of the stub has been set to the desired value.

The windowStub that stands in for the dependency is a stub, and not a mock, because the test wants to know the state of the dependency after a call to the function under test.

It's time to write the necessary code to make this test pass. Let's open the src/locateme.js file and implement the setLocation function right below the createURL function we wrote earlier:

tackle/locateme/src/locateme.js

```
var setLocation = function(window, url) {
  window.location = url;
};
```

The setLocation function is not only simple, but pretty innocent as well. It does not know anything about the total conspiracy that has been woven around it. It genuinely thinks that "the" window object was given to it and loyally updates the location property with the given url parameter. Unknown to it, the url is a fake one created for the test purpose and the window object is a stub and not the real one. Let's wipe those teary eyes—all that trickery is for a greater good and setLocation will fully understand and support our efforts if it ever comes to know about our plot.

This example nicely showed us the benefit of externalizing dependencies. During production runs the appropriate function or object can be passed to the target function for its use, and during test runs a test double can instead be provided—that's *dependency injection* in action.

For Ease of Testing, Inject the Dependencies

Deeply rooted dependencies are hard to replace for testing purposes. Instead of directly creating a dependent object or obtaining it from a global reference, consider passing the needed function or object as a parameter.

Test Interactions

We've tested and implemented the createURL and setLocation functions. That leaves three more functions to be tested and implemented from our modular design diagram. Let's pick the locate function next as that will help us explore a technique we've not seen so far in this book—testing interactions.

The tests we've written so far are all empirical tests. You call a method and assert that it returned a desired result—synchronously or asynchronously. When working with dependencies, often it's hard to predict the results. For example, if code depends on a service that returns the current temperature in Chicago, it's hard to write an empirical test for that code. Interaction tests are better for code with dependencies.

A test for a function is focused on that function's behavior, not the correctness of the dependencies. You want to know how the code behaves when its dependency succeeds. You also want to know that it handles gracefully the failures of its dependency. For these, the code really does not have to access the real dependency during testing. Checking to make sure the code is interacting with the dependency in the right way is sufficient to verify the behavior of the code under test.

Choose Between Empirical vs. Interaction Tests

If the result is deterministic, predictable, and easy to figure out, then use empirical tests.

If the code has intricate dependencies and if that makes the code nondeterministic, hard to predict, brittle, or slow, then use interaction tests.

Let's see why interaction testing is better than empirical testing for the locate function. Our program needs to call the getCurrentPosition function of the geolocation API. The spiking effort brought to light that this function is an asynchronous function that takes time to respond. Furthermore, the response depends on where in the world we are while running the code and the accuracy of the service that responds with the current location. In short, we can't predict the result we eventually get from the getCurrentPosition function. Since we can't rely on the result, there's no point taking the empirical test route.

In our desire to modularize we figured that the locate function can call getCurrentPosition and register two other functions—onSuccess and onError—as callbacks. Our goal is not to verify if getCurrentPosition is eventually returning the correct location—we're not testing getCurrentPosition after all. Our focus here is to test the behavior of the locate function. The responsibility of this function is to call getCurrentPosition and register the two callbacks—that's all we need to test, that interaction of locate with getCurrentPosition.

Let's open the test/locate-test.js file in the current project and add a new test suite and a test:

tackle/locateme/test/locate-test.js
```
describe('locate test', function() {
  it('should register handlers with getCurrentPosition', function(done) {

    var original = navigator.geolocation.getCurrentPosition;

    navigator.geolocation.getCurrentPosition = function(success, error) {
      expect(success).to.be.eql(onSuccess);
      expect(error).to.be.eql(onError);
      done();
    }

   locate();
   navigator.geolocation.getCurrentPosition = original;
  });
});
```

We want to verify that locate called getCurrentPosition, but we can't really let the function call the real geolocation functions during test—the test will get slow, unpredictable, and nondeterministic. We have to replace the getCurrentPosition function with a test double—a stub or a mock. Since we're mainly interested in knowing if locate called its dependency, it will be a mock instead of a stub.

When testing setLocation we injected the dependency. We could have taken the same approach here, but that's not necessary. The locate function gets the getCurrentPosition function from the window's navigator's geolocation property. Unlike the location property of window, the navigator's properties are relatively easy to mock out. That's exactly what we're doing in the test. We make a copy of the original getCurrentPosition function and then replace it with a mock function. At the end of the test, we replace the function within geolocation with the original function.

In the mock function, check that the passed-in values for the first two arguments are the references to the onSuccess and onError functions. These two functions and the locate function don't exist yet, but will come to life soon. The asserts—the calls to expect—are within the mock function. If the locate function never calls getCurrentPosition, then the asserts in the mock function would never run. That scenario should result in a failure. The call to done() is in place for that purpose. If locate calls getCurrentPosition and passes the expected callbacks, the test will pass. If it does not pass the correct parameters, then one of the asserts will fail. If locate does not call getCurrentPosition, then the test will time out since done won't be called to signal the test completion.

It's time to implement the locate method, but its implementation also needs the onSuccess and the onError functions. We can provide an empty implementation for these functions for the moment. Let's open the src/locateme.js file and write the following code right below the setLocation function we implemented earlier.

tackle/locateme/src/locateme.js
```
var locate = function() {
 navigator.geolocation.getCurrentPosition(onSuccess, onError);
};
var onError = function() {}
var onSuccess = function() {}
```

The locate function is pretty straightforward; it calls the getCurrentPosition function and passes the two callbacks that the test expects. We provided temporary placeholders for the event handler functions.

We saw how, instead of letting locate call the real getCurrentPosition function and checking for its results, we instead tested for locate's interaction with its dependency. The benefits of this approach are that the test is fast and predictable. Also, we did not have to deal with the issues of the browser granting or denying permission to access the geolocation.

There is, however, one thing unpleasant in what we did. The test replaced the function with a mock at the beginning of the test and reversed that in the end. This is not only tedious but also highly error prone. Next we'll see how Sinon, a popular mocking library, removes that burden nicely.

Use Sinon to Reduce Noise

The key to writing an automated test for locate was replacing the dependency with a test double. In the test in the file test/locate-test.js, we handmade the mock and manually replaced and restored the getCurrentPosition function. This approach can soon turn into drudgery and make tests verbose and error prone.

A good test doubles library can alleviate the pain significantly. Sinon is one such tool that can be used with any JavaScript testing tool. It's concise, fluent, and powerful—you'll see the tool shine in later chapters when we automate tests for Node.js, Express, and jQuery. Let's use Sinon test doubles instead of the handmade ones.

Set Up Sinon

Sinon complements Karma, Mocha, and Chai, the tool chain used for the tests so far. The Sinon module provides functions to create different types of

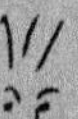

Joe asks:
When Should We Use Sinon Test Double vs. a Handmade Test Double?

Later in this book, you'll see examples that use Sinon to create test doubles, but a few examples will simply use handmade test doubles instead. Here are some guidelines for when to choose Sinon:

- When creating a test double by hand becomes arduous
- When the design and code structure seems to turn overly complex due to the use of a test double
- Where using Sinon may reduce the test size

In short, use Sinon when it brings true value. Don't hesitate to write your own test doubles for simple cases.

test doubles. In addition, the Sinon-Chai module makes the already fluent Chai library more expressive to verify calls on test doubles.

To use Sinon, we need four packages: sinon, sinon-chai karma-sinon, and karma-sinon-chai. When you did npm install, these packages were already installed since the package.json in the project you're working with included those in the devdependencies section.

In addition to installing these packages, we need to tell Karma to make use of them. Once again, the karma.conf.js file in the current project has been set up with the necessary change. Open the karma.conf.js file and notice the following configuration that tells Karma what plugins to load:

```
frameworks: ['mocha', 'chai', 'sinon', 'sinon-chai'],
```

Dip Into Sinon

Sinon makes creating test doubles concise and fluent. Also, if we choose to replace any of the existing functions with test doubles, Sinon sandbox streamlines the process of restoring the original functions.

With a series of code excerpts, let's quickly get a grasp of creating test doubles in Sinon.

While test doubles can directly be created using the sinon object, it's much better to use the sandbox since it gives us the peace of mind that any changes to existing objects are restored—it's a great way to guarantee that tests don't affect other tests, that they stay isolated.

As a first step to using Sinon, create a sandbox, like so:

```
var sandbox;

beforeEach(function() {
  sandbox = sinon.sandbox.create();
});
```

Right away, implement the function to restore the original objects, to undo any impact of test doubles, with the afterEach function.

```
afterEach(function() {
  sandbox.restore();
});
```

Now that we have a sandbox environment created for Sinon, let's explore creating and using spies, stubs, and mocks.

Create a spy for an existing function with a call to the spy function:

```
var aSpy = sandbox.spy(existingFunction);
```

Then to verify if the function was called, use

```
expect(aSpy.called).to.be.true;
```

That's an easy way to test if existingFunction was actually used by the code under test. But the syntax can be a lot more fluent, thanks to the magic of the Sinon-Chai module:

```
expect(aSpy).called;
```

To check if the function was called with an argument—let's say "magic"—express that expectation as

```
express(aSpy).to.have.been.calledWith('magic');
```

Let's move on to stubs. For a stub to stand in for a call to util.alias('Robert'), write

```
var aStub = sandbox.stub(util, 'alias')
                   .withArgs('Robert')
                   .returns('Bob');
```

This will create a stub for that function that will stand in only when the mentioned argument is passed and will then return to the caller the value passed to the returns function.

Finally, to create a mock for the same function, write

```
var aMock = sandbox.mock(util)
                   .expects('alias')
                   .withArgs('Robert');
```

Then, to check that the function under test actually interacted with the dependency for which the mock stands in, write

```
aMock.verify();
```

If the interaction did not happen, the verify call will fail and blow up the test.

We merely scratched the surface of what Sinon provides—you'll see examples of its usage throughout the rest of this book. For a comprehensive documentation of different functions available, refer to the Sinon documentation[3] and Sinon-Chai documentation.[4]

Use Sinon Mocks to Test Interactions

Now that you've learned about Sinon and how to use it, let's make use of Sinon for testing the locate function. First we need to create Sinon's sandbox before the test is called. Also, we have to restore any functions mocked or stubbed to their original state right after the test completes. A good place for these two operations will be in the beforeEach and the afterEach sandwich functions. Since more than one test suite may have a need for these functions, instead of placing these functions in one particular test suite, we'll write them in a separate file outside of any test suite. Then they become available for all test suites in the current project.

We'll put the Sinon setup and teardown operations in a separate file named sinon-setup.js. Let's open that pre-created empty file in the locateme project and add the following Sinon-related code:

tackle/locateme/test/sinon-setup.js

```
var sandbox;

beforeEach(function() {
  sandbox = sinon.sandbox.create();
});

afterEach(function() {
  sandbox.restore();
});
```

The sandbox variable will hold a reference to the Sinon sandbox object that will be the gateway to get stubs, mocks, and spies in the tests. The beforeEach function will promptly create and have ready a sandbox before each test. The afterEach will undo any effect of stubs and mocks on any objects—dependencies—created, through the sandbox, in the tests.

3. http://sinonjs.org/docs/
4. https://github.com/domenic/sinon-chai

Let's revisit the test we wrote for the locate function in the test/locate-test.js file.

tackle/locateme/test/locate-test.js
```
describe('locate test', function() {
  it('should register handlers with getCurrentPosition', function(done) {

    var original = navigator.geolocation.getCurrentPosition;

    navigator.geolocation.getCurrentPosition = function(success, error) {
      expect(success).to.be.eql(onSuccess);
      expect(error).to.be.eql(onError);
      done();
    }

   locate();
   navigator.geolocation.getCurrentPosition = original;
  });
});
```

We can make this test concise and expressive by using Sinon. We can remove the first and the last line within the test—no need to save the original and restore; Sinon does that for us. Instead of creating the mock function by hand and asserting that the arguments are as expected, we can use Sinon's mock function. Let's modify the previous test, the one we wrote earlier, in the test/locate-test.js file, to the following:

tackle/locateme/test/locate-test.js
```
describe('locate test', function() {
 it('should register handlers with getCurrentPosition', function() {
   var getCurrentPositionMock =
     sandbox.mock(navigator.geolocation)
            .expects('getCurrentPosition')
            .withArgs(onSuccess, onError);

  locate();

  getCurrentPositionMock.verify();
 });
});
```

As a net effect, the mock function will replace the getCurrentPosition function of geolocation with a function that will verify that the arguments passed are the ones mentioned in the call to withArgs. At the end of the test we ask the mock created by Sinon to verify that it was called as expected.

Not only is the modified version of the test concise, it also reveals its intention directly. More important, since we don't have to manually set and unset the mock, unlike the previous version, this version is not error prone.

Use Sinon Stubs to Test State

We saw a Sinon mock in action in the previous test. Let's get a feel for using a Sinon stub. Recall that a stub is useful to test for state whereas a mock can help to test interactions or behavior. We still have two functions in the design to complete the work for the problem at hand. Let's take on the onError function next as that will help you learn about stubs.

In the src/locateme.js file, we wrote the onError function as a blank function to get the implementation of locate done. It's time to replace that with the actual implementation, test first.

The onError function will be called by getCurrentPosition if it could not get the current position of the user. The failure could be due to one of several reasons, including the possibility that the user did not grant permission or the program is unable to access the network. In the spike we merely displayed a "unable to get your location" message. However, a good application should give users enough relevant useful details. It turns out that when the error function is called, the getCurrentPosition function passes on a PositionError object. which has, among other details, a human-readable message. Let's design the onError function to display that message on the DOM element with the id named error.

To test onError we need to pass in an instance of PositionError. However, the onError function needs only the message property of that object. We don't have to work hard to create a real PositionError instance. It will suffice for a simple JSON object with a message property to stand in. When a error object is passed, onError will ask for a DOM element with id error. Since we don't have such a DOM element while running the test, we'll stub that away as well.

That sounds exciting. Let's create a new test suite for the onError function. We'll call the new test suite "onError test," and this suite will readily have access to the Sinon object we created in the test/sinon-setup.js file. Let's enter the following code for the new test suite in the empty file test/onerror-test.js under the current project in the workspace.

tackle/locateme/test/onerror-test.js

```
describe('onError test', function() {
  it('should set the error DOM element', function() {
    var domElement = {innerHTML: ''};
    sandbox.stub(document, 'getElementById')
           .withArgs('error')
           .returns(domElement);

    var message = "you're kidding";
    var positionError = { message: message };

    onError(positionError);
```

```
    expect(domElement.innerHTML).to.be.eql(message);
  });
});
```

The variable domElement refers to a simple JSON object that stubs the DOM element the code under test expects. The stub for the getElementById function checks that the request came in for the id error and returns the domElement in response to the call. positionError is a lightweight JSON object standing in for the PositionError instance that the onError function expects. After calling the function to be verified, the test asserts the state of the domElement JSON object—it ensures that the object holds the error message that was passed in to the onError function.

Implementing the onError function is straightforward. Let's open the src/locateme.js file and change the existing empty onError function to make the test pass:

tackle/locateme/src/locateme.js

```
var onError = function(error) {
  document.getElementById('error').innerHTML = error.message;
};
```

The function gets the message property from the given argument and sets that value on the innerHTML property of the error DOM element obtained using the getElementById of the document object.

We saw Sinon mock and stub so far. We'll explore Sinon spy in the next example.

Use Sinon Spy to Intercept Calls

When testing locate we mocked out the getCurrentPosition function—that made sense because calling the real getCurrentPosition from the test would be preposterous and we wanted to test interaction. When testing onError we stubbed out getElementById because we wanted that object to maintain state and we were keen to verify what the function sets on its dependency. Sometimes, the dependency is benign and it's perfectly OK for the code under test to call it. However, we may still want to test for interactions. While a mock is usable in such a case, a spy may be a better fit as it will need much less effort. Let's explore this further and learn about spy by writing a test for the last function at hand, the onSuccess function.

The onSuccess function will be called by the getCurrentPosition function with details of the user's location. To fulfill its responsibility, the onSuccess function should extract the latitude and longitude values from the given position, call createURL to get the URL, and delegate to setLocation the task of setting the location on the window object. That tells us that the job of onSuccess is mostly interaction with two other functions and so the tests for this function will be interaction tests. However, we can get those done effectively with spies instead of mocks. Let's see how.

Let's open the test/onsuccess-test.js file and add a new test suite and the first test for onSuccess:

tackle/locateme/test/onsuccess-test.js

```
describe('onSuccess test', function() {
  it('should call createURL with latitude and longitude', function() {
    var createURLSpy = sandbox.spy(window, 'createURL');

    var position = { coords: { latitude: 40.41, longitude: -105.55 }};

    onSuccess(position);

    expect(createURLSpy).to.have.been.calledWith(40.41, -105.55);
  });
});
```

In the test, we first created a spy for the createURL function. The spy will merely intercept—sniff is probably a better way to think—and record the parameters passed to the real call. It will not, however, block or circumvent the call. The real function will be executed, which is quite fine in this test. At the end of the test we verify that the two expected arguments were passed by the code under test to its dependency, which has been replaced by the spy.

Also in the test, we passed a position local variable to the code under test. position is a JSON object with a coords property, which in turn holds the values for latitude and longitude. The reason for this nested format of data is that the real Position object that the geolocation API sends is in a similar format:

```
▼ Geoposition
  ▼ coords: Coordinates
      accuracy: 65
      altitude: 118.00774383544922
      altitudeAccuracy: 10
      heading: null
      latitude: 35.89259034437128
      longitude: -78.84664329787185
      speed: null
    ▶ __proto__: CoordinatesPrototype
    timestamp: 1440203820558
  ▶ __proto__: GeopositionPrototype
```

For the test we only need the data that the code under test cares about, so we provided minimum data for position, but in the necessary format.

Let's implement the minimum code to make this test pass. In the src/locateme.js file, let's change the current empty implementation of the onSuccess function to the following:

tackle/locateme/src/locateme.js

```
var onSuccess = function(position) {
  var latitude = position.coords.latitude;
  var longitude = position.coords.longitude;

  createURL(latitude, longitude);
}
```

The function extracts the latitude and longitude values from the given position argument and passes them down to the createURL function. That's the minimum code to make the test pass. However, the function needs to take the result of createURL and pass it to the setLocation function. Let's write a test for that.

The onSuccess function should receive whatever createURL returns and send that to the setLocation function. So, it does not matter, in the current context, what createURL actually returns. Ignoring that relieves us of the need to mess with the format of the URL. Instead, we can simply stub out the createURL function to return a canned URL value—no need to talk to the real createURL in this test. Let's add another test in the test/onsuccess-test.js file:

tackle/locateme/test/onsuccess-test.js

```
it('should call setLocation with URL returned by createURL', function() {
 var url = 'http://www.example.com';

 sandbox.stub(window, 'createURL')
        .returns(url);

 var setLocationSpy = sandbox.spy(window, 'setLocation');

 var position = { coords: { latitude: 40.41, longitude: -105.55 }};
 onSuccess(position);

 expect(setLocationSpy).to.have.been.calledWith(window, url);
});
```

In the test, we first created a canned url value and asked the stub for createURL to return that when it's called. Then we created a spy for the setLocation function—again, there's no harm if the real implementation is called. Right after that we called the onSuccess function with the same position as we did in the previous test. Finally, we verified that the spy for the setLocation intercepted calls to the function with the appropriate arguments.

To make this second test pass, along with the first, let's change the onSuccess function in the src/locateme.js:

tackle/locateme/src/locateme.js
```
var onSuccess = function(position) {
  var latitude = position.coords.latitude;
  var longitude = position.coords.longitude;

  var url = createURL(latitude, longitude);
  setLocation(window, url);
};
```

Save the file and ensure Karma reports the test as passing.

At this time, Karma should report all the nine tests we wrote so far as passing:

```
.........
Chrome 49.0.2623 (Mac OS X 10.10.5):
  Executed 9 of 9 SUCCESS (0.035 secs / 0.016 secs)
```

We've come a long way, developing the code incrementally using automated tests. Next, let's take a few minutes to review what we accomplished.

Review and Run

The journey started with a desire to write automated tests for the function with dependencies. In the end, in addition to the fast tests passing, the net result is a pretty good design compared to what we saw in the spike. Let's take a few minutes to review the tests we wrote.

- test/create-url-test.js: Here, we started with the tests for the createURL function. We avoided dealing with any dependencies while writing these tests.
- test/setlocation-test.js: In this file we wrote a test for the setLocation function. Since setLocation interacts with the window object, we mocked it using a lightweight JSON object with a location property.
- test/sinon-setup.js: We created this file to host the setup and teardown functions for Sinon sandbox.
- test/locate-test.js: Here, we wrote an interaction test to verify that locate calls getCurrentPosition with the proper callback functions. We first made a mock and then switched over to use Sinon mock for concise and fluent testing.
- test/onerror-test.js: The test for onError in this file helped us to learn about using stub instead of mock. We used Sinon to create the stub.
- test/onsuccess-test.js: Finally, the tests for onSuccess in this file showed us when and why to use a spy instead of a mock.

The problem we took was relatively small, but it had some intricate dependencies to the DOM and the geolocation API. It helped us to explore the use of mocks, stubs, and spies. At the end of the journey, we not only have automated tests, but also cohesive, modular, and easy-to-understand code.

Let's take a look at the spike we created—only a quick look. It's fully understandable if you don't want to see that code ever again:

tackle/spike/src/locateme.js

```
//This is a brute-force sample created during a spiking session
var locate = function() {
  navigator.geolocation.getCurrentPosition(
    function(position) {
      var latitude = position.coords.latitude;
      var longitude = position.coords.longitude;

      var url = 'http://maps.google.com/?q=' + latitude + ',' + longitude;
      window.location = url;
    },
    function() {
      document.getElementById('error').innerHTML =
        'unable to get your location';
    });
};
```

Let's not be harsh about that code; it gave us insight into the problem at hand. It's perfectly OK for spikes to look like this. It's when production code ends up like this—and unfortunately, it does on a lot of projects—that we should be truly sad.

Now, let's take the code written, for the same problem, using automated tests:

tackle/locateme/src/locateme.js

```
var createURL = function(latitude, longitude) {
  if (latitude && longitude)
    return 'http://maps.google.com?q=' + latitude + ',' + longitude;
  return '';
};

var setLocation = function(window, url) {
  window.location = url;
};

var locate = function() {
 navigator.geolocation.getCurrentPosition(onSuccess, onError);
};

var onError = function(error) {
  document.getElementById('error').innerHTML = error.message;
};

var onSuccess = function(position) {
```

```
  var latitude = position.coords.latitude;
  var longitude = position.coords.longitude;

  var url = createURL(latitude, longitude);
  setLocation(window, url);
};
```

Most of the functions are just one-liners. All the functions are short and are focused on the one responsibility each of them was born to fulfill. If you want to continue to admire the code we created, please feel free to take the time you need.

Test and Design, Best Buddies Forever

Automated testing brings along good design characteristics. Good design makes code testable. It invites automated tests.

Automated tests lead to modular, highly cohesive, loosely coupled, cleaner design. Those design characteristics in turn make it possible to write automated tests.

The tests pass, but you may wonder if the code actually works. Your inner voice may say "trust, but verify" and that's astute. Later in the book we will explore UI-level testing. For now, let's exercise the code manually, more with the intent to see the fruits of our effort than to verify. The index.html file in the current locateme project is identical to the file with the same name you saw in the spike project. It's shown here for your convenience:

tackle/locateme/index.html

```
<!DOCTYPE html>
<html>
  <head>
    <title>Locate Me</title>
  </head>
  <body>
    <button onclick="locate();">Locate Me</button>
    <div id="error"></div>
    <script src="src/locateme.js"></script>
  </body>
</html>
```

From the locateme directory, run the command

```
npm start
```

to start the web server:

```
> http-server -a localhost -p 8080 -c1

Starting up http-server, serving ./
```

```
Available on:
  http://localhost:8080
Hit CTRL-C to stop the server
```

If your system provides the capability to right-click on the displayed URL in the terminal or console window, make use of that capability to open it in the browser. Otherwise, open a browser and enter or copy and paste the URL http//localhost:8080 to see the browser display the index.html:

Click the "Locate Me" button, grant permission to access the location, and watch the program take you to Google Maps:

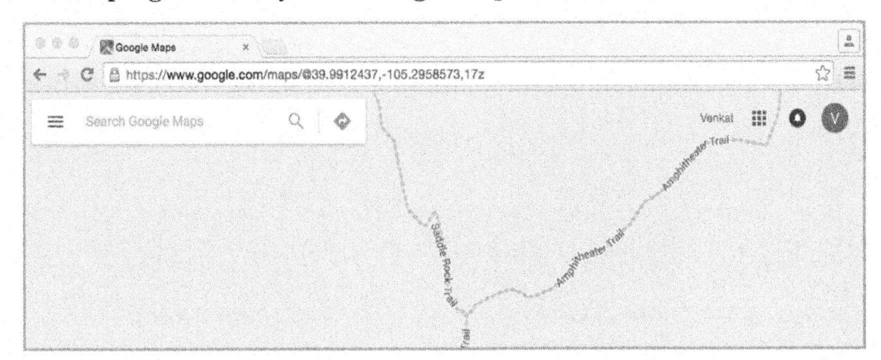

Now, turn off your Wi-Fi, disconnect your network cable or stop your dial-up modem (just kidding), and then visit the URL http://localhost:8080 once more. Click the button again to see a message like

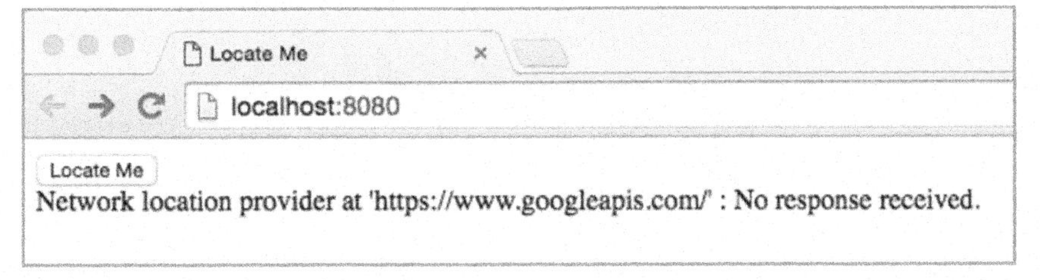

Seeing a program working is satisfying. Seeing a well-tested, well-written program working? Now that's blissful.

Wrapping Up

We tackled some hard topics in this chapter. Dependencies can make testing very hard. You first learned to separate dependencies, where possible, and bring the function down to pure computations so it can be easily tested.

To deal with an intrinsic dependency, first decouple and inject the dependency into the code being tested. Then replace the dependency during test runs with a test double. You explored the use of spies, stubs, and mocks while writing automated tests for a problem with a dependency. Also you learned how to use Sinon and its benefits compared to handmade test doubles.

You will be applying the techniques learned in this chapter throughout the rest of the book and in your own projects. We have covered some of the most important fundamentals in this part. In the next part we'll take a closer look at working with server-side code.

Part II

Real-World Automated Testing

In this part, we'll pull together all the different pieces that we covered in Part 1 by building practical examples. You will test-drive fully functional applications that use Node.js, Express, jQuery, and AngularJS. For the most part, you won't have to spin up web servers or browsers—that means fast and deterministic feedback loops.

You'll explore testing the models that talk to databases, the routes that handle URL paths, the code that manipulates the DOM, and functions that serve as AngularJS controllers. You'll also write and exercise end-to-end integration tests, from the UI, through the controllers, routes, and models, all the way to the database.

Finally, this part ends with a discussion on test-driving the design and the levels of testing at different application layers.

CHAPTER 5

Test-Drive Node.js Apps

In part 1, we covered various techniques for writing automated tests, verifying the behavior of asynchronous functions, and tackling dependencies. We're now ready to put them all together as we test-drive the design and implementation of an entire Node.js application, from start to finish.

Node.js has emerged as a popular JavaScript runtime for the server side. It's a powerful environment and a lot of fun to code. But how do you tell if the code actually works, for various inputs, the different edge cases, through network failures, and when some required files go missing? Running the application manually and trying out different scenarios is not an option you've come here for. This chapter will walk you through, step by step, how to create a practical fully functional Node.js application using tests to drive the design.

We'll create an application that will report the prices of various ticker symbols. We'll build the app in two stages: as a standalone program first, and then extended to provide a web interface. The application will read a list of ticker symbols from a file, get the stock prices from Yahoo finance, and print the latest prices for each symbol in sorted order. The program will also gracefully handle errors from file operations and network access.

With the skills gained to test drive a full-fledged application, you'll be ready to apply these techniques to your everyday programming projects.

Start with a Strategic—Just Enough—Design

In the yesteryears of waterfall development, we did big up-front design and tried to figure out a lot of the details before coding started, but that didn't go well. Today the world is agile, but does that means no design? Sadly that's how it has turned out for some developers, but it's not helping. Both extremes—big up-front versus little design—are dangerous and counterproductive.

It's better to start with a strategic design—a high-level design that will help us assess the overall problem at hand and get a big picture, with just enough details. The details that emerge are not set in stone. The strategic design will give us an idea of the complexity, help us identify important areas for the detailed design, and set us on a direction to start coding.

Following a short strategic design step, we'll move forward to a more detailed, tactical design—this is the design that lives in code and involves both thinking and typing. This is where we spend most of our time and effort; tests will guide us through the fine-grained details of design as the code emerges and evolves.

Let's create a strategic design for the stock application. First conceptualize the overall logic or flow of the program: read a file, say tickers.txt; collect the price for each symbol; and finally print the result. Along the way the program should gracefully handle errors. Let's sketch those details in a diagram.

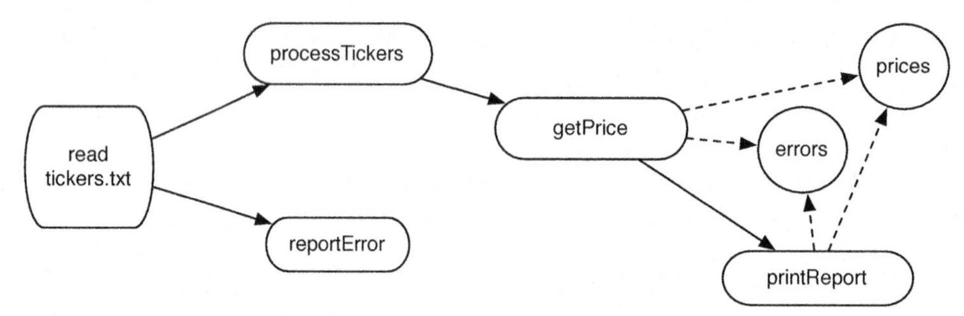

In the figure, the solid lines represent function calls and the dotted lines indicate the operation of updating a variable. Most of the operations for this program are asynchronous and the overall flow nicely falls into a function pipeline or chain. The read function reads the tickers.txt file and reports any errors to the reportError function. The reportError function will print the error details for the user to see and exit the program. On the other hand, if the read went well, then the read function will send a list of ticker symbols to the processTickers function. This function iterates over the list of symbols and calls a getPrice function for each ticker. getPrice gets the data from the web service and stores the price values in a prices collection. If it runs into an error, then it stores the error details in an errors collection. The function also notifies a printReport function, which waits for all symbols to be processed. Once all the data is ready, the printReport function will print the prices and errors.

With the strategic design in front of us, it's time to think of the next step. It should get us coding since that's when we get valuable feedback—both from automated tests and from exercising the application. At this level of the design we have five functions. Let's jot down some high-level tests for these functions.

Leap Into Tactical—Test First—Design

From the initial design we'll move on to the tactical design, the act of making fine-grained design decisions and implementing code. We'll use the strategic design as a starting point and pick a few functions to begin the design with tests. We'll write positive, negative, and exception tests and along the way make detailed design decisions. As we transition from one function to the next, you will see the design and the code for the program take shape, one piece at a time.

Let's start by jotting down a series of tests.

Create an Initial Test List

Jot down the tests that come to mind, on a piece of paper—don't worry about right or wrong at this time:

- read invokes processTickers if the file is valid
- read invokes an error handler if the file is invalid
- processTickers calls getPrice for each ticker symbol
- getPrice calls the web service
- For valid response, getPrice updates the prices collection
- For failed response, getPrice updates the errors collection
- getPrice calls printReport in the end
- printReport prints the results in sorted order

These are some initial tests that come to mind. They will change once the detailed design and implementation starts. As we write code, new tests will emerge and we'll add them to this list. As new ideas for the design emerge—and they will—those ideas should readily go in the list as new tests. Once a test is implemented, we'll check it off the list.

Start with a test list, but don't spend too much time on the list. Once you jot down what comes to mind, break the inertia and get started with the first test. You don't have to follow the sequence in the list. Pick any test you're comfortable with, but favor something interesting and useful to start with.

Write the First Test

We'll use the stockfetch project under the tdjsa/testnode directory in your workspace. Change to the tdjsa/testnode/stockfetch directory and take a look at the package.json file to see the modules that we need. We'll use Mocha, Chai, Istanbul, and Sinon in this project. Run npm install to get these installed for the current project.

Now let's write the first test. It makes little sense to start with a test for printReport or reportError. The read, processTickers, and getPrice functions all seem interesting and important. We could pick any one of them. We'll pick the read function as it's first in line and may be a good starting point to think logically about the flow of control.

Since we decided to focus on the read function first, the first two tests seem like a good idea, but we still have to pick one. Let's start with the second test in the list—read a file that does not exist.

Before we write that test, let's write the traditional canary test we write when we start on a new project. Open the empty file named stockfetch-test.js that's located under the tdjsa/testnode/stockfetch/test directory and enter the following code:

testnode/stockfetch/test/stockfetch-test.js

```
var expect = require('chai').expect;

describe('Stockfetch tests', function() {
  it('should pass this canary test', function() {
    expect(true).to.be.true;
  });
});
```

Run the command npm test to ensure the canary test is passing and to confirm everything is ready for us to work on this project.

Let's now prepare the test suite with the setup and teardown functions.

testnode/stockfetch/test/stockfetch-test.js

```
var expect = require('chai').expect;
var sinon = require('sinon');
var fs = require('fs');
var Stockfetch = require('../src/stockfetch');

describe('Stockfetch tests', function() {

  var stockfetch;
  var sandbox;

  beforeEach(function() {
    stockfetch = new Stockfetch();
    sandbox = sinon.sandbox.create();
  });

  afterEach(function() {
    sandbox.restore();
  });

  it('should pass this canary test', function() {
    expect(true).to.be.true;
  });
});
```

We added a require for Sinon to facilitate easy stubbing and mocking. Also, we set up the sandbox and restored or cleared out the stubs/mocks after each test, using the beforeEach and afterEach functions.

Let's now proceed to write the test for the read function, right below the canary test within the "Stockfetch tests" test suite in the stockfetch-test.js file:

testnode/stockfetch/test/stockfetch-test.js

```
it('read should invoke error handler for invalid file', function(done) {
  var onError = function(err) {
    expect(err).to.be.eql('Error reading file: InvalidFile');
    done();
  };

  sandbox.stub(fs, 'readFile', function(fileName, callback) {
    callback(new Error('failed'));
  });

  stockfetch.readTickersFile('InvalidFile', onError);
});
```

We made a few design decisions while writing this test: asynchrony, the function's signature, and the function's name. In the strategic design, we called the function read but here we gave it a more detailed name: readTickersFile.

The first test for readTickersFile passes an invalid filename, along with a callback, and verifies that the callback was invoked. Since accessing a file is an asynchronous operation, the test has to wait for the callback to complete. We can convey that the callback was executed with a call to done(), right there in the callback. We also ensure that readTickersFile fails with a proper error message. Since reading a file is a brittle operation, we don't want to depend on the actual readFile function of the fs module. Instead, we stubbed out the readFile function to send an error to its callback to indicate an invalid file was received.

The test is in place; it's time to implement the function. The code will go into the stockfetch.js file in the src directory. Edit the empty file provided:

```
var Stockfetch = function() {
  this.readTickersFile = function(filename, onError) {
    onError('Error reading file: ' + filename);
  };
};

module.exports = Stockfetch;
```

Remember the first few tests should help us tease out the interface and the later tests should lead us through the implementation. So, there's no rush to do all the coding yet; we just want to get something minimal in place to make the test pass. We need a series of interrelated functions for this program, with some possible state, so we created a class Stockfetch to hold the functions. The readTickersFile function takes the two parameters, but merely invokes the callback synchronously. Even though the real implementation will be more complex, this is sufficient for now to make the test pass. The tests we write as we move forward will fill in the details of the implementations.

Ask mocha to run the tests by running the command npm test. Observe the output:

```
Stockfetch tests
  ✓ should pass this canary test
  ✓ read should invoke error handler for invalid file
2 passing (9ms)
```

Mocha picked up the test file from the test directory and executed the test suite contained in the file. It reported that both the canary test and the negative test for readTickersFile are passing. Kudos—our application has taken life with that first test.

Write a Positive Test

Now let's write a test to take a valid file and extract the ticker symbols from it. While thinking of this test, you'll realize that a valid file may be empty or contain data in the wrong format. Instead of jumping on these issues immediately, jot them down into the test list—the list will grow and shrink as we code, but keep the focus on the test at hand. Here's the updated test list; it shows one completed test and the two new tests:

- …
- ✓ read invokes an error handler if the file is invalid
- …
- printReport prints the results in sorted order
- ⇒ read handle empty file
- ⇒ read handle file content in unexpected format

Let's turn to the positive test we set out to write. Think through the behavior of the readTickersFile function for the happy path. Given a valid filename, this function should read the content of the file, parse it, and send a list of ticker symbols to processTickers, which is the next function in the function pipeline.

But think SRP—the single responsibility principle. readTickersFile should focus on one thing: reading the file. It's better for this function to delegate the responsibility of parsing to another function, say parseTickers. We don't want to think about parsing now, so jot down a test for it in the test list as a reminder.

- ...
- read handle file content in unexpected format
- ⇒ parseTickers receives a string and returns a list of tickers

Once again, let's turn our attention back to the test at hand—we'll implement the test based on how the design has evolved so far in our mind. We'll write the next test in the stockfetch-test.js file, right below the previous test:

testnode/stockfetch/test/stockfetch-test.js

```
it('read should invoke processTickers for valid file', function(done) {
  var rawData = 'GOOG\nAAPL\nORCL\nMSFT';
  var parsedData = ['GOOG', 'AAPL', 'ORCL', 'MSFT'];

  sandbox.stub(stockfetch, 'parseTickers')
         .withArgs(rawData).returns(parsedData);

  sandbox.stub(stockfetch, 'processTickers', function(data) {
    expect(data).to.be.eql(parsedData);
    done();
  });

  sandbox.stub(fs, 'readFile', function(fileName, callback) {
    callback(null, rawData);
  });

  stockfetch.readTickersFile('tickers.txt');
});
```

The current goal is to implement the read function in a way it uses the parseTickers and processTickers functions, but without actually implementing those functions. We'll achieve this goal by stubbing out those functions in the test.

In the test we create stubs for the parseTickers and processTickers functions. The first stub is created only for the expected argument, which is the content of the file we'll pass to the readTickersFile function. The stub, if and when called with the expected argument, will return an array of ticker symbols as canned data. In the second stub, for the processTickers function, we assert that the parameter received is equal to the canned data that was returned by the parseTickers stub. In this stub we also invoke done() to signal completion of the asynchronous callback. We stub the readFile function like in the previous test, but this time return the canned rawData to the callback. Finally we call the code under test, the readTickersFile function. Since we're on a happy path in this test and don't expect the function to fail, we don't need to send the second argument, the onError callback.

We need to change the code under test to make this test pass. Let's write the minimum code so that both the new test and the previous negative test that was passing are happy. Edit the file stockfetch.js, like so:

```
var fs = require('fs');

var Stockfetch = function() {
  this.readTickersFile = function(filename, onError) {
    var self = this;

    var processResponse = function(err, data) {
      if(err)
        onError('Error reading file: ' + filename);
      else {
        var tickers = self.parseTickers(data.toString());
        self.processTickers(tickers);
      }
    };

    fs.readFile(filename, processResponse);
  };

  this.parseTickers = function() {};
  this.processTickers = function() {};
};

module.exports = Stockfetch;
```

The code evolved quite a bit to make this new test pass. We use the readFile function of the fs module, sending it the filename and an internal function as a callback. In the internal function, if the response is an error we call the onError callback. Otherwise, we pass the data to the yet-to-be-implemented parseTickers function, which is stubbed in the test and implemented as an empty function in the Stockfetch class. Then we take the result of that function and pass it to the soon-to-be-written processTickers function.

Since our focus right now is on designing the readTickersFile function, we don't need to bother about the implementations of the parseTickers and processTickers functions. They appear as empty functions in code, but the test provides the necessary stub for those—all good.

We don't need the tickers.txt file mentioned in the test. The stubbed-out readFile function will pretend to have read the file and return the canned value. Run the tests and make sure they're passing:

```
Stockfetch tests

  ✓ should pass this canary test

  ✓ read should invoke error handler for invalid file

  ✓ read should invoke processTickers for valid file

3 passing (13ms)
```

That's two tests, in addition to the canary test, that are passing. Currently there are nine more tests in the test list. Let's move on to the next.

Continue the Design

We covered the happy path for the readTickersFile function, but along the way we added two tests to the test list to handle cases where the file may be empty or contain data in an invalid format. We'll take care of those scenarios next.

Negative Tests for readTickersFile

At this stage of the design, the readTickersFile function calls parseTickers to parse the content of the file into an array of ticker symbols. If the file were empty, then the content would also be empty. In that case this helper function should return an empty array—let's jot down a test in the test list to ensure that behavior of parseTickers is handled when we come around to design that function. That begs the question, what if the content, instead of being empty, is a bunch of white spaces? We want parseTickers to return an empty array for this scenario too. Then, the scenario of white spaces need not be tested on readTickersFile, but we'd need a test for this on the parseTickers function. Update the test list for these scenarios:

- ...
- parseTickers receives a string and returns a list of tickers
- ⇒ parseTickers returns an empty array if content is empty
- ⇒ parseTickers returns an empty array for white spaces–only content

Let's get back to the test on readTickersFile for the scenario of an empty file. Since we're stubbing the readFile function, we don't really need to create an empty file. We'll write the test first for this scenario, again in the stockfetch-test.js file:

testnode/stockfetch/test/stockfetch-test.js

```
it('read should return error if given file is empty', function(done) {
  var onError = function(err) {
    expect(err).to.be.eql('File tickers.txt has invalid content');
    done();
  };

  sandbox.stub(stockfetch, 'parseTickers').withArgs('').returns([]);

  sandbox.stub(fs, 'readFile', function(fileName, callback) {
    callback(null, '');
  });

  stockfetch.readTickersFile('tickers.txt', onError);
});
```

The canned error handler verifies that an "invalid content" message is sent by readTickersFile. The stub for parseTickers returns an empty array when called with empty raw data. After setting up the stubs, call the function under test.

Tests document design decisions. In this test we expressed that if parseTickers returns no ticker symbols, then readTickersFile will report an error. Change the readTickersFile function in the file stockfetch.js to make this test pass.

```
this.readTickersFile = function(filename, onError) {
  var self = this;

  var processResponse = function(err, data) {
    if(err)
      onError('Error reading file: ' + filename);
    else {
      var tickers = self.parseTickers(data.toString());
      if(tickers.length === 0)
        onError('File ' + filename + ' has invalid content');
      else
        self.processTickers(tickers);
    }
  };

  fs.readFile(filename, processResponse);
};
```

Run the tests and ensure all current tests pass.

We took care of the scenario of the file being empty, but we have another test in our test list for file content in unexpected format. If we design the parseTickers function to return an empty array for this scenario too, then the current implementation of readTickersFile is adequate. We don't need any more tests for the readTickersFile function, but we have to add another test for parseTickers. Let's reflect this knowledge in the test list:

- ...
- ~~read handle file content in unexpected format~~
- parseTickers receives a string and returns a list of tickers
- parseTickers returns an empty array if content is empty
- parseTickers returns an empty array for white spaces–only content
- ⇒ parseTickers handles content with unexpected format

The tests we jotted down for readTickersFile are done—one was removed; we can now move on to test other functions. The readTickersFile function depends on two functions that were stubbed out in the tests. They are good candidates to visit next.

Design the parseTickers Function

parseTickers has no dependencies; it's a synchronous function, and verifying its behavior is straightforward. There are four tests for this function in the test list. Implement them, one at a time, with minimum code after writing each test. Once you're done, compare your tests with the code listed next:

testnode/stockfetch/test/stockfetch-test.js

```
it('parseTickers should return tickers', function() {
  expect(stockfetch.parseTickers("A\nB\nC")).to.be.eql(['A', 'B', 'C']);
});

it('parseTickers should return empty array for empty content', function() {
  expect(stockfetch.parseTickers("")).to.be.eql([]);
});

it('parseTickers should return empty array for white-space', function() {
  expect(stockfetch.parseTickers(" ")).to.be.eql([]);
});

it('parseTickers should ignore unexpected format in content', function() {
  var rawData = "AAPL   \nBla h\nGOOG\n\n    ";
  expect(stockfetch.parseTickers(rawData)).to.be.eql(['GOOG']);
});
```

The first test is a positive test whereas the other three are negative tests. The positive test verifies that, given a content in good format, the function parses and returns the ticker symbols. The second test ensures that the function returns an empty list if the input is empty; the third verifies the same for purely white spaces.

The last test ensures that if the ticker symbol has spaces in its name or an empty line, then the function ignores them. If you'd rather reject all ticker symbols even if one of them is ill-formatted, change the test and code to meet that expectation. Here's the code, in stockfetch.js, that satisfies all these tests, created incrementally with each test:

```
this.parseTickers = function(content) {
  var isInRightFormat = function(str) {
    return str.trim().length !== 0 && str.indexOf(' ') < 0;
  };
  return content.split('\n').filter(isInRightFormat);
};
```

This code replaces the empty placeholder for parseTickers in Stockfetch. Remember to run the tests and ensure all tests are passing. We're making good progress, so let's move on to design the next function.

Design the processTickers Function

We designed readTickersFile to invoke processTickers with a list of ticker symbols. In turn, the latter function should invoke a getPrice function once for each ticker symbol. Also, for later use, we need to keep track of the number of ticker symbols processed. A return result is not expected from a call to processTickers. So, to verify that function's behavior we only need interaction tests. Let's add these tests to the stockfetch-test.js file:

testnode/stockfetch/test/stockfetch-test.js
```
it('processTickers should call getPrice for each ticker symbol', function() {
  var stockfetchMock = sandbox.mock(stockfetch);
  stockfetchMock.expects('getPrice').withArgs('A');
  stockfetchMock.expects('getPrice').withArgs('B');
  stockfetchMock.expects('getPrice').withArgs('C');

  stockfetch.processTickers(['A', 'B', 'C']);
  stockfetchMock.verify();
});

it('processTickers should save tickers count', function() {
  sandbox.stub(stockfetch, 'getPrice');

  stockfetch.processTickers(['A', 'B', 'C']);
  expect(stockfetch.tickersCount).to.be.eql(3);
});
```

In the first test we mock the yet-to-be-written getPrice function of Stockfetch with the expectation that it will be called with arguments 'A', 'B', and 'C'. Then we call the function under test and verify that processTickers interacts with getPrice as expected. The second test checks that processTickers sets tickersCount to the number of ticker symbols passed as the argument.

processTickers will be a simple loop. Let's write that next, in the stockfetch.js file:

```
this.processTickers = function(tickers) {
  var self = this;
  self.tickersCount = tickers.length;
  tickers.forEach(function(ticker) { self.getPrice(ticker); });
};

this.tickersCount = 0;

this.getPrice = function() {}
```

In addition to implementing processTickers, we initialized the property tickersCount to 0 and created a placeholder for getPrice.

Since readTickersFile calls processTickers only if it has ticker symbols, no negative tests are needed for processTickers. Run all the tests written so far and confirm they all pass. We've designed three functions so far. Let's move on to the fourth.

Create a Spike to Gain Insight

The next logical step is the design of the getPrice function. This function should visit Yahoo Finance to get the stock data for a given ticker symbol, parse the data for price, and invoke printReport. It also should handle errors that may occur. There's a lot going on and it sounds like it involves a few moving parts.

The function is complex enough that most of us can't write it in one shot, let alone write the tests first. We need to change our approach. We'll create a spike to gain much needed insights about this function.

Spike for getPrice

Let's think through the tests for getPrice. It may feel like a struggle and that's because it's quite hard to envision the full implementation of getPrice. When the implementation's not clear, it's hard to *test first*. When in doubt, create a quick isolated spike before returning to writing tests.

Spikes can give much needed insight into the implementation, how to approach the problem, the dependencies to deal with, and the different issues to test for.

Leverage Spikes

Learn from creating the spike; then discard the spike and continue with the test-driven approach.

While creating the spike for getPrice, we should consider three different scenarios: response for a ticker symbol, response for an invalid ticker symbol, and response when the connection to the network is lost. We'll create a quick and dirty, standalone spike for the function—keep the spike in a separate directory away from the test-driven project code.

Once you've created a spike for the function, compare your efforts to this spike:

testnode/spike/getprice.js

```
//A quick and dirty prototype
var http = require('http');

var getPriceTrial = function(ticker) {
  http.get('http://ichart.finance.yahoo.com/table.csv?s=' + ticker,
    function(response) {
    if(response.statusCode === 200) {
      var data = '';
      var getChunk = function(chunk) { data += chunk; };
      response.on('data', getChunk);
      response.on('end', function() {
        console.log('received data for ' + ticker);
        console.log(data);
      });
```

```
    } else {
      console.log(ticker + ' - error getting data : ' + response.statusCode);
    }
  }).on('error', function(err) {
    console.log(ticker + ' - error getting data : ' + err.code);
  });
};

getPriceTrial('GOOG');
getPriceTrial('INVALID');
//Also try running after disconnecting from the network
```

The spike is a ball of mud—just the way it should be—but it serves its purpose, to given us insight and clarity about a possible implementation. The spike has clarified quite a few things: how to handle the response, how to deal with an invalid ticker symbol, and what happens if there's a network connection error.

Design the getPrice Function

With the new insight from the spike, we can replace one of the tests in the test list—shown stricken—with a few other tests: three for getPrice and two for the handlers it needs:

- ~~getPrice calls the web service~~
- getPrice calls get on http with valid URL
- getPrice calls get with a response handler as argument
- getPrice registers handler for failure to reach host
- Response handler gathers data and updates price collection
- Error handler updates errors collection

Joe asks:

Can't We Take the Easy Route?

Why can't we write just one test for getPrice instead of so many tests? After all, the tests now are depending on the implementation of the function. If we decide to change the implementation, these related tests would have to change, wouldn't they?

That perceived easy route is not really easy in the long run. getPrice depends on an external service. We can't predict what that service will return. Furthermore, we have to properly deal with the invalid symbol and failure to connect. These fine-grained tests will force us to decouple the getPrice function from the service, thus making the code easier to test and more robust along the way. Having to change these tests if and when the implementation changes is a small price for the peace of mind we get knowing the code is actually doing the right things.

The three tests for getPrice will greatly modularize the function. Let's write these three tests and the minimum code for these tests to pass—again take small steps, one test at a time.

We'll start with the first test—call getPrice and assert that http's get is called with the proper URL. Since we can't predict the actual response from the service, during the test the code under test should not talk to the real service. For the test to be deterministic, the code should talk to a test double instead of the real http get function. Instead of an empirical test, we'll write an interaction test here again. To stub out the get function of http, we have to externalize the dependency. One option is to pass an instance of http as an argument to getPrice. Another option is to make http a property of Stockfetch for getPrice to access. The first option will increase the burden on the caller of getPrice, which is the already designed processTicker. Let's go with the second option—here's the test, in stockfetch-test.js:

testnode/stockfetch/test/stockfetch-test.js

```
it('getPrice should call get on http with valid URL', function(done) {
  var httpStub = sandbox.stub(stockfetch.http, 'get', function(url) {
    expect(url)
      .to.be.eql('http://ichart.finance.yahoo.com/table.csv?s=GOOG');
    done();
    return {on: function() {} };
  });

  stockfetch.getPrice('GOOG');
});
```

Since http is now a property of Stockfetch, it's easy to stub out that dependency. In the stub for the http.get function, we verify that it's called with the proper URL from within getPrice. From the spike we can glean that the get function should return an object with an on property. So, the stub returns a JSON object that has a dummy on function.

Let's implement getPrice to make this test pass. We'll call this.http.get and pass the appropriate URL. We'll take a look at the code after writing a few more tests. Once the test passes, proceed to write the next test.

Think through a few things before the next test. In the spike for getPrice, pay close attention to what's being passed to http.get as the second parameter. That's an anonymous function that does the significant work of gathering the data that arrives in chunks or bursts from the web service. We don't want to deal with that logic now, in the middle of testing and designing getPrice—we need to modularize.

Let's use a function, processResponse, as the handler for the responses. The getPrice function needs to register this function as the handler with http.get. Here's the test to verify that:

testnode/stockfetch/test/stockfetch-test.js

```
it('getPrice should send a response handler to get', function(done) {
  var aHandler = function() {};

  sandbox.stub(stockfetch.processResponse, 'bind')
         .withArgs(stockfetch, 'GOOG')
         .returns(aHandler);

  var httpStub = sandbox.stub(stockfetch.http, 'get',
    function(url, handler) {
      expect(handler).to.be.eql(aHandler);
      done();
      return {on: function() {} };
    });

  stockfetch.getPrice('GOOG');
});
```

In this test, we stub the bind function of the processResponse function, assert that it receives the correct context object (the first parameter) and the symbol (the second parameter). If the arguments to bind are received as expected, then we return a stub to represent the result of the call to bind. As a next step, we stub the http.get function and in the stub we ensure that what the handler received is what bind returned. For this test to work correctly, the code under test, getPrice, should bind the given symbol to the processResponse function and register it as a handler to the http.get function. Proceed to implement enough code for this test to pass.

processResponse will take care of dealing with good responses and any potential errors from the web service. However, if the service can't be reached in the first place, http will fail much earlier with an error event. We need to register a handler for this—let's test to verify this behavior:

testnode/stockfetch/test/stockfetch-test.js

```
it('getPrice should register handler for failure to reach host',
  function(done) {
  var errorHandler = function() {};

  sandbox.stub(stockfetch.processHttpError, 'bind')
         .withArgs(stockfetch, 'GOOG')
         .returns(errorHandler);

  var onStub = function(event, handler) {
    expect(event).to.be.eql('error');
    expect(handler).to.be.eql(errorHandler);
    done();
  };
```

```
  sandbox.stub(stockfetch.http, 'get').returns({on: onStub});

  stockfetch.getPrice('GOOG');
});
```

In the test we stubbed the bind function of the error handler processHttpError and set up the expectation that it will be called with the proper context object and symbol. This is pretty similar to what we did for the processResponse's bind function in the earlier test. We created a stub for the on function and, in turn, used it as the return value in the stub for http.get. When the code under test calls http.get(), the stub will step in to return the on function. Upon the call to that function in the code under test, once again the stub for the on function will verify that the proper error handler was registered.

Change the getPrice function to make this test pass. Let's take a look at the implementation of this function, in stockfetch.js, to make all three tests pass:

```
this.http = http;

this.getPrice = function(symbol) {
  var url = 'http://ichart.finance.yahoo.com/table.csv?s=' + symbol;
  this.http.get(url, this.processResponse.bind(this, symbol))
          .on('error', this.processHttpError.bind(this, symbol));
};
this.processResponse = function() {};
this.processHttpError = function() {};
```

Remember to add

```
var http = require('http');
```

to the top of the file stockfetch.js to bring in the http module.

Take a few minutes to go over each of the tests for getPrice and see how they verify the behavior of getPrice. It takes some thinking, so don't let the tests intimidate you—it's only a few lines of code in each test. Once you think through the sequence, you'll get the hang of it in no time.

Compare the implementation of getPrice that we arrived at using tests with the spike created earlier. Though the code is not doing everything the spike did—parts of it will be in other functions—the code is concise, expressive, modular, and cohesive, and it takes on a single responsibility. Furthermore, it has delegated the rest of the details to two other functions yet to be written. That's a significant departure in design from the spike.

The new design that emerged has some significant benefits compared to the design in the spike. The behavior of the modular code is much easier to verify with automated tests. We did pay a small price for that. It took effort to write these tests, but it's a skill that gets better with practice. In addition, once written, the tests pay high dividends through rapid feedback.

Modularize to Facilitate Testing

The complex getPrice in the spike turned out to be only a few lines of code in stockfetch.js, but a significant part of implementation that was in the spike is not done yet. Let's continue to modularize, making each piece of code cohesive, narrow, and focused on a single responsibility.

Design the processResponse and processError Functions

Let's turn our attention to the two new functions called from within getPrice. We can think through the tests for these functions now a lot better than when we focused on getPrice. Let's add a few more tests for these functions:

- …
- ✓ getPrice calls get on http with valid URL
- ✓ getPrice calls get with a response handler as argument
- ✓ getPrice registers handler for failure to reach host
- ~~response handler gathers data and updates price collection~~
- ~~error handler updates errors collection~~
- processResponse calls parsePrice with valid data
- processResponse calls processError if response failed
- processHttpError calls processError with the error details
- …

Let's write the first test for the processResponse function. processResponse has a few moving parts—it has to register a 'data' event to gather the data chunks that comes from the HTTP responses, and another event 'end' that would signal that there's no more data. Once all the data is received, the processResponse has to call a parsePrice function. Here's the test for this behavior:

testnode/stockfetch/test/stockfetch-test.js

```
it('processResponse should call parsePrice with valid data', function() {
  var dataFunction;
  var endFunction;

  var response = {
    statusCode: 200,
    on: function(event, handler) {
      if(event === 'data') dataFunction = handler;
      if(event === 'end') endFunction = handler;
    }
  };

  var parsePriceMock =
```

```
    sandbox.mock(stockfetch)
           .expects('parsePrice').withArgs('GOOG', 'some data');

  stockfetch.processResponse('GOOG', response);
  dataFunction('some ');
  dataFunction('data');
  endFunction();

  parsePriceMock.verify();
});
```

In the test we grab the references to the callbacks that processResponse registers with the on event of the response object. We then call these functions with some sample data, simulating the actions of an HTTP response session. Finally verify that parsePrice was called from within the processResponse with the appropriate simulated data.

To make this test pass we don't have to check the response status yet. Instead set the proper event handlers on response and invoke parsePrice when the end event is received. Implement that minimum code and run the test to ensure it passes. We'll see the code for processResponse in a short while.

Let's proceed now to the next test for processResponse—it should call processError if the status code is not 200. Write a positive and a negative test, one with status code 200 and the other with status code, say, 404:

testnode/stockfetch/test/stockfetch-test.js

```
it('processResponse should call processError if response failed',
  function() {
  var response = { statusCode: 404 };

  var processErrorMock = sandbox.mock(stockfetch)
                              .expects('processError')
                              .withArgs('GOOG', 404);

  stockfetch.processResponse('GOOG', response);
  processErrorMock.verify();
});

it('processResponse should call processError only if response failed',
  function() {
  var response = {
    statusCode: 200,
    on: function() {}
  };

  var processErrorMock = sandbox.mock(stockfetch)
                              .expects('processError')
                              .never();

  stockfetch.processResponse('GOOG', response);
  processErrorMock.verify();
});
```

In the first test we set the statusCode to 404 and confirm that when processResponse is called, it in turn calls processError as expected. In the second test we send a good status code and ensure that the error function is not called. Here's the code for processResponse that makes the tests pass:

```
this.processResponse = function(symbol, response) {
  var self = this;

  if(response.statusCode === 200) {
    var data = '';
    response.on('data', function(chunk) { data += chunk; });
    response.on('end', function() { self.parsePrice(symbol, data); });
  } else {
    self.processError(symbol, response.statusCode);
  }
};

this.parsePrice = function() {};

this.processError = function() {};
```

Again compare this code with the corresponding part in the spike—clarity emerges from chaos.

Design processHttpError

We have one unfinished item. In the getPrice function, if there was trouble reaching the host we invoked a processHttpError function. We've not implemented that yet. This function should extract the details of the error and send it to the processError function. Let's write the test for that:

testnode/stockfetch/test/stockfetch-test.js

```
it('processHttpError should call processError with error details',
  function() {
  var processErrorMock = sandbox.mock(stockfetch)
                                .expects('processError')
                                .withArgs('GOOG', '...error code...');

  var error = { code: '...error code...' };
  stockfetch.processHttpError('GOOG', error);
  processErrorMock.verify();
});
```

The test checks to make sure that processHttpError extracts the code from the error and passes it to processError—again take a glance at the spike to glean what the test should expect. The code to make this test pass is simple:

```
this.processHttpError = function(ticker, error) {
  this.processError(ticker, error.code);
};
```

We have come a long way, but there are a few more steps to finish this program. Take a break before you continue on to the last few steps—stepping away from the code and looking at it after a break may give you not only a breather, but also a fresh perspective on the problem.

Design parsePrice and processError

parsePrice and processError have to update shared data structures and invoke a printReport function. Let's write tests for these—again even though multiple tests are listed here, write one test at a time and minimum code to make each test pass before moving on to the next test.

To parse the data we need sample data in the format returned by the web service. Since we have a spike, we can run it to get a sample and use the data in the test, like so:

testnode/stockfetch/test/stockfetch-test.js

```
var data = "Date,Open,High,Low,Close,Volume,Adj Close\n\
2015-09-11,619.75,625.780029,617.419983,625.77002,1360900,625.77002\n\
2015-09-10,613.099976,624.159973,611.429993,621.349976,1900500,621.349976";

it('parsePrice should update prices', function() {
  stockfetch.parsePrice('GOOG', data);

  expect(stockfetch.prices.GOOG).to.be.eql('625.77002');
});

it('parsePrice should call printReport', function() {
  var printReportMock = sandbox.mock(stockfetch).expects('printReport');

  stockfetch.parsePrice('GOOG', data);
  printReportMock.verify();
});

it('processError should update errors', function() {
  stockfetch.processError('GOOG', '...oops...');

  expect(stockfetch.errors.GOOG).to.be.eql('...oops...');
});

it('processError should call printReport', function() {
  var printReportMock = sandbox.mock(stockfetch).expects('printReport');

  stockfetch.processError('GOOG', '...oops...');
  printReportMock.verify();
});
```

The tests are pretty straightforward and the code to make these tests pass should be easy to write as well. Let's get the code implemented in stockfetch.js:

```
this.prices = {};

this.parsePrice = function(ticker, data) {
  var price = data.split('\n')[1].split(',').pop();
  this.prices[ticker] = price;
  this.printReport();
};

this.errors = {};

this.processError = function(ticker, error) {
  this.errors[ticker] = error;
  this.printReport();
};

this.printReport = function() {};
```

Now to the final step, to design and implement the printReport function.

Separate Concerns

The test list now has one incomplete test, "printReport prints the results in sorted order," which seemed like a good test at the end of the strategic design. But looking at the code we've designed so far, that appears like a giant step. We need to break it into smaller functions. Print and sort are two separate concerns—a good design keeps separate concerns apart. Also, we don't want printReport to write to the console; it's better to send the data to the caller so they can decide where to print it. Let's jot down the tests that just emerged:

- ...
- ~~printReport prints the results in sorted order~~
- printReport sends price, errors once all responses arrive
- printReport does not send before all responses arrive
- printReport sorts prices based on the tickers
- printReport sorts errors based on the tickers

Design printReport

We'll implement the first two tests and then look at the sort feature after that.

testnode/stockfetch/test/stockfetch-test.js

```
it('printReport should send price, errors once all responses arrive',
  function() {
  stockfetch.prices = { 'GOOG': 12.34 };
  stockfetch.errors = { 'AAPL': 'error' };
  stockfetch.tickersCount = 2;

  var callbackMock =
    sandbox.mock(stockfetch)
          .expects('reportCallback')
          .withArgs([['GOOG', 12.34]], [['AAPL', 'error']]);
```

```
  stockfetch.printReport();
  callbackMock.verify();
});

it('printReport should not send before all responses arrive', function() {
  stockfetch.prices = { 'GOOG': 12.34 };
  stockfetch.errors = { 'AAPL': 'error' };
  stockfetch.tickersCount = 3;

  var callbackMock = sandbox.mock(stockfetch)
                            .expects('reportCallback')
                            .never();

  stockfetch.printReport();
  callbackMock.verify();
});
```

The first test confirms that the callback was called with the right data while the second test confirms that the callback was not called if all symbols have not been processed. Implement the minimum code to make these two tests pass before continuing to the next step.

Design sortData

The last two tests in the test list say that the printReport function should sort prices and errors. On second thought, implementing that code in printReport may lead to duplication. Let's revisit these tests:

- ...
- ✓ printReport does not send before all responses arrive
- ~~printReport sorts prices based on the tickers~~
- ~~printReport sorts errors based on the tickers~~
- printReport calls sortData, once for prices, once for errors
- sortData sorts the data based on the symbols

Time to roll out the last few tests:

testnode/stockfetch/test/stockfetch-test.js

```
it('printReport should call sortData once for prices, once for errors',
  function() {
  stockfetch.prices = { 'GOOG': 12.34 };
  stockfetch.errors = { 'AAPL': 'error' };
  stockfetch.tickersCount = 2;

  var mock = sandbox.mock(stockfetch);
  mock.expects('sortData').withArgs(stockfetch.prices);
  mock.expects('sortData').withArgs(stockfetch.errors);

  stockfetch.printReport();
  mock.verify();
});
```

```
it('sortData should sort the data based on the symbols', function() {
  var dataToSort = {
    'GOOG': 1.2,
    'AAPL': 2.1
  };

  var result = stockfetch.sortData(dataToSort);
  expect(result).to.be.eql([['AAPL', 2.1], ['GOOG', 1.2]]);
});
```

In those two short tests we verified first, that printReport calls sortData twice, and second, that sortData does its business as expected. The implementation should not take much effort; let's take care of that next.

```
this.printReport = function() {
  if(this.tickersCount ===
    Object.keys(this.prices).length + Object.keys(this.errors).length)
  this.reportCallback(this.sortData(this.prices), this.sortData(this.errors));
};

this.sortData = function(dataToSort) {
  var toArray = function(key) { return [key, dataToSort[key]]; };
  return Object.keys(dataToSort).sort().map(toArray);
};

this.reportCallback = function() {};
```

All the tests in the test list are now complete. We started with the readTickersFile function and walked through all the functions needed up through the printReport function. The tests are passing, but we can't call this done until we run the program and see the result on the console.

Integrate and Run

We need one final function that integrates all the functions together and for that, we need a few integration tests. Let's start with the integration tests; you can also key these into the stockfetch-test.js file:

```
it('getPriceForTickers should report error for invalid file',
  function(done) {
  var onError = function(error) {
    expect(error).to.be.eql('Error reading file: InvalidFile');
    done();
  };
  var display = function() {};

  stockfetch.getPriceForTickers('InvalidFile', display, onError);
});

it('getPriceForTickers should respond well for a valid file',
  function(done) {
```

```
  var onError = sandbox.mock().never();

  var display = function(prices, errors) {
    expect(prices.length).to.be.eql(4);
    expect(errors.length).to.be.eql(1);
    onError.verify();
    done();
  };

  this.timeout(10000);

  stockfetch.getPriceForTickers('mixedTickers.txt', display, onError);
});
```

The second test reads a file named mixedTickers.txt. Since this is an integration test, we need this file—we don't have the option of mocking file access this time. You can readily use the file provided in your workspace, with the following content:

```
GOOG
AAPL
INVALID
ORCL
MSFT
```

The new tests exercise an integrating function getPriceForTickers, which takes three arguments: a filename, a callback to display prices and errors, and finally a callback to received errors related to file access. The first test checks to make sure the integrating function wires the error handler properly to the rest of the code. The second test ensures that it wires the display callback function properly. Add the following short integrating function to the StockFetch class in the stockfetch.js file:

```
this.getPriceForTickers = function(fileName, displayFn, errorFn) {
  this.reportCallback = displayFn;
  this.readTickersFile(fileName, errorFn);
};
```

That was quite easy. Run the tests and ensure all the tests are passing:

```
Stockfetch tests
  ✓ should pass this canary test
  ✓ read should invoke error handler for invalid file
  ✓ read should invoke processTickers for valid file
  ✓ read should return error if given file is empty
  ✓ parseTickers should return tickers
  ✓ parseTickers should return empty array for empty content
  ✓ parseTickers should return empty array for white-space
  ✓ parseTickers should ignore unexpected format in content
  ✓ processTickers should call getPrice for each ticker symbol
  ✓ processTickers should save tickers count
```

```
  ✓ getPrice should call get on http with valid URL
  ✓ getPrice should send a response handler to get
  ✓ getPrice should register handler for failure to reach host
  ✓ processResponse should call parsePrice with valid data
  ✓ processResponse should call processError if response failed
  ✓ processResponse should call processError only if response failed
  ✓ processHttpError should call processError with error details
  ✓ parsePrice should update prices
  ✓ parsePrice should call printReport
  ✓ processError should update errors
  ✓ processError should call printReport
  ✓ printReport should send price, errors once all responses arrive
  ✓ printReport should not send before all responses arrive
  ✓ printReport should call sortData once for prices, once for errors
  ✓ sortData should sort the data based on the symbols
  ✓ getPriceForTickers should report error for invalid file
  ✓ getPriceForTickers should respond well for a valid file (1181ms)

27 passing (1s)
```

That was quite a journey. It's great to see all the tests pass, but we also want to see the program run and print the results. Let's write a driver program to run the code. Open the file src/stockfetch-driver.js in the current project in the workspace and enter the following code:

testnode/stockfetch/src/stockfetch-driver.js

```
var Stockfetch = require('./stockfetch');

var onError = function(error) { console.log(error); };

var display = function(prices, errors) {
  var print = function(data) { console.log(data[0] + '\t' + data[1]); };

  console.log("Prices for ticker symbols:");
  prices.forEach(print);

  console.log("Ticker symbols with error:");
  errors.forEach(print);
};

new Stockfetch().getPriceForTickers('mixedTickers.txt', display, onError);
```

The code is not much different from the last integration tests we wrote, except we log the output to the console instead of programmatically asserting the response. To run the driver, use the following command:

```
node src/stockfetch-driver.js
```

Take a look at the output—of course, the data will be different when you run it, depending on the current market and network connectivity:

```
Prices for ticker symbols:
AAPL     105.260002
GOOG     758.880005
MSFT     55.48
ORCL     36.529999
Ticker symbols with error:
INVALID 404
```

We took a test-driven approach to design this application—it's great to see the fruits of that effort in action. Let's next take a look at the code coverage.

Review the Coverage and Design

A total of twenty-seven tests came together to influence the design of the code. Since we wrote the tests first, the behavior of every single line of code is verified by one or more tests. We'll confirm that's true by taking a peek at the code coverage and then discuss how the design has evolved.

Measure Code Coverage

Each time we ran npm test, the command has been quietly measuring the coverage, thanks to Istanbul. If you'd like to know the exact command to create the coverage report, take a look at the test command, under scripts, in the package.json file. You'll find the following command in there:

```
istanbul cover node_modules/mocha/bin/_mocha
```

Take a look at the coverage report produced as part of running the npm test command:

```
  Stockfetch tests
...
  27 passing (1s)

============================= Coverage summary =============================
Statements   : 100% ( 59/59 )
Branches     : 100% ( 10/10 )
Functions    : 100% ( 19/19 )
Lines        : 100% ( 55/55 )
============================================================================
```

If you'd like to see the line-by-line coverage report, open the file coverage/lcov-report/index.html in a browser.

In contrast to 307 lines in stockfetch-test.js, the source code is 96 lines in stockfetch.js. That's a 3-1 test/code ratio—quite typical. For example, in an e-commerce system in production at my organization, the ratio is 3.9-1.

Test/Code Ratio

Applications that are test driven typically have three to five lines of test for each line of code.

Excluding the integration test, all the tests run pretty fast, are deterministic, and don't need a network connection to provide quick feedback that the code behaves as expected. While the two integration tests rely on a network connection, they too are deterministic in the way they're written. Next, we'll discuss the design that resulted from the test-driven effort.

The Design in Code

The tests and code evolved incrementally and it's hard to see the overall design from short code snippets. Download the electronic version of the test file[1] and the source code.[2] Take a few minutes to study both.

We started with a strategic design—see the figure in *Start with a Strategic—Just Enough—Design*, on page 91. That design gave us an initial direction, and the tests shaped that initial idea into a practical design with several good qualities. Each function is modular and concise, and does one thing. Along the way we applied many design principles—single responsibility principle (SRP), Don't Repeat Yourself (DRY), high cohesion, low coupling, modularity, separation of concerns, dependency injection... Let's visualize the resulting design.

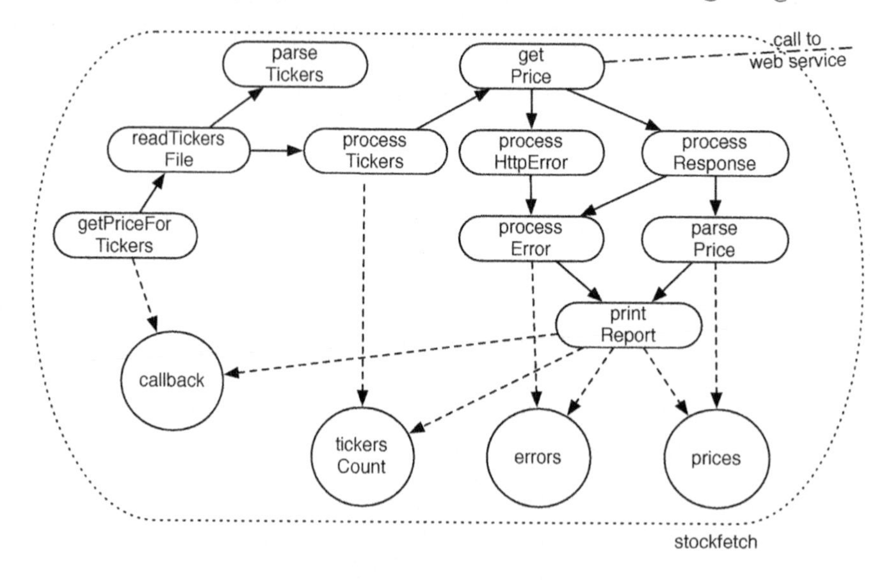

1. https://media.pragprog.com/titles/vsjavas/code/testnode/stockfetch/test/stockfetch-test.js
2. https://media.pragprog.com/titles/vsjavas/code/testnode/stockfetch/src/stockfetch.js

Compare the tactical design diagram with the strategic design diagram. While the tactical design diagram has more details and modular functions, you can see the original functions we identified in the strategic design—readTickersFile, processTickers, getPrice, printReport—in their new enhanced forms. The interfaces of these methods evolved significantly during the tactical design. New supporting functions also cropped up during the design, mainly to make the code cohesive, modular, and above all testable.

It did take a lot more effort than it would to simply hack the code. However, we know the consequence of hacking code: it leads to unmaintainable code. When we invest the time to create better-quality code, it yields better dividends when the code changes to add features or fix bugs. We don't have to manually exercise every piece of code to know things behave as expected. Quick feedback equals greater confidence and agility.

Providing HTTP Access

The code we created runs on Node.js as a standalone program. Providing HTTP access for this program is relatively easy as well.

Let's create a rudimentary web access—a single route, '/', that receives a GET request, with a query of the form ?s=SYM1,SYM2. Here's a short snippet of code that gets the query string from an HTTP request and delegates the bulk of the work to Stockfetch, which we designed earlier. Create this code in the file src/stockfetch-service.js in the current project in the workspace:

testnode/stockfetch/src/stockfetch-service.js

```
var http = require('http');
var querystring = require('querystring');
var StockFetch = require('./stockfetch');

var handler = function(req, res) {
  var symbolsString = querystring.parse(req.url.split('?')[1]).s || '';

  if(symbolsString !== '') {
    var stockfetch = new StockFetch();
    var tickers = symbolsString.split(',');

    stockfetch.reportCallback = function(prices, errors) {
      res.end(JSON.stringify({prices: prices, errors: errors}));
    };

    stockfetch.processTickers(tickers);
  } else {
    res.end('invalid query, use format ?s=SYM1,SYM2');
  }
};

http.createServer(handler).listen(3001);
```

To run this service, type the following at a command prompt:

```
node src/stockfetch-service.js
```

Then point a browser to the URL http://localhost:3001?s=GOOG,JUNK,AAPL to see the response.

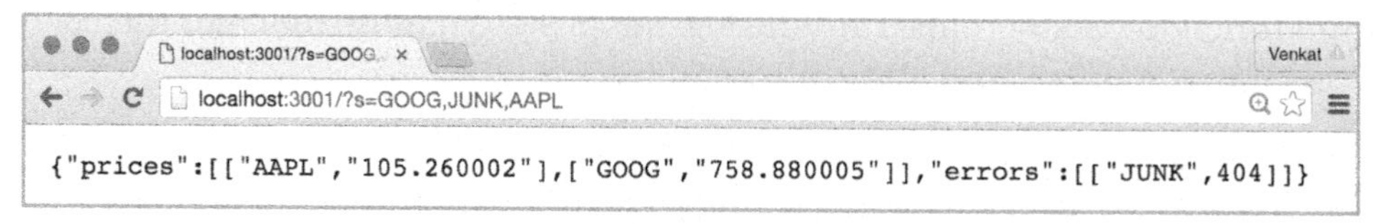

The output shows the prices for valid ticker symbols and error message for the invalid one. But wait a minute—Stockfetch is thoroughly automated and tested, but what about this little piece of code?

To write automated tests you'd have to design the code in stockfetch-service.js file differently. First, move the handler function to a separate file so it can be isolated and tested. The tests would verify that the function is handling various query strings, like an empty query string or one with no symbols, and so on. To test these we'd stub out req and res. Then the tests can verify that the function is interacting correctly with Stockfetch—we'd have to pass Stockfetch as a parameter for easy stubbing. Finally, we can test that the service file registers the handler function properly with the http.createServer function. That would test this piece of code, but in reality a typical web app would use different HTTP methods, like GET, POST, and DELETE, and multiple routes, like /, /stocks, and so on. How do we methodically test all of those methods and routes handlers? We'll answer that in the next chapter, but using Express.

Wrapping Up

This chapter pulled together lessons from prior chapters. We created a practical example to get a good feel for how to test drive a fully working Node.js app—from strategic design to fine-grained tactical design and implementation.

We saw that writing tests is an act of applying good design principles. The result is concise, modular, cohesive, and well-maintainable code. We also explored when and how to spike and the benefits of the insights it gives, especially when it's not clear how to proceed with tests. You can now apply the techniques explored in this chapter to write automated tests for back-end services. Realistically, though, writing full-fledged web apps on Node.js to support multiple routes or endpoints is tedious. You'd most likely use a tool like Express for that. In the next chapter you'll learn how to write automated tests for web apps that use Express, including writing tests for routes and various HTTP methods.

CHAPTER 6

Test-Drive Express Apps

Express is lightweight and makes writing Node.js web apps a breeze. With Express you don't have to write any code to read and render HTML files. You don't need to parse the query strings or manually map the URL paths or routes to handler functions. Simply configure the necessary details and the framework takes care of the rest for you.

It's great that Express does so much, but it may not always be clear how to automate the tests for code written in Express. That's because, when a request arrives, Express invokes the appropriate routes function and pushes the response to the client after the function completes. The code we write to handle the requests is not called directly from an application's code. Instead, it's invoked by Express when requests arrive. It's for such code we want to write automated tests that run fast and can be repeated easily.

Furthermore, the routes functions often invoke model functions that interact with the database. When that happens, we want to verify that the model functions properly perform their logic and correctly interact with the database.

In this chapter you'll learn to set up and test the database connection for MongoDB. You will then learn to design the model functions to interact with the database in a way that it can be stubbed out easily during testing. Once you master automated testing of the models, you'll learn to verify the behavior of the routes functions. With these techniques under your belt, you'll soon be on your way to fully automating and verifying your own Express apps.

Design for Testability

With frameworks like Express that make life easy, we can get apps up and running within minutes. But they seem to make it so easy to code that how to write the tests may not be clear. As we've discussed before, testability is a design issue. By carefully structuring code, we can perform fully automated testing of Express apps. Let's see an example.

Maintenance Cost Is Part of Development Cost

Frameworks like Express reduce the time and cost of creating code. Automated verification has the same benefit when changing code. To lower the overall development cost, we want to reduce both the coding cost and the maintenance cost.

We're going to test-drive a TO-DO Express app. It's intentionally small so we can keep the focus on learning test automation. The program will maintain a persistent list of task names along with the expected date of their completion. The application will respond to a `/tasks` URL route with one of the following HTTP methods:

- *GET*: return a list of all tasks in the database
- *GET*: given an `id`, return the task for that `id`
- *POST*: add a task to the database
- *DELETE*: remove a task with a given `id` from the database

Let's create a high-level design first.

Create the Strategic Design

We'll need one file, `tasks.js`, to register the routes and one model file, `task.js`, with functions to interact with the database. We'll use MongoDB for persistence, with one collection named `tasks` that will contain tasks with the following format:

`{'name': string, 'month': number, 'day': number, 'year': number}`.

Only the model will depend on the database; the routes should have no knowledge about persistence. This is a good idea, but we have to go a step further. It's better to avoid tight coupling of the model to the database as well. That's because, if the model were to directly depend on the database connection, it would be really hard to automate the tests of the model functions. To avoid this problem, we need dependency injection to decouple the model from the actual database connection. Then, the application can inject a connection to the production database, while the tests can inject a connection to the test database. When put that way it sounds complicated, but thankfully it's really easy to code.

The figure on page 123 shows the big picture of the strategic design.

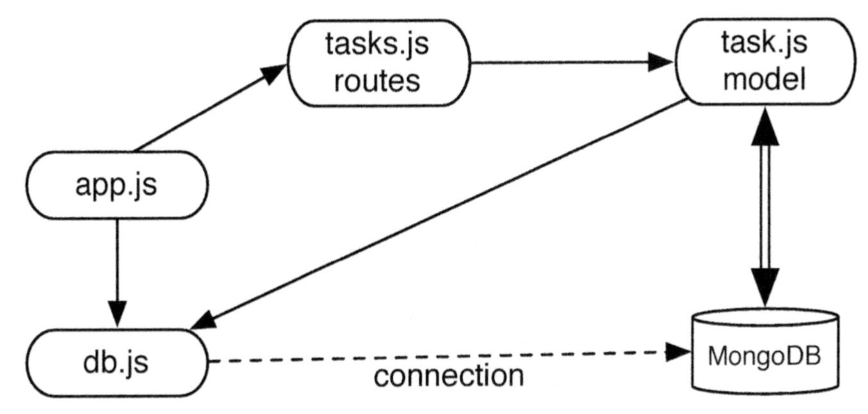

When the application starts up, the code in app.js will call a connect() function in the db.js file to create a connection to the production database. During testing, since we won't invoke the app.js file, the tests, where necessary, will call the db.js file to create a connection to the test database—we'll dig into this further when we get to the tactical design. In short, a connection to the appropriate database is set at the start of the application or the test run.

When a web request arrives for the URL /tasks, Express will call the appropriate callback function registered in tasks.js. Depending on the operation, the routes function will call the necessary model functions in task.js. The model will get the preset database connection from db.js to interact with the database.

Let's get down to the tactical design next.

Create the Tactical Design with Tests

We have three files or groups of functions to design: the database connection functions in db.js, the model functions in task.js, and the routes functions in tasks.js. app.js is mostly Express-generated code that will need some minor change. Let's start with a list of initial tests—positive, negative, and exception. Jot down on a piece of paper the tests that come to mind. Here are some:

- db: get returns null initially for the connection
- db: close will set the connection to null
- db: close will close the existing connection
- db: connect, given a valid database name, sets the connection
- db: connect, when no database name is given, returns an error
- task: all returns an array of tasks from the tasks collection
- task: get returns a task with a given id
- task: get returns a {} for an invalid id
- task: add adds a task to the tasks collection
- task: add will return an error if the input is invalid

- task: delete will delete a task with the given id
- task: delete will return an error if the task with id is not found
- tasks: ...we'll get to these later...

We have some initial tests on our hands. Let's move forward to the fine-grained design and implementation using the tests.

Set Up the Express App and Run a Canary Test

Before we can write any tests we need to prepare the Express application and install necessary modules, including MongoDB. A pre-created project directory is provided for you in the workspace—this was created using the express-generator.[1] Let's change to the tdjsa/testexpress/todo directory and take a look at the package.json file. The development dependencies include Mocha, Chai, Sinon, Istanbul—the testing-related modules we've come to expect.

Since we'll use MongoDB for this application, we need the MongoDB module—this is specified in the dependencies section in the package.json file. To get the dependencies installed for this project, let's run npm install.

In addition, we need the actual database. If you don't have it yet, download[2] and install MongoDB on your system. For this example we'll use a db directory under the tdjsa/testexpress/todo directory to store the database—an empty directory is already provided in the workspace. Once the installation of MongoDB is complete, start the MongoDB daemon with the command

```
mongod --dbpath db
```

Leave the mongod daemon running—you may move that command prompt window aside and out of the way. If you're running the daemon already on your system as a forked process, you may make use of that instead of those steps.

Under the todo directory, a test/server directory is already provided—this is where the tests will go. We'll start automated testing for this project by writing the canary test in the file named db-test.js that's under the test/server directory:

testexpress/todo/test/server/db-test.js

```
var expect = require('chai').expect;

describe('db tests', function() {
  it('should pass this canary test', function() {
    expect(true).to.be.true;
  });
});
```

1. http://expressjs.com/en/starter/generator.html
2. https://www.mongodb.org/downloads

Let's once again take a look at the package.json file in the current project in the workspace, but this time focus on the test command. It says mocha --watch --recursive test/server. The --watch option asks Mocha to rerun the tests when it sees a file change. The --recursive option explores all the subdirectories, in this case the server directory—right now we don't have any tests in the subdirectories of server, but soon we will.

Let's run npm test and make sure the canary test passes. We're ready to write tests for the database-related functions.

Design the Database Connection

The app.js file will call a connect function to set the database connection on application start. The rest of the code may call a get function to get the connection. The close function will help to close the database connection. The application may not have a use for the close function during normal execution—the connection is created on start-up and is kept throughout the execution. However, we'll still design this function because it will be needed to ensure the connections in the connection pool are closed properly during testing. Let's design those functions, test first, starting with the get function. In the test list, the first test says the get function will return null by default. Let's write the test to verify that in the db-test.js file, right after the canary test:

testexpress/todo/test/server/db-test.js

```
it('get should return null connection by default', function() {
  expect(db.get()).to.be.null;
});
```

The test calls the get function on db. For this we need to require the db.js file, in the top of the db-test.js file:

testexpress/todo/test/server/db-test.js

```
var db = require('../../db');
```

We'll next implement the minimum code to make the test pass, in the file db.js under the todo directory:

testexpress/todo/db.js

```
module.exports = {
  connection: null,

  get: function() { return this.connection; },
};
```

As soon as you save the files, Mocha should report two tests passing.

Let's design the close function next. The test list has two tests for this function. We'll start with the first test—open the file db-test.js and enter the following:

testexpress/todo/test/server/db-test.js

```
it('close should set connection to null', function() {
  db.close();
  expect(db.connection).to.be.null;
});
```

The test verifies that the connection is set to null after close is called. To make this test pass, we have to create a function named close, in the file db.js, right below the get function:

testexpress/todo/db.js

```
close: function() {
    this.connection = null;
},
```

Now let's write the second test:

testexpress/todo/test/server/db-test.js

```
it('close should close existing connection', function(done) {
  db.connection = { close: function() { done(); } };
  db.close();
  expect(db.connection).to.be.null;
});
```

The second test goes further to verify that close actually closed the connection instead of merely setting it to null. To avoid relying on the real connection, we stubbed out the connection's close function in this test.

Let's change the close function in db.js to make both tests pass:

testexpress/todo/db.js

```
close: function() {
  if(this.connection) {
    this.connection.close();
    this.connection = null;
  }
},
```

The next function, connect, should set the connection property to the database connection if a valid database name is given. MongoClient's connect function, which we'll use to get a connection to the MongoDB database, is an asynchronous function. So connect will need asynchronous tests. Here's the test to verify the function's behavior, the happy path:

testexpress/todo/test/server/db-test.js

```
it('connect should set connection given valid database name',
  function(done) {
    var callback = function(err) {
      expect(err).to.be.null;
      expect(db.get().databaseName).to.be.eql('todotest');
      db.close();
      done();
    };

    db.connect('mongodb://localhost/todotest', callback);
});
```

The test calls the connect function with a todotest database name, then waits for the callback. Within the callback, the test checks that there was no err and the connection object, returned by a call to get, is correct. To implement the function, we must remember to bring in the mongodb module at the top of the db.js file:

testexpress/todo/db.js

```
var MongoClient = require('mongodb').MongoClient;
```

Now, let's implement the connect function minimally for the happy path:

```
connect: function(dbname, callback) {
  var self = this;

  var cacheConnection = function(err, db) {
    self.connection = db;
    callback(null);
  }

  MongoClient.connect(dbname, cacheConnection);
}
```

That was straightforward. Let's think about the negative tests—the test list asks us to verify an invalid database name. On second thought, more than the database name may be invalid. For example, the schema name, instead of being mongodb, may be wrong. Let's test for both scenarios, with an incorrect schema name first.

In the test we'll send a badschema instead of the correct mongodb schema. The MongoClient's connect function will blow up with an exception if an invalid schema name is provided. We'll design the connect function to catch that exception and pass the details through the callback. Here's the test to verify that behavior:

testexpress/todo/test/server/db-test.js

```
it('connect should reject invalid schema', function(done) {
  var callback = function(err) {
    expect(err).to.be.instanceof(Error);
    done();
  };

  db.connect('badschema://localhost/todotest', callback);
});
```

To pass this test, let's place a try-catch around the call to MongoClient.connect(...) and in the catch block invoke the callback, passing the exception caught as the argument to the function. Then, after making sure the test passes, we can move on to the next negative test—send no name for the database and verify the code returns an error.

testexpress/todo/test/server/db-test.js

```
it('connect should reject invalid name', function(done) {
  var callback = function(err) {
    expect(err).to.be.instanceof(Error);
    done();
  };

  db.connect('mongodb', callback);
});
```

Here's the complete connect method to pass all three tests:

testexpress/todo/db.js

```
connect: function(dbname, callback) {
  var self = this;

  var cacheConnection = function(err, db) {
    self.connection= db;
    callback(err);
  };

  try {
    MongoClient.connect(dbname, cacheConnection);
  } catch(ex) {
    callback(ex);
  }
}
```

We've designed the functions in the db.js file to create a connection to the database. The connect function will be used by the app.js file to open a connection and the get function will be used by the model functions to access the database. The close function will be used by the database-related tests to close the connection after the tests—this function was written exclusively to facilitate automated testing. Now, let's move on to design the functions for the model.

Design for Testability from the Ground Up

Deliberately design with automated verification in mind. Structure code so the tests can be FAIR—fast, automated, isolated, and repeatable.

Design the Model

The model-related functions are the only functions that will interact with the database. We need four functions: an all function to get all the tasks from the database, a get to fetch a task with an id, an add to insert a task, and a delete to remove a task. We identified a few tests related to these functions in the test list. Before we can write them, we have to set up a connection to the database in a new task-test.js file.

Since the model functions update a database, we'll run into an issue with repeating the tests if we're not careful. Suppose we perform an add task on an empty database. Now we can verify that the number of persistent records is 1. If we run the test again, the test would fail since the count is no longer 1. Likewise, repeating a test that deletes a persistent task would fail since the data was removed on the first run. To solve this problem, we'll use test fixtures—the beforeEach and afterEach methods are great places to set up and clean up these data for each test. Also, we don't need to create a connection repeatedly for each test; instead we can initialize the connection in the before function, which is run once before the first test in the suite.

Take a Pragmatic Approach

In a puristic view, models don't talk to the database during testing. In this book, we take a pragmatic approach—we care more about writing deterministic and fast-running tests. If that goal can be achieved with a dependency in place, then that's fine. If, on the other hand, the dependency prevents us from realizing that goal, only then will we isolate it.

Set Up Connection and Test Fixture

Let's get the test setup code in place before looking at the first model test.

An empty directory named models is provided under the testexpress/todo directory with an empty file named task.js. Also, an empty test file named task-test.js is provided under the test/server/models directory.

Let's edit the task-test.js file to add the setup functions:

testexpress/todo/test/server/models/task-test.js

```
var expect = require('chai').expect;
var db = require('../../../db');
var ObjectId = require('mongodb').ObjectId;
var task = require('../../../models/task');
describe('task model tests', function() {
  var sampleTask;
  var sampleTasks;

  before(function(done) {
    db.connect('mongodb://localhost/todotest', done);
  });

  after(function() {
    db.close();
  });
});
```

The before function creates a database connection before any tests run. The after function takes care of closing the connection at the end of the last test. This is helpful when running Mocha with the watch option—it keeps database connections open only when necessary.

In addition to the previous setup functions, we need a few more functions. Let's create those, in task-test.js right below the after function, and learn what they do:

testexpress/todo/test/server/models/task-test.js

```
var id = function(idValue) {
  return new ObjectId(idValue);
};

beforeEach(function(done) {
  sampleTask = {name: 'a new task', month: 12, day: 10, year: 2016};

  sampleTasks = [
    {_id: id('123412341240'), name: 'task1', month: 10, day: 5, year: 2016},
    {_id: id('123412341241'), name: 'task2', month: 11, day: 2, year: 2016},
    {_id: id('123412341242'), name: 'task3', month: 12, day: 8, year: 2016},
  ];

  db.get().collection('tasks').insert(sampleTasks, done);
});

afterEach(function(done) {
  db.get().collection('tasks').drop(done);
});
```

The id function, which goes right below the after function in task-test.js, is a helper function to create an id of the proper type expected by MongoDB. In beforeEach we create a test fixture of some sample tasks and insert them into the tasks collection of the database. The afterEach function promptly wipes out the collection at the end of each test. These two functions work together to guarantee that each test gets a fresh slate of data to work with. Rerunning the tests should be quite easy with this setup in place.

The beforeEach function also initializes a variable sampleTask with a single canned task data. This will be useful for testing the add function, which we'll design after the all and get functions.

Design the all Function

With the setup completed in the task-test.js file, let's write the test for the all function:

testexpress/todo/test/server/models/task-test.js

```
it('all should return all the tasks', function(done) {
  var callback = function(err, tasks) {
    expect(tasks).to.be.eql(sampleTasks);
    done();
  };

  task.all(callback);
});
```

The test sends a callback to the task.all function and in the callback verifies that the get fetched all the tasks in the tasks collection of the database. Now, let's implement the all function in the task.js file to make this test pass:

testexpress/todo/models/task.js

```
var db = require('../db');
var ObjectId = require('mongodb').ObjectId;

var collectionName = 'tasks';

module.exports = {
  all: function(callback) {
    db.get().collection(collectionName).find().toArray(callback);
  },

};
```

The function makes an asynchronous call through the MongoClient's database connection. It gets the tasks collection, performs a query using the find function, and requests that an array be returned. Once MongoDB completes the query, it will invoke the callback. The all function passes the callback function it receives as a parameter to the toArray function, so in effect MongoClient will directly send back the response to the caller of the all function.

Let's glance at Mocha—running in the watch mode—to ensure all the tests, including the ones in db-test.js, pass. The db-test.js is in the test/server directory while the file task-test.js is in the test/server/models directory, but Mocha will run them all because of the --recursive option.

If you can think of negative tests for the all function, write those, and then make the necessary changes to the all function. When you're done, we can move on to design the get function next.

Design the get Function

Unlike the all function, which returned all the values from the tasks collection, the get function will return only the task with a matching id. If none are found, it will return a null. Keep in mind that the model functions are asynchronous since the MongoClient functions are asynchronous.

Here's the first test for the get function:

testexpress/todo/test/server/models/task-test.js

```
it('get should return task with given id', function(done) {
  var callback = function(err, task) {
    expect(task.name).to.be.eql('task1');
    expect(task.month).to.be.eql(10);
    done();
  };

  task.get('123412341240', callback);
});
```

The test sends a valid id and verifies that the value returned is equal to one of the canned tasks from the test fixture. Here's the code for the get function, to make the test pass:

testexpress/todo/models/task.js

```
get: function(taskId, callback) {
  db.get().collection(collectionName)
    .find({'_id': new ObjectId(taskId)}).limit(1).next(callback);
},
```

That's one short function to get the job done. While the all function used the find function with no arguments, this one uses the function with the details of the expected object's id. Then it limits the value to a single value, using the limit function.

Let's now write the second test:

testexpress/todo/test/server/models/task-test.js

```
it('get should return null for non-existing task', function(done) {
  var callback = function(err, task) {
    expect(task).to.be.null;
    done();
  };

  task.get(2319, callback);
});
```

The second test sends an arbitrary id—a value not present in any of the canned data—and verifies that the result is a null. Let's quickly confirm that this test passes along with all the current tests.

Let's move on to the tests for the add function.

Address the add Function

Unlike the prior functions, the add function will rely on user-entered data. When user input is involved, we need more error checking. The add function should take a task and add it to the database if valid. Otherwise, it should return an error. Since a task has multiple parameters, multiple things could go wrong. We need to check that each of the parameters is valid, but there's a catch.

Where possible, it would be better to perform the checks on the client side. This will be faster and will require fewer round-trips to the server. However, a check is still needed on the server side; it's possible that the data is sent to the server, bypassing the client-side checks. But duplicating code is an act of criminal negligence. We need to share the validation code between the two sides to honor good design.

Keep Data Validation Code DRY

Avoid duplicating any validation code between the client side and the server side. Duplication increases the cost of maintaining code and fixing errors.

Here's how we'll approach the design of validation. If a check can be performed only on the server side, we'll do it right within the add function. If a check may be performed on either sides, then we'll do it in a validateTask function, which will be common and shared by both sides. We'll focus on the validateTask function after we complete the tests for the model functions. For now, all we need to verify is that add calls validateTask properly.

We now have a fairly good idea on how to approach the design of the add function. We'll start with a positive test, then walk through a few negative tests, followed by tests for new tasks validation.

Start with a Positive Test

Let's get to the design of the add function. We'll first look at the positive test:

testexpress/todo/test/server/models/task-test.js

```
it('add should return null for valid task', function(done) {
  var callback = function(err) {
    expect(err).to.be.null;
    task.all(function(err, tasks) {
      expect(tasks[3].name).to.be.eql('a new task');
      done();
    });
  };

  task.add(sampleTask, callback);
});
```

We need to verify two things in this test: first, that the add function did not return any error, and second, that the data was actually added to the database. For this, in the callback passed to the add function we verify that the err parameter is null. Then, we invoke the all function to check if the new task is present in the database.

Let's write the minimum code to make this test pass. Add the following to the add function in task.js:

testexpress/todo/models/task.js

```
add: function(newTask, callback) {
      db.get().collection(collectionName).insertOne(newTask, callback);
},
```

In the add function we get the connection to the database and invoke the insertOne function, passing the given newTask and the given callback. The insertOne function will insert the given task to the database and invoke the callback to let us know all went well. Ensure that Mocha reports that all tests are passing as soon as the task.js file is saved.

Write Negative Tests

Let's now focus on a series of negative tests for the add function. First, we'll check that a duplicate task can't be added to the database. This is a test appropriate for the server side only since the data on the client side may be stale at any time.

testexpress/todo/test/server/models/task-test.js

```
var expectError = function(message, done) {
  return function(err) {
    expect(err.message).to.be.eql(message);
    done();
  };
};

it('add should return Error if task already exists', function(done) {
  sampleTask = sampleTasks[0];
  delete sampleTask._id;
  task.add(sampleTask, expectError('duplicate task', done));
});
```

expectError is a helper function that checks if the proper error message is received and also signals the completion of a test. The test tries to add an existing task to the database and verifies that the request gracefully fails. Let's modify the add function to pass this test:

testexpress/todo/models/task.js

```
add: function(newTask, callback) {

  var found = function(err, task) {
    if(task)
      callback(new Error('duplicate task'));
    else
      db.get().collection(collectionName).insertOne(newTask, callback);
  };

    db.get().collection(collectionName).find(newTask).limit(1).next(found);
},
```

The add function has evolved to meet the challenges of the new test. It calls the find function on the connection to first check if the given task exits. The new internal function found acts as a callback function for the find function. If a task is found, this internal function invokes the given callback with an error of "duplicate task." If not found, then it performs the intended insert operation.

That takes care of duplicate tasks, but more things may go wrong. Let's address task validation next.

Validate New Tasks

The name of a task may be missing or one of the date parameters may be messed up. Validation of these fields should be done on both the client side and the server side. That task should be delegated to a validateTask function. Let's write a few tests to check that add properly uses the validateTask function. We'll start with the first test for this purpose.

It's hard to replace the validateTask function with a stub or a mock if the add function directly depends on it. We will apply dependency injection to solve this. The task, which holds the model functions, can have a validate property that simply refers to the validateTask function. It's easy to replace this reference with a test double. We'll soon see how.

First, let's create a test to verify that the validate property refers to the validateTask function:

testexpress/todo/test/server/models/task-test.js

```
it('task.validate should refer to validateTask', function() {
  expect(task.validate).to.be.eql(validateTask);
});
```

Also, remember to add a require for the file that will hold the validateTask function:

testexpress/todo/test/server/models/task-test.js

```
var validateTask =
  require('../../../public/javascripts/common/validate-task');
```

To pass the previous test, we'll add the validate property to the task in task.js:

testexpress/todo/models/task.js

```
validate: validateTask,
```

We need the validateTask function. However, we're not yet ready to implement it—we need tests for it but we're in the middle of testing the task-related model functions. For now, let's change task.js to require the file that will hold the validateTask function:

testexpress/todo/models/task.js

```
var validateTask = require('../public/javascripts/common/validate-task');
```

Also, in the file todo/public/javascripts/common/validate-task.js we'll place the following temporary code:

testexpress/todo/public/javascripts/common/validate-task.js

```
var validateTask = function(task) {
  return true;
}

(typeof module !== 'undefined') && (module.exports = validateTask);
```

This file will be shared by the server side and the client side. The client side does not use require to gain access to functions in other files. Instead, it gets them through the window object. The check for the presence of module and exports will make this code available properly for both sides. Feel free to use any other techniques you like to share code between the two sides.

The current implementation of validateTask is a placeholder that will evolve to validate a task when we write tests for it later.

Now, let's turn our attention back to the tests for the add function—to verify that add calls validate when a new task is given.

testexpress/todo/test/server/models/task-test.js

```
it('add should call validate', function(done) {
      validateCalled = false;

      task.validate = function(task) {
              expect(task).to.be.eql(sampleTask);
              validateCalled = true;
              return validateTask(task);
      };

      task.add(sampleTask, done);

      expect(validateCalled).to.be.true;

      task.validate = validateTask;
});
```

The test creates a spy for the validate property. The spy asserts that the attached function is called with the task sent to the add function. The spy signals it was called by setting the validateCalled flag and returns the result of the validateTask function. The test then calls the add function, sending a sample task and a no-op/empty callback function. It then asserts that the validateTask function was actually called by checking the validateCalled flag. Finally, it replaces the spy with the original reference to the validateTask function. Update the add function to make this test pass. Make the call to find only if the given task is valid:

testexpress/todo/models/task.js

```
if(this.validate(newTask))
  db.get().collection(collectionName).find(newTask).limit(1).next(found);
```

That takes care of the happy path when a given task is valid, but we need to also test for the case when the given task is not valid—that is, if validateTask returns false. Let's write a test for that:

testexpress/todo/test/server/models/task-test.js

```
it('add should handle validation failure', function(done) {
  var onError = function(err) {
    expect(err.message).to.be.eql('unable to add task');
    done();
  };
  task.validate = function(task) { return false; };

  task.add(sampleTask, onError);

  task.validate = validateTask;
});
```

The test stubs the validate property and returns false to pretend that the given task is invalid. Then the test asserts that a proper error message is received in the callback passed to the add function. We need to write the else part in the add function to make this test pass:

testexpress/todo/models/task.js

```
if(this.validate(newTask))
  db.get().collection(collectionName).find(newTask).limit(1).next(found);
else
  callback(new Error("unable to add task"));
```

Designing the code for adding a new task took more effort than the work needed for previous operations. Let's take a look at the code created.

Review the Created Function

We created the add function using a few tests. Let's step back and take a look at the complete add function created using these tests:

testexpress/todo/models/task.js

```
add: function(newTask, callback) {

  var found = function(err, task) {
    if(task)
      callback(new Error('duplicate task'));
    else
      db.get().collection(collectionName).insertOne(newTask, callback);
  };

  if(this.validate(newTask))
    db.get().collection(collectionName).find(newTask).limit(1).next(found);
  else
    callback(new Error("unable to add task"));
},
```

The add function does significant work and the tests we wrote fully verify its behavior. That takes us to the design of the last model function—delete.

Handle delete

The delete function should take a task id and delete the task with that id. Add a positive and a couple of negative tests for that. Start with the positive test:

testexpress/todo/test/server/models/task-test.js

```
it('delete should send null after deleting existing task', function(done) {
  var callback = function(err) {
    expect(err).to.be.null;
    task.all(function(err, tasks) {
      expect(tasks.length).to.be.eql(2);
      done();
    });
```

```
  };
  task.delete('123412341242', callback);
});
```

The positive test verifies that the delete function removed the existing data and returned a null through the callback. In the callback, the response to the all function call will confirm that the number of tasks in the database is one less than what was created during the setup. Here's the minimum code, in the task.js file, to pass the test:

testexpress/todo/models/task.js

```
delete: function(taskId, callback) {
  var handleDelete = function(err, result) {
      callback(null);
  };

  db.get().collection(collectionName)
    .deleteOne({'_id': new ObjectId(taskId)},  handleDelete);
},
```

The delete function calls the deleteOne function using the connection object and passes the given id and a reference to an internal function. When deleteOne calls the internal function, it turns around and calls the given callback function, passing a null to indicate success.

That takes care of the happy path. Let's write a negative test to take care of an invalid id for task to be deleted:

testexpress/todo/test/server/models/task-test.js

```
it('delete should return Error if task not found', function(done) {
  task.delete('1234123412341234123423 19',
    expectError('unable to delete task with id: 123412341234123412342319',
     done));
});
```

The test passes a nonexistent id value and asserts that the error message indicates that the task with the given id could not be deleted. Let's change the delete function to make this test pass:

testexpress/todo/models/task.js

```
delete: function(taskId, callback) {
  var handleDelete = function(err, result) {
    if(result.deletedCount != 1)
      callback(new Error("unable to delete task with id: " + taskId));
    else
      callback(null);
  };

  db.get().collection(collectionName)
    .deleteOne({'_id': new ObjectId(taskId)},  handleDelete);
},
```

In the handleDelete internal function, if the delete count returned by deleteOne is not equal to 1, then we send an error message back to the caller through the given callback. Let's write one more negative test, to check that the code behaves well if no id was given:

testexpress/todo/test/server/models/task-test.js
```
it('delete should return Error if task id not given', function(done) {
  task.delete(undefined,
    expectError('unable to delete task with id: undefined', done));
});
```

The code we wrote should handle this case already and all tests should be passing at this time. Let's verify that and move forward.

The necessary functions for the model are now in place. A modular design, inversion of dependency to the database connection, and proper setup of the test fixture made the gnarly steps of testing into something pleasantly approachable.

The validate function relies on validateTask. Let's design that function next.

Design Shared Validation Code

The validateTask will check that a provided task has all the necessary properties. We need a number of tests to verify the behavior of validateTask. We'll write the tests in the todo/test/server/common/validate-task-test.js file.

Create Test Suite and Setup Code

Let's start with the necessary setup code:

testexpress/todo/test/server/common/validate-task-test.js
```
var expect = require('chai').expect;
var validateTask =
  require('../../../public/javascripts/common/validate-task');

describe('validate task tests', function() {
  var sampleTask;

  var expectFailForProperty = function(property, value) {
    sampleTask[property] = value;
    expect(validateTask(sampleTask)).to.be.false;
  };

  beforeEach(function() {
    sampleTask = {name: 'a new task', month: 12, day: 10, year: 2016};
  });
});
```

We brought the validate-task.js file into the test file using the require call. In the test suite, we created a helper function, expectFailForProperty, that will set a property on a sample task object to a given value and assert that the validateTask function returns false. In the beforeEach function we create a sample task, named sampleTask, which has all the essential properties. Instead of repeatedly creating a task in each test, we will use the sampleTask instance in each of the tests.

Write a Positive Test

Let's write the first test for validateTask, a positive test that confirms the sample task is valid:

testexpress/todo/test/server/common/validate-task-test.js

```
it('should return true for valid task', function() {
  expect(validateTask(sampleTask)).to.be.true;
});
```

The test simply calls the validateTask function with the good sampleTask as an argument. Recall that the current fake implementation of validateTask we created when designing the add function returns true. So, this test will pass without any change to the function under test. Let's start with negative tests next.

Write Negative Tests

The first negative test we'll write will verify that validateTask will return false if the argument to the function is missing.

testexpress/todo/test/server/common/validate-task-test.js

```
it('should return false for undefined task', function() {
  expect(validateTask()).to.be.false;
});
```

For this to pass, we have to make a small change to the validateTask function:

testexpress/todo/public/javascripts/common/validate-task.js

```
var validateTask = function(task) {
  if(task)
    return true;
  return false;
}
```

The validateTask function should also check that a null argument is not valid—let's test for that next:

testexpress/todo/test/server/common/validate-task-test.js

```
it('should return false for null task', function() {
  expect(validateTask(null)).to.be.false;
});
```

This test will pass without any change to the code. Next, we'll verify that validateTask returns false if the name property for a task is undefined.

testexpress/todo/test/server/common/validate-task-test.js
```
it('should return false for undefined name', function() {
  expectFailForProperty('name');
});
```

For this test to pass, we need to make yet another change to the validateTask function:

testexpress/todo/public/javascripts/common/validate-task.js
```
var validateTask = function(task) {
  if(task && task.name)
    return true;
  return false;
}
```

That was a small change—we added task.name to the if condition. Next, we'll verify the function's behavior when the name property is null.

testexpress/todo/test/server/common/validate-task-test.js
```
it('should return false for null name', function() {
  expectFailForProperty('name', null);
});
```

This test does not require any change to the code, the condition we added suffices for this test too. We've verified the function's behavior if the name property is undefined or null. But we should decide what to do if the value of this property is an empty string. Let's lean toward considering the task to be invalid if the name is empty. Here's the test for that:

testexpress/todo/test/server/common/validate-task-test.js
```
it('should return false for empty name', function() {
  expectFailForProperty('name', '');
});
```

Surprisingly, as soon as save the file, Mocha will report all the tests, including this test, as passing. The implementation we wrote has us covered for this condition too, so there's no need for anymore code to handle the name property. Let's turn our attention to the month property.

Keep the Tests DRY

The month property should not be undefined, null, or an arbitrary text—it should be a number. The same rule applies to the day and the year properties as well. We don't want to duplicate the tests for these three properties. We'll create the test for validating the presence of month in a way it's reusable for the other two properties.

testexpress/todo/test/server/common/validate-task-test.js

```
['month'].forEach(function(property) {
  it('should return false for undefined ' + property, function() {
    expectFailForProperty(property);
  });

  it('should return false for null ' + property, function() {
    expectFailForProperty(property, null);
  });

  it('should return false for non number ' + property, function() {
    expectFailForProperty(property, 'text');
  });
});
```

We've written three tests, but we embedded the tests into a forEach iteration over an array that contains a single element, 'month'. This form will create a set of three tests for each value in the array—currently we only have one value, but we'll add two more soon.

These tests will require the validateTask function to change yet again:

testexpress/todo/public/javascripts/common/validate-task.js

```
var validateTask = function(task) {
  if(task && task.name &&
    task.month && !isNaN(task.month))
    return true;
  return false;
}
```

Now the validateTask function checks that the month property exists and that it is a number as well. Let's change the array that holds 'month' to include the two other properties, like so:

testexpress/todo/test/server/common/validate-task-test.js

```
['month', 'day', 'year'].forEach(function(property) {
```

Let's change the validateTask function, one final time, to make all the tests pass:

testexpress/todo/public/javascripts/common/validate-task.js

```
var validateTask = function(task) {
  if (task && task.name &&
    task.month && !isNaN(task.month) &&
    task.day && !isNaN(task.day) &&
    task.year && !isNaN(task.year))
    return true;

  return false;
};
```

validateTask is a synchronous function and its implementation was pretty straightforward. The code is passing all the tests written so far. It's now time to design the routes functions.

Design the Routes

A routes function is a callback registered with Express. It's registered for a URI path and an HTTP method. The callback functions typically take three parameters: HTTP request (req), HTTP response (res), and a next routes handler (next). Unlike the model functions that we typically call from a routes function, we never directly call any of the routes functions in the application code. Instead, Express calls them with an HTTP request. In response, a handler typically renders data to the HTTP response object. This can leave us confused—how in the world can we test a function that's never called directly from the application code?

Well, our test can pretend to be Express and make the calls to verify the functions' behavior—it's that simple. JavaScript makes it incredibly easy to substitute JSON objects in place of real objects, so we can pass a JSON object instead of req, res, and next, with the canned behavior needed to make the tests pass.

Rely on Test Doubles when Testing Routes

When testing routes, by relying on test doubles, we can avoid having the server or the database up and running.

Let's Revisit Routes

Before coding the first test for a routes callback function, let's refresh our memory of what goes on in a routes file. We'll start on familiar ground—take a look at the index.js file, under the routes directory, in the todo project, that was created by the Express generator.

testexpress/todo/routes/index.js

```
var express = require('express');
var router = express.Router();

/* GET home page. */
router.get('/', function(req, res, next) {
  res.render('index', { title: 'Express' });
});

module.exports = router;
```

Let's study the content of the file so we can understand the effect of each line.

First, it brings in a reference to the express module. Then the Router function on the express object is called to get a router instance. It's this instance that is returned from this module at the end of this file. The file creates a callback, an anonymous function that is the second argument to the router.get call. In essence, the file registers the callback as a routes handler for a GET request on the URI / suffix.

The tasks.js file we'll create for the tasks routes is going to look very similar. The net effect of all the routes files—like index.js—is the following:

- For each method, like GET, POST, and DELETE, register a callback handler by passing two arguments: a path suffix and a callback.
- Each registered callback handler will optionally read some parameters from the req object, interact with the model functions, and make some calls on the res object. They may also call functions on next.

Now that we've refreshed what goes on in a routes file, let's think about testing for behavior of the code in these files.

The tests for the routes functions should focus on two things:

1. Verify that a handler for an expected HTTP method, like GET, is registered.
2. Verify that the registered handlers interact with the request, response, and model functions properly.

To verify the registration, we can mock out the functions like get on the router instance and verify the interactions of the code in the routes file with these functions.

To verify the behavior of the handlers, we can stub or mock out the req, res, and optionally the next instance. That way while the stubs can return canned data, the mocks can confirm proper interaction of the code with its dependencies like HTTP response.

Using these approaches we can fully verify that the necessary callbacks have been registered for the HTTP methods and the handlers are performing the necessary actions. That shouldn't be hard; let's give it a shot.

For the program at hand we need to register the following paths and methods:

- /—GET: will be used to get all the tasks
- /:id—GET: used to get task for the given id
- /—POST: used to create a new task
- /:id—DELETE: used to delete a task with the given id

Let's get started with the tests.

Start with the Stubs for Router

The test for the routes function will go into the file named tasks-test.js under the testexpress/todo/test/server/routes directory. The routes functions will go into a file named tasks.js under the testexpress/todo/routes directory. Both of these are provided as empty files in the workspace for your convenience.

As a first step, let's bring the necessary files into the test file tasks-test.js, using the require function calls:

testexpress/todo/test/server/routes/tasks-test.js
```
var expect = require('chai').expect;
var sinon = require('sinon');
var task = require('../../../models/task');
var express = require('express');
```

The most important part of the code segment is what's not there—no require to the routes/tasks.js file, not just yet. Don't require it now—let's postpone that until after we get a chance to stub out the express.Router function. The beforeEach function is a perfect place to create the stubs; that way the afterEach function can restore and get things back to a pristine state for the next tests.

testexpress/todo/test/server/routes/tasks-test.js
```
describe('tasks routes tests', function() {
  var sandbox;
  var router;

  beforeEach(function() {
    sandbox = sinon.sandbox.create();

    sandbox.stub(express, 'Router').returns({
      get: sandbox.spy(),
      post: sandbox.spy(),
      delete: sandbox.spy()
    });

    router = require('../../../routes/tasks');
  });

  afterEach(function() {
    sandbox.restore();
  });
});
```

The beforeEach function replaces the Router function of express with a stub that returns a JSON object with three properties: get, post, and delete. Each of these three properties, in turn, refers to a spy function—an empty function which will simply record the parameters when called. Only after the Router function is stubbed, the call to require is run to bring in the routes/tasks.js file. When this file performs a require(express), however, the code in routes/tasks.js will use the stub instead of the original Router function. That's because the test has already required this file and stubbed the Router. That's slick, eh?

Test the GET Method for Path /

The / path should handle an HTTP GET request. Let's write a test to verify the registration for this route. This test will go right below the afterEach function in the file tasks-test.js.

testexpress/todo/test/server/routes/tasks-test.js
```
it('should register URI / for get', function() {
  expect(router.get.calledWith('/', sandbox.match.any)).to.be.true;
});
```

For what appeared to be very complex at the outset, this test turned out to be shockingly simple, thanks to the ability to stub out the Router function.

Let's understand how this would work. The routes/tasks.js file is required in the beforeEach function. When loaded, the code in that file will require express and then call express.Router(); to get an instance of the router. Those steps are much like what you saw in the index.js file earlier. The router instance it receives, however, will be the canned value returned by the Router stub created in the test suite. As a result, when the code in routes/tasks.js calls the get function on router, it will be intercepted by the spy created in the test suite.

Let's implement the minimum code to make this test pass. The code for our routes functions will go into the testexpress/todo/routes/tasks.js file:

testexpress/todo/routes/tasks.js
```
var express = require('express');
var task = require('../models/task');

var router = express.Router();

router.get('/', undefined);

module.exports = router;
```

Since the test so far only checks if the GET method was registered for the path suffix /, the code does only that. The code invokes the get function with / for the path and an undefined argument for the handler. Let's confirm that Mocha, which is running in the watch mode, reports all the tests as passing, including the one for the routes.

Registering the method for the path suffix is only half the story. When Express calls the callback handler, upon receiving an HTTP GET request to the / path, we want the handler to get all the tasks from the database and return an array of JSON objects. This leads us to two issues we have to deal with in order to test the handler.

First, to test the handler we need to get hold of it. But the handler will be passed as the second argument to the get function—currently undefined in the code being tested. At first glance, the handler seems hard to reach from the tests. Thankfully the spy that stands in for the get function can come to the rescue.

Second, the handler will talk to the model functions in model/task.js—but this will drag us into setting up the database. Oh no, not that mess again. We don't have to; we can stub out the methods of the model in the test so the callback handler can be tested without the actual database.

Let's apply these ideas to the test for the GET / routes handler:

testexpress/todo/test/server/routes/tasks-test.js

```
var stubResSend = function(expected, done) {
  return { send: function(data) {
    expect(data).to.be.eql(expected);
    done();
  }};
};

it("get / handler should call model's all & return result",
  function(done) {
  var sampleTasks = [{name: 't1', month: 12, day: 1, year: 2016}];

  sandbox.stub(task, 'all', function(callback) {
    callback(null, sampleTasks);
  });

  var req = {};
  var res = stubResSend(sampleTasks, done);

  var registeredCallback = router.get.firstCall.args[1];
  registeredCallback(req, res);
});
```

Before the test, we created a helper function that returns a stub for the send function of res. The stub verifies that the data it receives is equal to an expected value and signals a completion of the test by calling done().

The test first creates a stub for the task.all function and returns a canned array of tasks. Recall from the model design that all gets a list of tasks from the database. The stub circumvents that call to the database for ease of testing.

Before the test can verify the behavior of a routes handler, it needs to get a reference to the handler. In the routes file, the handler we're interested in will be registered as the second argument to the get function. It's not hard to get access to this second argument—we'll simply ask the spy of the router.get function to give us the second argument passed to its call. That's done using firstCall to get the details of the first call to the get function—right now there's only one call, but there will be more later. Once we get the details of the first call, we can get the second argument from the args property. Finally, to complete the test, the obtained routes handler is called with the JSON stub for req and a stub for the res object.

With a few lines to set up the stubs, we totally avoided making database calls, reached into the routes handler, and verified it does exactly what we want. Now, let's implement the callback handler that we left undefined:

testexpress/todo/routes/tasks.js

```
router.get('/', function(req, res, next) {
  task.all(function(err, tasks) {
    res.send(tasks);
  });
});
```

All we needed was a call to the task.all function and in its callback, we direct the tasks array received to the res object's send function. In effect, the routes handler renders a JSON response of an array of tasks. If the response were HTML instead of JSON, then we'd call render instead of send like the code in the index.js file you saw earlier. That takes care of the / path for the GET method. Next let's take care of another GET method, but this time for the /:id path.

Test the GET Method for Path /:id

While the suffix / for the GET method will return all tasks, a GET request to a path suffix like /42 should return only a single task with that id. The model function get is capable of returning that data from the database. The corresponding routes callback handler needs to receive the id from the web request, make the call to the model task.get, check for errors, and return an appropriate response. Let's think through the tests for this routes function.

As a first test, let's assert that get is called with the path /:id—a short and simple test:

testexpress/todo/test/server/routes/tasks-test.js

```
it('should register URI /:id for get', function() {
  expect(router.get.calledWith('/:id', sandbox.match.any)).to.be.true;
});
```

The test does not expect much from the implementation we're about to write. It is mostly teasing out the initial declaration of the method. In the file routes/tasks.js we already have a call to the get method for the / path. Now, we'll add another call to get, but this time for the /:id path:

```
router.get('/:id', function(req, res, next) {});
```

After this change to the tasks.js file, ensure all tests are passing, including the new one.

The next test should help us get the necessary implementation into the empty callback function we registered with get function. For this, we will obtain a reference to the callback from the get function, invoke it, and assert it fulfilled its responsibility.

testexpress/todo/test/server/routes/tasks-test.js

```
it("get /:validid handler should call model's get & return a task",
  function(done) {
  var sampleTask = {name: 't1', month: 12, day: 1, year: 2016};

  sandbox.stub(task, 'get', function(id, callback) {
    expect(id).to.be.eql(req.params.id);
    callback(null, sampleTask);
  });

  var req = {params: {id: 1}};
  var res = stubResSend(sampleTask, done);

  var registeredCallback = router.get.secondCall.args[1];
  registeredCallback(req, res);
});
```

The earlier test used firstCall.args[1] to get the callback handler, but the latest test uses secondCall.args[1]. The reason for this is the file routes/tasks.js will make two calls to router.get, but with two different paths and handlers. Both calls will be received by the get's spy during testing, and we decide to pick whichever call details we're interested in.

There's one caveat. The tests expect the routes handlers to be registered in a certain order, the / first and /:id next. If you change the order of their registration in code, the tests would fail. This is a reminder that despite our good intentions, the tests rely on the implementation of the code to some extent. The good news, though, is that the feedback of such failure will be rather fast.

There are no surprises in the test. The test we just wrote is much like the tests for the / path. Let's implement the minimum code for the get call to make the test pass, again in the routes/tasks.js file:

```
router.get('/:id', function(req, res, next) {
  task.get(req.params.id, function(err, task) {
    res.send(task);
  });
});
```

The handler registered with get now calls the model task's get function. When the function returns a task instance, it's sent to the response object res.

We need to take care of one more issue here. The model task.get function returns a null if an invalid id is provided. Instead of a null we should nicely return an empty JSON object. Let's write the last test for this routes handler to verify that it gracefully converts the null to a friendly {} to indicate there's no data with that id.

testexpress/todo/test/server/routes/tasks-test.js

```
it("get /:invalidid handler should call model's get & return {}",
  function(done) {
  var sampleTask = {};

  sandbox.stub(task, 'get', function(id, callback) {
    expect(id).to.be.eql(req.params.id);
    callback(null, null);
  });

  var req = {params: {id: 2319}};
  var res = stubResSend(sampleTask, done);

  var registeredCallback = router.get.secondCall.args[1];
  registeredCallback(req, res);
});
```

Let's change the callback to the get function to make all three tests we've written so far pass:

testexpress/todo/routes/tasks.js

```
router.get('/:id', function(req, res, next) {
  task.get(req.params.id, function(err, task) {
    if(task)
      res.send(task);
    else
      res.send({});
  });
});
```

Let's quickly take a look at the Mocha test run to ensure all tests are passing. It's time to move on to design the routes handler for the POST method for path suffix /.

Handle POST Method for Path /

The path suffix / may receive an HTTP POST request in addition to a GET request. The POST method is for adding a new task. We first need to test that the path is registered. Then we need to verify that the handler calls the model task.add and returns success if all went well. We should also verify that the function gracefully returns any error if the add operation were to fail. That's three tests for the POST routes. Let's start with the first one:

testexpress/todo/test/server/routes/tasks-test.js
```
it('should register URI / for post', function() {
  expect(router.post.calledWith('/', sandbox.match.any)).to.be.true;
});
```

Just like the test for the get's :/id path route, this test simply verifies that the path / is registered for a post method. The implementation needed for the post method registration is much like the registration for the get. Take a few minutes to implement the code in tasks.js to make the latest test pass. Once you're done, let's proceed to the next test—to verify the behavior of the handler registered to handle the post method for the / route:

testexpress/todo/test/server/routes/tasks-test.js
```
it("post / handler should call model's add & return success message",
  function(done) {
  var sampleTask = {name: 't1', month: 12, day: 1, year: 2016};

  sandbox.stub(task, 'add', function(newTask, callback) {
    expect(newTask).to.be.eql(sampleTask);
    callback(null);
  });

  var req = { body: sampleTask };
  var res = stubResSend('task added', done);

  var registeredCallback = router.post.firstCall.args[1];
  registeredCallback(req, res);
});
```

This test fetches the registered callback and verifies that it calls the add function of the task model. This test will bring in the implementation into the handler registered for post—give that a shot and then move on to the last test for the post method.

testexpress/todo/test/server/routes/tasks-test.js
```
it("post / handler should return error message on failure", function(done) {
  var sampleTask = {month: 12, day: 1, year: 2016};

  sandbox.stub(task, 'add', function(newTask, callback) {
    expect(newTask).to.be.eql(sampleTask);
    callback(new Error('unable to add task'));
  });

  var req = { body:  sampleTask };
  var res = stubResSend('unable to add task', done);

  var registeredCallback = router.post.firstCall.args[1];
  registeredCallback(req, res);
});
```

This test verifies the behavior of the handler when an invalid task is added—it expects the handler to gracefully fail with an error message.

Let's take a look at the implementation of the post method for the / route that will satisfy all three tests:

testexpress/todo/routes/tasks.js
```
router.post('/', function(req, res, next) {
  task.add(req.body, function(err) {
    if(err)
      res.send(err.message);
    else
      res.send('task added');
  });
});
```

If the model task.add returns an error, pass the error's message as the response. If all went well, send back a success message. That completes the POST method handling. Implementing the routes handler for DELETE should be easy now.

Complete with the DELETE Method for Path /:id

The tests for DELETE method for the path suffix /:id should be a lot like the tests for the POST method—we need to verify path registration, check for success of the delete operation, and then check for the possibility of the failure of delete operation. Let's write the first test:

testexpress/todo/test/server/routes/tasks-test.js
```
it('should register URI /:id for delete', function() {
  expect(router.delete.calledWith('/:id', sandbox.match.any)).to.be.true;
});
```

This test verifies that a handler is registered for the DELETE method. Take a minute to implement the code in tasks.js to make this test pass; then proceed to the next test—the function will be like the code for the POST method handling.

The next test is on the handler, to verify it calls the delete function of the model and passes back the result of that call appropriately through the res object:

testexpress/todo/test/server/routes/tasks-test.js
```
it("delete /:validid handler should call model's delete & return success",
  function(done) {
  sandbox.stub(task, 'delete', function(id, callback) {
    expect(id).to.be.eql(req.params.id);
    callback(null);
  });

  var req = {params: {id: 1}};
  var res = stubResSend('task deleted', done);

  var registeredCallback = router.delete.firstCall.args[1];
  registeredCallback(req, res);
});
```

Once you get this test passing, by adding the minimum code in tasks.js, we can proceed to the final test for the DELETE method handling:

testexpress/todo/test/server/routes/tasks-test.js

```
it("delete /:invalidid handler should return error message",
  function(done) {
  sandbox.stub(task, 'delete', function(id, callback) {
    expect(id).to.be.eql(req.params.id);
    callback(new Error('unable to delete task with id: 2319'));
  });

  var req = {params: {id: 2319}};
  var res = stubResSend('unable to delete task with id: 2319', done);

  var registeredCallback = router.delete.firstCall.args[1];
  registeredCallback(req, res);
});
```

The last test verifies that any attempt to delete a nonexistent task is handled properly. The implementation is a lot like the handler for the POST method, except for the model functions used and the success message. Let's take a look at the DELETE method handling code in tasks.js, which is sufficient to pass all three DELETE-related tests:

testexpress/todo/routes/tasks.js

```
router.delete('/:id', function(req, res, next) {
  task.delete(req.params.id, function(err) {
    if(err)
      res.send(err.message);
    else
      res.send('task deleted');
  });
});
```

Take a minute to ensure that all the tests are passing, and we're done. That was quite a ride, but our code is fully automated and tested. You may be curious about the code coverage; we'll take a look at that next.

Measure Code Coverage

We didn't write any code without writing failing tests first. Hence, the coverage should hold no surprises. Let's take a couple of minutes to view the code in the online resources on the website for this book. We wrote the following tests:

- code/testexpress/todo/test/server/db-test.js
- code/testexpress/todo/test/server/models/task-test.js
- code/testexpress/todo/test/server/common/validate-task-test.js
- code/testexpress/todo/test/server/routes/tasks-test.js

With the help of these tests, we designed the functions in the following files:

- code/testexpress/todo/db.js
- code/testexpress/todo/models/task.js
- code/testexpress/todo/public/javascripts/common/validate-task.js
- code/testexpress/todo/routes/tasks.js

Let's measure the code coverage using Istanbul, which is already installed for this project. So far we've been observing the test run that was produced as a result of running the npm test command—this command was running Mocha in the watch mode. To run the coverage, we have to ask Istanbul to instrument the code and then run the tests. To save you some typing the necessary command is already provided in the package.json—it's in the scripts section under the command name cover. Let's take a look at that command:

```
"cover":
  "istanbul cover node_modules/mocha/bin/_mocha -- --recursive test/server"
```

The command calls istanbul and passes the command-line arguments cover and _mocha. Then the double dash, --, specifies that the options that follow are for Mocha and not for Istanbul.

To run this script, let's enter the following command on the command prompt:

```
npm run-script cover
```

This command will run the tests and produce the coverage report. Here's the output from the command:

```
  validate task tests
    ✓ should return true for valid task
    ✓ should return false for undefined task
    ✓ should return false for null task
    ✓ should return false for undefined name
    ✓ should return false for null name
    ✓ should return false for empty name
    ✓ should return false for undefined month
    ✓ should return false for null month
    ✓ should return false for non number month
    ✓ should return false for undefined day
    ✓ should return false for null day
    ✓ should return false for non number day
    ✓ should return false for undefined year
    ✓ should return false for null year
    ✓ should return false for non number year

  db tests
    ✓ should pass this canary test
    ✓ get should return null connection by default
    ✓ close should set connection to null
```

```
    ✓ close should close existing connection
    ✓ connect should set connection given valid database name
    ✓ connect should reject invalid schema
    ✓ connect should reject invalid name

  task model tests
    ✓ all should return all the tasks
    ✓ get should return task with given id
    ✓ get should return null for non-existing task
    ✓ add should return null for valid task
    ✓ add should return Error if task already exists
    ✓ task.validate should refer to validateTask
    ✓ add should call validate
    ✓ add should handle validation failure
    ✓ delete should send null after deleting existing task
    ✓ delete should return Error if task not found
    ✓ delete should return Error if task id not given

  tasks routes tests
    ✓ should register URI / for get
    ✓ get / handler should call model's all & return result
    ✓ should register URI /:id for get
    ✓ get /:validid handler should call model's get & return a task
    ✓ get /:invalidid handler should call model's get & return {}
    ✓ should register URI / for post
    ✓ post / handler should call model's add & return success message
    ✓ post / handler should return error message on failure
    ✓ should register URI /:id for delete
    ✓ delete /:validid handler should call model's delete & return success
    ✓ delete /:invalidid handler should return error message


  44 passing (355ms)

=============================== Coverage summary ===============================
Statements   : 100% ( 59/59 )
Branches     : 100% ( 26/26 )
Functions    : 100% ( 19/19 )
Lines        : 100% ( 59/59 )
================================================================================
```

The output shows all the tests running and also the code coverage. If you'd like to view the line-by-line coverage report for each JavaScript source file, then open the HTML version of the report: coverage/lcov-report/index.html.

As a final step, we'll get the app running as a server.

Take It for a Drive

The tests are passing but we have not yet run the app as a server, though we did have to run the mongod database process, but only for the tests for the model. We'll explore end-to-end testing, from the UI down to the database, later in the book. In the interim, having designed the server-side code, leaving it with the tests running is rather unsettling. We can't celebrate the efforts until we see the fruits of the efforts run as a true Express app. We need one more thing before that can happen; let's take care of that small bit.

We designed the db.js file, the model functions in model/task.js, and the routes in routes/tasks.js. The routes are all wired to a handful of path suffixes, but we need to assign a prefix to the paths. Let's choose a prefix of /tasks so that a GET request to the URL http://localhost:3000/tasks will go to the GET method callback handler for the suffix / we wrote in the routes/tasks.js file. To do this, right below this line in app.js:

testexpress/todo/app.js
```
app.use('/users', users);
```

add the following two lines:

testexpress/todo/app.js
```
var tasks = require('./routes/tasks');
app.use('/tasks', tasks);
```

The first line gets an object of router from the routes/tasks.js file—the one we designed to register the four paths. The second line sets the prefix as /tasks for all the routes we created in that file.

Oh, one more thing—we need to tell Express to connect to a database on start. For that, let's add the following, also to the app.js file, right after the previous two lines you added:

testexpress/todo/app.js
```
var db = require('./db');

db.connect('mongodb://localhost/todo', function(err) {
  if(err) {
    console.log("unable to connect to the database");
    throw(err);
  }
});
```

We call the connect method and send a database named mongodb://locahost/todo. This is the production/development database instead of the test database we used during testing. If there was an error, we report the failure on the console and throw an exception, to bring down the application. Let's hope all goes well for our test drive.

Now, let the drums roll; make sure that process you started earlier with the command

```
mongod --dbpath db
```

is still running—after all, we'd need the database for our app to work. Now, keep those drums rolling...run on the command prompt, from the todo directory, the command

```
npm start
```

Express should report that node ./bin/www is running and quietly wait. Let's fire up a request to the service and see the output. Oh, darn it—we did not create any HTML pages to interact with the app. In addition to creating HTML pages, we have to create some client-side code to make HTTP requests. But before we create any client-side code we'd have to write the test first. What gives? We're focused on the server here and don't want to get dragged into the client-side details now.

Thankfully, to see the application in action we can use some third-party programs that send HTTP requests with various verbs/methods.

We will use two different tools to exercise the server side: one is command line based and the other is browser based. You may use either one or both based on your preference.

Using Curl

For command-line types, *Curl* is an awesome tool. It's readily available on Unix-like systems and also on Windows through Cygwin. That's the tool we'll use here. Type in the following commands on a command line and see the app in action:

```
> curl -w "\n" -X GET http://localhost:3000/tasks
[]
> curl -w "\n" -X POST -H "Content-Type: application/json" \
  -d '{"name": "Practice TDD", "month": 8, "day": 10, "year": 2016}' \
  http://localhost:3000/tasks
task added
> curl -w "\n" -X GET http://localhost:3000/tasks
[{"_id":"568da96758102f0914bc93a6",
  "name":"Practice TDD","month":8,"day":10,"year":2016}]
> curl -w "\n" -X DELETE http://localhost:3000/tasks/568da96758102f0914bc93a6
task deleted
>
```

We'll discuss the response after we take a look at using the browser to do the same.

Using Chrome Extensions

Depending on the browser you're using, you may use a REST client extension for the browser that will allow you to create and send custom HTTP requests and observe the response from websites. We'll use the Advanced REST client Chrome extension to manually exercise the server side of the application. If you don't already have it installed in your Chrome browser, download it from the Chrome Web Store.[3]

Let's open the Chrome ARC application. In the text field for the URL, enter the URL http://localhost:3000/tasks, make sure that GET radio button is selected for the methods section, and click the Send button. The response in the bottom should show [] for the list of tasks, which is empty.

Next, change the methods radio button selection to POST, keep the same URL as before in the text field, change the "Headers" to Content-Type: application/json, and enter {"name": "Practice TDD", "month": 8, "day": 10, "year": 2016} into the Payload text area. Finally, clicking the Send button should display the message that the task was added, like in this figure:

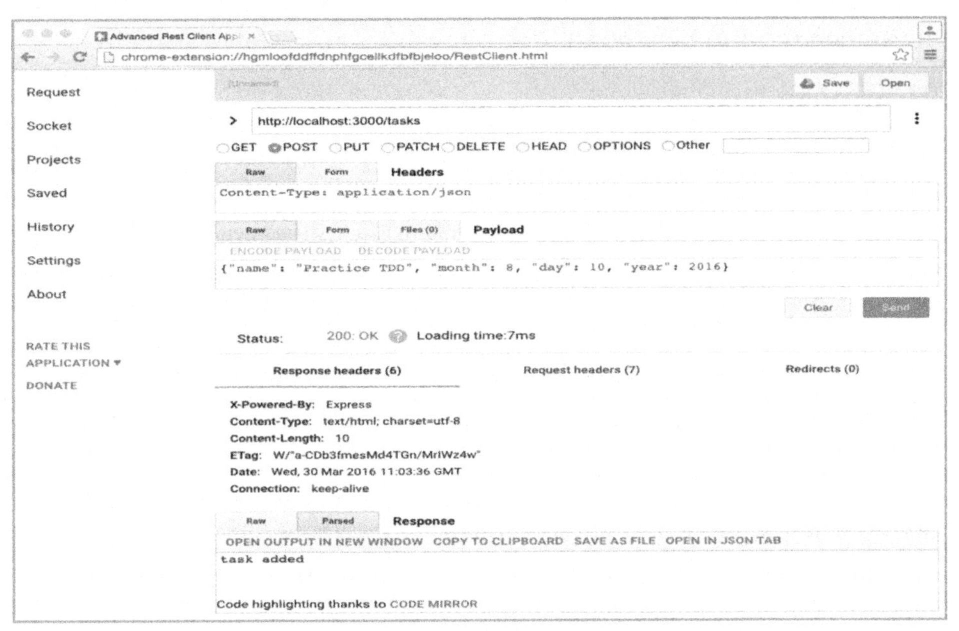

Next, let's change the methods section to select GET radio button again, keep the same URL, and click the Send button. The response will now show a JSON object of the task we added. Copy the value for the _id property into the clipboard. Then click the Clear button to clear the fields. Now, in the URL text field, enter the URL http://localhost:3000/tasks/THEID, replacing the "THEID" with the id you copied to the clipboard. Select DELETE in the methods radio button and click Send to observe the response from the server.

---

3. https://chrome.google.com/webstore/category/extensions

Observe the Response

Whether you used Curl or the browser extension, the response from the program should be the same. Let's take a look at how the program behaved to the four requests.

The app responded with `[]` to signal no values for the first HTTP `GET` request to the URL `http://localhost:3000/tasks`. The `POST` request to add a new task went well, with a response of `task added` received after the second request. The third request confirms that the task was actually added, and finally the last request to delete the data was handled favorably too. That shows the application in action, with the routes functions handling the routes, the model functions handling persistence, and with the data sitting in an instance of MongoDB.

While the quick runs showed us things are working on the server side, it's a manual process. Once you create the UI, you'll learn how to automate the integration test through the UI.

Wrapping Up

This chapter walked you through the steps to fully automate the design and implementation of the server side of an Express application. We started with a strategic design and saw the implementation unfold with each test. You learned how to configure the database and design the model functions for automated verification. We also explored how to fully test the Express routes functions with the help of stubs, spies, and mocks. Along the way we also created a validation function that will be shared with the client side. The code has a 100 percent test coverage and the automated verification was achieved without actually starting the web server.

In the next chapter we'll explore automated verification of the client side of this application. We'll look at two versions of the UI: one that uses the built-in functions to manipulate the DOM and the other that uses jQuery.

CHAPTER 7

Working with the DOM and jQuery

JavaScript on the client side is not new. But the demand for rich user interactions and improved computing power on the client side have spearheaded extensive and intense front-end development with the language. That has led to a greater need for automated verification of code running in browsers.

Verifying the behavior of client-side code poses some extra challenges. Coding on the client side is predominantly manipulating the DOM and interacting with services. This translates to a lot of moving parts. That in turn increases the chances for errors. If we take on manual verification, it soon will get tiring—we'll have to constantly type stuff into a browser to check if the code being developed is working as expected.

We can greatly reduce the pain of verifying client-side code by adopting a few techniques. By applying the techniques you'll learn in this chapter, you can continuously verify code while writing it. You also won't have to rush to create HTML files, or manually fire up browsers, or even spin up the web server. All this translates into greater productivity during development and peace of mind whenever you change code.

In this chapter, we'll create a client side to accompany the server side of the TO-DO program from the previous chapter. The server accepts JSON and provides a handful of routes to manipulate tasks. First we'll look at automated testing of code that uses functions readily available in browsers, to manipulate the DOM and interact with the back end. After that, we'll see how the tests change when we use jQuery to perform those operations.

Create a Strategic Design

We'll incrementally built a front end to the TO-DO service. The main features the UI will provide are list tasks, add a task, and delete a task.

A GET request to the URL /tasks of the TO-DO service returns an array of tasks in JSON format. A POST request to the same URL adds a task, while a DELETE request removes an existing task. Let's visualize a front end for this service—here's a sketch of a simple UI for the three operations:

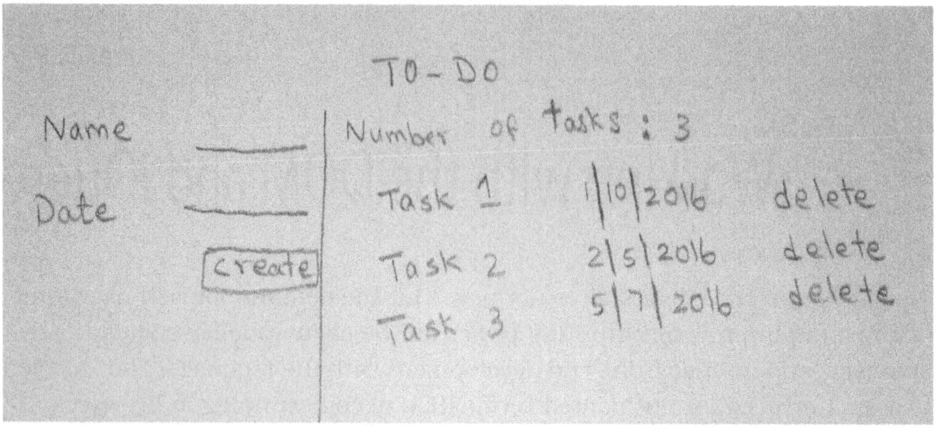

The view could be a pure HTML file with ids for dynamically updatable DOM elements, and it can reference a JavaScript file that holds the client-side code. Upon loading the browser should make a request to the service for a list of tasks and update the view when the data arrives. When the user asks to add a task, the UI should send the request to the server and update the view with the returned message or an error. It should perform the delete task operation as well.

We don't need the HTML file until we have written and tested the code for listing tasks. Nor do we need the server to be running at this time. Let's think through some tests to start the detailed design.

Create the Tactical Design with Tests

We will create a test list for the coding task at hand and set up the project to get ready for writing the first test.

Create a Test List

For the three operations we have, let's list some initial tests that come to mind. Remember, this is not a complete or a perfect list, but just an initial list of ideas:

- getTasks updates taskscount
- getTasks updates tasks table
- call getTasks on window onload

- addTask updates message
- addTask calls getTasks
- register add task click event on window onload
- deleteTask updates message
- deleteTask calls getTasks

More tests will come to mind once we start coding. We're ready to start with the first test, but we need to get the project prepared for client-side coding.

Set Up the Project

The client code will be part of the todo app, which we wrote for the server side in the previous chapter. For your convenience, the fully working server-side code is saved under the todo project in the tdjsa/testdomjquery directory in your workspace. As you may notice, this is a different directory than the workspace you used in the previous chapter. In addition, directories and empty files for writing client-side code and tests are provided in this workspace. Take a minute to change to this directory and get familiar with the subdirectories and files there, before we start writing tests for the client side.

The tests for the server side are in the test/server directory—these are copies of the tests we wrote in the previous chapter. We'll place the tests for the client side in the test/client directory. The client-side code will go into the public/javascripts/src directory. Empty files are provided in the appropriate directories for you to use.

For the client side, we'll use Mocha, Chai, Sinon, Karma, and Istanbul for running the automated tests. Let's run npm install to get the packages installed for this project.

A Karma configuration file, karma.conf.js, created using the command karma init, is already under the todo directory. Let's examine a small part of that file to see what's been set up specifically for this project:

testdomjquery/todo/karma.conf.js

```
frameworks: ['mocha', 'chai', 'sinon', 'sinon-chai'],

// list of files / patterns to load in the browser

files: [
  'public/javascripts/jquery-2.1.4.js',
  './test/client/**/*.js',
  './public/javascripts/**/*.js',
],
```

The frameworks configuration tells Karma to load the listed plugins. The files configuration lists the JavaScript files that Karma should load into the browser before running any test. By specifying **/*.js we're asking Karma to load up any JavaScript code—source and test—it finds under the mentioned directories test/client and public/javascripts, and their subdirectories. We also included the jQuery file—we'll talk about this file later.

Now, let's edit the client-side test file test/client/tasks-test.js to start with a canary test, to help us to verify that all things we need for the client-side testing are set up properly.

testdomjquery/todo/test/client/tasks-test.js

```
describe('tasks-with builtin functions-tests', function() {
  it('should pass this canary test', function() {
    expect(true).to.be.true;
  });
});
```

The package.json file contains a new scripts command to run the client-side tests: "test-client": "karma start --reporters clear-screen,dots". To exercise this command, from the command line, we'll run

```
npm run-script test-client
```

The canary test should pass. We'll start with tests for listing tasks next.

Evolve Code in Small Steps

The first client-side feature we'll implement will list all tasks when the page opens in a browser. For this we need a getTasks function. We listed three test in our test list for this function, but let's analyze before starting to code.

getTasks should request tasks from the service, but it's not the only function that will call the service. To keep the code DRY and cohesive, and to make testing easier, we'd want to delegate the task of calling the service to a separate function, say callService. getTasks would then invoke callService and register a callback, say updateTasks. The latter function would take on the responsibility to update a message DOM element if there was an error. Otherwise, it would update a taskscount DOM element and a div with a table of tasks. Those are reasonable goals for getTasks and updateTasks. Let's see what callService should do.

The main job of callService would be to call the back end and handle the response it receives. When a response arrives, it should forward both the status and the response text to the provided callback.

Finally, we need to register an event handler with the window onload event and in that handler call getTasks so that it automatically lists tasks after the page loads.

The three tests we jotted down initially now change to multiple tests in the test list:

- ~~getTasks updates taskscount~~
- ~~getTasks updates tasks table~~
- ~~call getTasks on window onload~~
- getTasks calls callService
- getTasks registers updateTasks with callService
- updateTasks updates message if status != 200
- updateTasks updates taskscount
- updateTasks updates tasks table
- callService makes call to service
- callService sends xhr status code to callback
- callService sends response to callback
- callService only sends when the final response is received
- register initpage handler with window onload
- initpage calls getTasks
- ...

We have our work cut out for us. Let's start with the first test.

Design getTasks

Let's start with the first test for getTasks—this test will go right under the canary test in the file todo/test/client/tasks-test.js. All we want to verify is that this function invokes callService and passes the necessary options. For this we can mock out the invoked function, like so:

testdomjquery/todo/test/client/tasks-test.js

```
it('getTasks should call callService', function(done) {
  sandbox.stub(window, 'callService',
    function(params) {
    expect(params.method).to.be.eql('GET');
    expect(params.url).to.be.eql('/tasks');
    done();
  });

  getTasks();
});
```

The test is using sinon to stub out the callService function of the window object—the global functions in tasks.js are available through the window object. The test verifies that when getTasks is called, it internally invokes callService with the GET method and /tasks as the url.

For this test, we need to set up sandbox using the beforeEach and afterEach functions in the test suite, like so:

testdomjquery/todo/test/client/tasks-test.js
```
var sandbox;

beforeEach(function() {
  sandbox = sinon.sandbox.create();
});

afterEach(function() {
  sandbox.restore();
});
```

It's time to write the minimum code to make the test pass. Add the following code for getTasks in the file todo/public/javascripts/src/tasks.js:

testdomjquery/todo/public/javascripts/src/tasks.js
```
var getTasks = function() {
  callService({method: 'GET', url: '/tasks'});
}

var callService = function() {}
```

As soon as you save the files, Karma, which is monitoring the code and tests, should report that the new test is passing.

The next test should verify that getTasks registers the callback updateTasks with callService. That's similar to the previous test:

testdomjquery/todo/test/client/tasks-test.js
```
it('getTasks should register updateTasks with callService', function() {
  var callServiceMock = sandbox.mock(window)
      .expects('callService')
      .withArgs(sinon.match.any, updateTasks);

  getTasks();
  callServiceMock.verify();
});
```

This test incrementally changes the getTasks function so it passes an extra argument to the callService function. Let's again edit getTasks:

testdomjquery/todo/public/javascripts/src/tasks.js
```
var getTasks = function() {
  callService({method: 'GET', url: '/tasks'}, updateTasks);
}

var callService = function() {}
var updateTasks = function() {}
```

That's all we expect of the getTasks function—single responsibility. Let's move forward to test updateTasks.

Update the DOM

getTasks passed updateTasks as the callback to callService. When a response arrives from the service, updateTasks should set the proper DOM elements. It has to handle two scenarios: update a message element if there was an error, or update the taskscount and a tasks table otherwise.

Let's test for the error scenario first:

testdomjquery/todo/test/client/tasks-test.js
```
it('updateTasks should update message if status != 200', function() {
  updateTasks(404, '..err..');

  expect(domElements.message.innerHTML).to.be.eql('..err.. (status: 404)');
});
```

The test calls updateTasks with 404 for the response status and a sample response text. After the call it verifies if the document's element with id message has the proper value set for its innerHTML property. But we haven't created an HTML file yet, so there are no DOM elements. No worries—we can quite easily stub out the document. In the test file, todo/test/client/tasks-test.js, let's change beforeEach to accommodate this:

testdomjquery/todo/test/client/tasks-test.js
```
//...
var domElements;

beforeEach(function() {
  sandbox = sinon.sandbox.create();

  domElements = {
  };

  sandbox.stub(document, 'getElementById', function(id) {
    if(!domElements[id]) domElements[id] = {};
    return domElements[id];
  });
});
```

In the beforeEach function we created a stub for the document's getElementById function. The stub creates an empty JSON object and assigns it to the stub domElements if it does not already exist. It then returns the fake JSON object in response to the getElementById call.

To make the new test pass, we should change the empty function for updateTasks to hold the following code:

testdomjquery/todo/public/javascripts/src/tasks.js
```
var updateTasks = function(status, response) {
  var message = response + ' (status: ' + status + ')';
  document.getElementById('message').innerHTML = message;
}
```

The code merely sets the message on the desired DOM element—that's enough for now. We can bring in more implementation with the next few tests.

For the next test, let's verify that updateTasks checks if the status is 200 and sets the appropriate DOM elements with tasks count and a tasks table. But before we write that test, let's think through the format of the response. The todo app back end sends a JSON response to the GET request at the /tasks URL. When callService receives the response from the service, it would be encoded as a string. So, the second argument to updateTasks would be a string—let's keep that in mind when writing the tests. Let's write the test to verify that updateTasks updates the tasks count:

testdomjquery/todo/test/client/tasks-test.js
```
it('updateTasks should update taskscount', function() {
  updateTasks(200, responseStub);

  expect(domElements.taskscount.innerHTML).to.be.eql(3);
});
```

In the test, the second argument passed to updateTasks is a string representation of a JSON array of tasks—we'll create that shortly. The next step verifies that the DOM element taskscount has the length of the array as its value. Let's change beforeEach to meet the needs of this test:

testdomjquery/todo/test/client/tasks-test.js
```
//...
var responseStub;

beforeEach(function() {
  //...
  responseStub = JSON.stringify([
    {_id: '123412341201', name: 'task a', month: 8, day: 1, year: 2016},
    {_id: '123412341202', name: 'task b', month: 9, day: 10, year: 2016},
    {_id: '123412341203', name: 'task c', month: 10, day: 11, year: 2017},
  ]);
});
```

We have everything in place for the test. Let's change updateTasks to make the new test pass:

testdomjquery/todo/public/javascripts/src/tasks.js
```
var updateTasks = function(status, response) {
  if(status === 200) {
    var tasks = JSON.parse(response);

    document.getElementById('taskscount').innerHTML = tasks.length;
  } else {
    var message = response + ' (status: ' + status + ')';
    document.getElementById('message').innerHTML = message;
  }
}
```

If the status is 200 the function manipulates the DOM to update the tasks count on the view. Let's write the final test for updateTasks. If the status is 200, the function should also update the view with a table of tasks:

testdomjquery/todo/test/client/tasks-test.js
```
it('updateTasks should update tasks table', function() {
  updateTasks(200, responseStub);

  expect(domElements.tasks.innerHTML).contains('<table>');
  expect(domElements.tasks.innerHTML).contains('<td>task a</td>');
  expect(domElements.tasks.innerHTML).contains('<td>8/1/2016</td>');
  expect(domElements.tasks.innerHTML).contains('<td>task b</td>');
});
```

The test checks to see if the generated table, in the DOM element with id tasks, has some sample expected HTML fragments. Here's the code for updateTasks that passes all three tests:

testdomjquery/todo/public/javascripts/src/tasks.js
```
var updateTasks = function(status, response) {
  if(status === 200) {
    var tasks = JSON.parse(response);

    document.getElementById('taskscount').innerHTML = tasks.length;

    var row = function(task) {
      return '<tr><td>' + task.name + '</td>' +
        '<td>' + task.month + '/' + task.day + '/' +task.year + '</td>' +
        '</tr>';
    }

    var table = '<table>' + tasks.map(row).join('') + '</table>';
    document.getElementById('tasks').innerHTML = table;
  } else {
    var message = response + ' (status: ' + status + ')';

    document.getElementById('message').innerHTML = message;
  }
}
```

We have one more function, fairly critical, on our hands for the loading of tasks feature. Let's take care of that next.

Call the Service

getTasks has a fairly specific expectation on the interface and behavior of the callService function—it should take two parameters: the first includes the method and the URL, whereas the second specifies the callback. The function should invoke the back-end service using the method and the URL given. Let's write a test to verify that small step.

But, before we do, let's think through the workflow for callService. The function will create an XMLHttpRequest object, set the method and the URL using the open method, and finally call the send function—that's the normal Ajax call sequence when using XMLHttpRequest. We don't have the back-end server running at this time and we certainly don't want to start it now. Making calls to the actual service during test runs will make the tests nondeterministic and brittle. We need to mock the XMLHttpRequest for testing purposes.

Verify the Client in Isolation

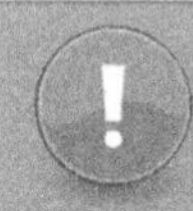

Running automated tests for the client-side code should not require the server to be up and running. Needing the server will make the tests brittle, nondeterministic, and hard to run.

Sinon has a powerful way to mock out XMLHttpRequest in place—FakeXMLHttpRequest. We'll make use of this facility here. Let's change the beforeEach and afterEach functions to bring in the XMLHttpRequest mocking facility:

testdomjquery/todo/test/client/tasks-test.js

```
//...
var xhr;

beforeEach(function() {
//...

  xhr = sinon.useFakeXMLHttpRequest();
  xhr.requests = [];
  xhr.onCreate = function(req) { xhr.requests.push(req); }
});

afterEach(function() {
  sandbox.restore();
  xhr.restore();
});
```

In beforeEach we called sinon.useFakeXMLHttpRequest—don't call this function on sandbox, which doesn't actually mock XMLHttpRequest—and instructed the onCreate function to gather the requests received into a local array. Any reference to

XMLHttpRequest in code now will use this constructor function referenced by xhr instead of the original. afterEach restores the original XMLHttpRequest at the end, which in effect removes the interception by the mock.

Now, let's write the test to verify that callService makes a request to the service and sets the method and URL as expected.

testdomjquery/todo/test/client/tasks-test.js

```
it('callService should make call to service', function() {
  callService({method: 'GET', url: '/tasks'}, sandbox.spy());

  expect(xhr.requests[0].method).to.be.eql('GET');
  expect(xhr.requests[0].url).to.be.eql('/tasks');
  expect(xhr.requests[0].sendFlag).to.be.true;
});
```

The test calls callService and checks the xhr.request, the array we populated in the onCreate function, for the expected values of method and url. In the code, these values will be set upon a call to open, but the actual request should end with a call to send—this is verified with a check for sendFlag to be true. Now, we'll implement the callService function, with just enough code to make this test pass:

testdomjquery/todo/public/javascripts/src/tasks.js

```
var callService = function(options, callback) {
  var xhr = new XMLHttpRequest();
  xhr.open(options.method, options.url);
  xhr.send();
}
```

This code is nowhere near complete, but we won't write more than what the current tests demand. Once Karma reports the test is passing, move on to the next test: when callService receives a response from the server, it should send the status and the response text to its callback. Here's a test to verify that:

testdomjquery/todo/test/client/tasks-test.js

```
it('callService should send xhr status code to callback', function() {
  var callback = sandbox.mock().withArgs(200).atLeast(1);

  callService({method: 'GET', url: '/tasks'}, callback);
  xhr.requests[0].respond(200);

  callback.verify();
});
```

The callback mock passed to callService verifies that callService sends it a proper status code. The callService function, however, will simply pass through the status code it receives from the web service. But, during the test runs, we're not talking to the real back end. Sinon solves this issue elegantly—you can instruct the mock to send a canned response much like the way a real service would. That's the purpose of the call to respond in the test.

In addition to the previous change, instead of merely calling verify on the mock, we use atLeast(1); this is because the event handler may be called multiple times during an XHR processing cycle. We'll write a test soon to limit the number of times the handler is called, but at this time multiple calls should be permissible.

Let's change the callService function to satisfy this test, like this:

testdomjquery/todo/public/javascripts/src/tasks.js

```
var callService = function(options, callback) {
  var xhr = new XMLHttpRequest();
  xhr.open(options.method, options.url);

  xhr.onreadystatechange = function() {
    callback(xhr.status);
  }

  xhr.send();
}
```

We know that callService sends back the status, but we also need the response. Here's a test to verify that:

testdomjquery/todo/test/client/tasks-test.js

```
it('callService should send response to callback', function() {
  var callback = sandbox.mock().withArgs(200, '..res..').atLeast(1);

  callService({method: 'GET', url: '/tasks'}, callback);
  xhr.requests[0].respond(200, {}, '..res..');

  callback.verify();
});
```

This test will result in a very small change to the code:

testdomjquery/todo/public/javascripts/src/tasks.js

```
var callService = function(options, callback) {
  var xhr = new XMLHttpRequest();
  xhr.open(options.method, options.url);

  xhr.onreadystatechange = function() {
    callback(xhr.status, xhr.response);
  }

  xhr.send();
}
```

Both the previous two tests checked for status code 200. But what if something went wrong—say, if the status was 404? Let's write a test to verify the code handles error situations properly as well.

testdomjquery/todo/test/client/tasks-test.js

```
it('callService should send error response to callback', function() {
  var callback = sandbox.mock().withArgs(404, '..err..').atLeast(1);

  callService({method: 'GET', url: '/tasks'}, callback);
  xhr.requests[0].respond(404, {}, '..err..');

  callback.verify();
});
```

The test passes and the code handles this situation. Later when we look at using jQuery, we'll need some extra code for this test—stay tuned.

There's one glitch—XMLHttpRequest is a chatty API. It may trigger the callback onreadystatechange multiple times, to let us know the connection was established, the request was received, the request is being processed, and finally that the request finished and the response is ready. Very rarely do we care about all these events; only the last one—which has a readyState value of 4—is of interest. Let's write a test to verify that the callback is called only when the final response is ready.

testdomjquery/todo/test/client/tasks-test.js

```
it('callService should only send when final response received', function() {
  var callback = sandbox.spy();
  callService({method: 'GET', url: '/tasks'}, callback);

  expect(callback.callCount).to.be.eql(0);
});
```

The test will fail right now since the callback to callService is called when any of the events are raised by xhr—at least one will be raised when the code calls send. Let's change the implementation of callService to trigger the callback only if the readyState is 4 and watch the test pass.

Here's the current implementation of callService to call the back end, created fully test driven, without the actual server running. Pretty nifty, eh?

testdomjquery/todo/public/javascripts/src/tasks.js

```
var callService = function(options, callback) {
  var xhr = new XMLHttpRequest();

  xhr.open(options.method, options.url);

  xhr.onreadystatechange = function() {
    if(xhr.readyState === 4)
      callback(xhr.status, xhr.response);
  }

  xhr.send();
}
```

The getTasks and the related functions to implement the tasks listing are done, but something has to call getTasks. That's the next step in our design.

Register window onload Event

When a user visits the view page, we want the list of tasks to appear right away without requiring any clicks or commands. In other words, getTasks should be run automatically. We may be able to achieve this by calling getTasks at the bottom of the script file public/javascript/src/tasks.js. But where the script file reference is placed in the HTML file will affect the correctness of the execution sequence. Instead of relying on that, we can implement the initialization using the window onload event—besides, it's not really hard. Let's write a couple of tests for this.

In the first test, we'll verify that the initpage function is assigned to the onload property.

testdomjquery/todo/test/client/tasks-test.js

```
it('should register initpage handler with window onload', function() {
  expect(window.onload).to.be.eql(initpage);
});
```

For this test to pass, we just need to make a simple code change. In public/javascripts/src/tasks.js we need to define an empty function initpage and assign it to window.onload. Let's write the second test, to verify that initpage calls getTasks.

testdomjquery/todo/test/client/tasks-test.js

```
it('initpage should call getTasks', function(done) {
  sandbox.stub(window, 'getTasks', done);

  initpage();
});
```

The test verifies, with the help of a stub, that the initpage function calls getTasks. Since getTasks is stubbed out with the reference to the done function, if initpage does not call getTasks, this test will time out and fail. Let's take a look at the code in tasks.js that makes these tests pass.

testdomjquery/todo/public/javascripts/src/tasks.js

```
var initpage = function() {
  getTasks();
}

window.onload = initpage;
```

That completes the code needed for listing tasks, all test driven. Take a look at the command window where Karma is running and you'll see that all the tests written so far are passing. But we can't really call this part done until we see the code in real action—that's next.

Take the UI for a Short Drive

We've only implemented code to get a list of tasks, but let's not write more code until we integrate the current code into an HTML page and see it live in action. You saw a design sketch for the UI in *Create a Strategic Design*, on page 161, it's a good time to put that into an HTML file.

testdomjquery/todo/public/tasks.html

```
<!DOCTYPE html>
<html>
  <head>
    <title>TO-DO</title>
    <link rel="stylesheet" href="/stylesheets/style.css">
  </head>
  <body>
    <div class="heading">TO-DO</div>
    <div id="newtask">
      <div>Create a new task</div>
      <form>
        <label>Name</label><input type="text" id="name" />
        <label>Date</label><input type="text" id="date"/>
        <input type="submit" id="submit" value="create"/>
      </form>
    </div>
    <div id="taskslist">
      <p>Number of tasks: <span id='taskscount'></span>
      <span id='message'></span>
      <div id='tasks'></div>
    </div>
    <script src="javascripts/src/tasks.js"></script>
    <script src="javascripts/common/validate-task.js"></script>
  </body>
</html>
```

There's nothing special in this file; it depicts the design from the sketch, except for the delete link—that will come in later. There's a placeholder div element for the tasks table. You can download[1] the stylesheet referenced from the media link for the book. The script tag refers to the source code we designed using the tests.

Before we can view the page, we need to start the server and get sample data into the database; let's do that next.

Start the mongod daemon using the following command, under the todo directory. The steps are the same as the ones you followed in *Set Up the Express*

1. https://media.pragprog.com/titles/vsjavas/code/testdomjquery/todo/public/stylesheets/style.css

App and Run a Canary Test, on page 124, except we will run the command in the todo directory under tdjsa/testdomjquery.

```
mongod --dbpath db
```

We'll leave that daemon running.

Also start the Express server using the command

```
npm start
```

We need sample data to view when we visit the HTML page. Populate the database with a sample task using the same steps you did in *Take It for a Drive*, on page 156, except leave the task in the database—don't delete the data.

Now take the bold step to fire up your favorite browser and point it at the URL http://localhost:3000/tasks.html. The browser should display the one task we added in the previous step.

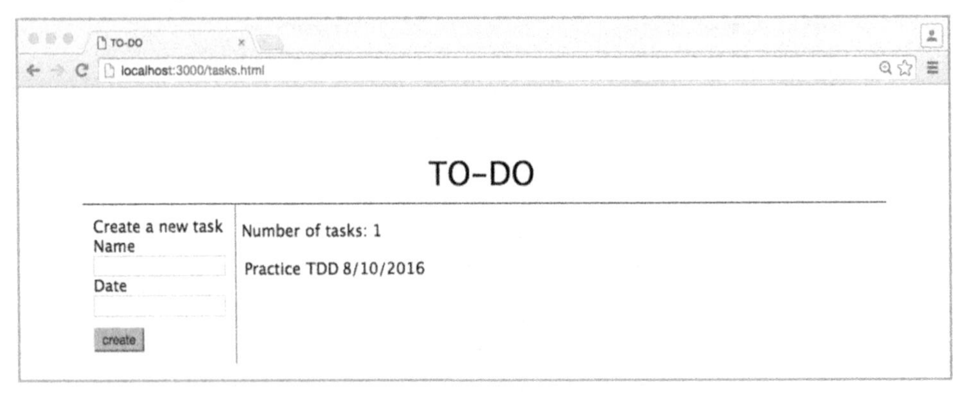

The complexities of communicating with the web service and manipulating the DOM are all hidden in the JavaScript source file and have been verified using the automated tests. Of course, for the code to integrate well with the browser, the ids of the DOM elements on the HTML page have to be right and the JavaScript source file has to be referenced correctly.

We completed the feature to list the tasks, but we have two more features to write. Feel free to stop the Node.js Express server that's running at this time. Take a break and continue on to those two tasks—bring along your favorite beverage for the next part.

Complete the Design

We completed about a dozen tests and all the efforts so far have gone toward fetching a list of tasks from the server and displaying them in the view. We still have two major features on our hands: to add a task and to delete a task. Both of these features need to communicate with the server. However, unlike getTasks these will have to send some data to the server in addition to getting a response. Let's work on adding a task first and then look at the delete operation after that.

Design addTask

Let's start by looking at the current test list:

- ...
- ✓ register onready handler with document
- ✓ initpage calls getTasks
- addTask updates message
- addTask calls getTasks
- register add task click event on window load

We can expect the tests for the addTask function to evolve much like the tests for getTasks did. Let's explore addTask further.

Analyze addTask

addTask needs to call the service—for that, we can use callService. But callService currently does not send any data—the send call passes no arguments. We need to evolve callService so it meets the needs of getTasks plus the additional needs of addTask. Thankfully, as we change callService the existing tests will give quick feedback that what worked before still works.

After addTask gets the response from the service, it needs to update the message DOM element with the response. Finally, it should update the list of tasks by calling getTasks to reflect the newly added task.

When a user clicks the create submit button, we need to call the addTask function. The initpage function we wrote earlier is a great place to register this event. Finally, addTask should return false—this is needed to prevent the browser from submitting the form. Otherwise, the browser, after executing the click event, will post a request to the server, which would be redundant since we've already handled that in code.

Oh, one final thing—there's no point in sending a request to the service if the task is not valid. For example, if the month were a string instead of being a number, it'd be better to let the user know without making a round-trip to the server. Thankfully, we already created a reusable function, validateTask, for that in the previous chapter. Instead of duplicating the efforts here, addTask can simply call that function. We will add a test to verify that behavior.

The test list should reflect the new understanding and the details of the design that's emerging from this analysis.

- …
- ~~addTask updates message~~
- ~~addTask calls getTasks~~
- ~~register add task click event on window load~~
- addTask calls callService
- callService sends data to the service
- callService has default content type
- callService sets content type if present
- addTask callback updates message
- addTask callback calls getTasks
- initpage registers add task click event
- addTask return false
- addTask for invalid task should skip callServiceMock, call updateMessage

Most of the work will be to evolve the callService function—which is good, since it's better to extend than duplicate. Changing a key function is often a risky business, but we have tests to cover our backs, no worries. Let's get started with the first test, for addTask.

Test for addTask

The addTask function should do a few things. It should create a new task JSON object from the data in the HTML input fields. Then we pass that data, as a string, to callService with a POST method, and also set a contentType property. We don't have to change the callService function yet—we can mock it out to test addTask—but we also have to create a stub for the necessary document elements. Let's get that done first. Change the beforeEach function in the test suite, like so:

testdomjquery/todo/test/client/tasks-test.js

```
beforeEach(function() {
  //...
  domElements = {
    name: {value: 'a new task'},
    date: {value: '12/11/2016'},
  };
  //...
});
```

We added stubs for the DOM elements name and date. The test should verify that addTask passes the necessary details to callService. Let's write that.

testdomjquery/todo/test/client/tasks-test.js

```
it('addTask should call callService', function(done) {
  sandbox.stub(window, 'callService',
    function(params, callback) {
      expect(params.method).to.be.eql('POST');
      expect(params.url).to.be.eql('/tasks');
      expect(params.contentType).to.be.eql("application/json");

      var newTask = '{"name":"a new task","month":12,"day":11,"year":2016}';
      expect(params.data).to.be.eql(newTask);
      expect(callback).to.be.eql(updateMessage);
      done();
    });

  addTask();
});
```

That's a lot of parameters for addTask to send. To make this test pass, let's add the addTask function and an empty updateMessage function in the tasks.js file.

testdomjquery/todo/public/javascripts/src/tasks.js

```
var addTask = function() {
  var date = new Date(document.getElementById('date').value);
  var newTask = {
    name: document.getElementById('name').value,
    month: date.getMonth() + 1,
    day: date.getDate(),
    year: date.getFullYear() };

  callService({method: 'POST', url: '/tasks',
    contentType: 'application/json',
    data: JSON.stringify(newTask)}, updateMessage);
}

var updateMessage = function() {}
```

The addTest function gets the values from the DOM input elements based on their ids, creates a JSON object, converts it to a string, and then sends it off to callService along with the appropriate options. It also registers a new updateMessage function as the callback with callService. Make sure the test is passing, and then move on to the next test.

Extend callService

We need to change callService. It served the getTasks function earlier, but now it also needs to satisfy the needs of the addTask function we just designed. Let's extends callService with the help of three tests.

In the first test we'll verify that callService passes on the given data to the web service:

testdomjquery/todo/test/client/tasks-test.js

```
it('callService should send data to the service', function() {
  callService({method: 'POST', url: '/tasks', data: '...some data...'});

  expect(xhr.requests[0].requestBody).to.be.eql('...some data...');
});
```

Update the callService function in tasks.js to make this test pass. Then proceed to the next test.

Extend Code by Writing Tests First

As we add features to the application, existing functions will have to evolve. Extend functions by adding new tests—write a test first, and then make a minimum change to the existing code to make the tests pass.

It's not enough to send the data; the data also has to be sent with the correct content type. If no content type is given, we would want a default value to be sent—let's verify that in the next test.

testdomjquery/todo/test/client/tasks-test.js

```
it('callService should have default content type', function() {
  callService({method: 'POST', url: '/tasks', data: '...some data...'});

  expect(
    xhr.requests[0].requestHeaders["Content-Type"]).contains("text/plain");
});
```

The callService function will have to evolve a bit to make this test pass. Confirm all tests pass after your change to the function, and then proceed to the next test. Let's verify that if a content type is given to the call to callService, then it passes that information along to the web service.

testdomjquery/todo/test/client/tasks-test.js

```
it('callService should set content type if present', function() {
  callService({method: 'POST', url: '/tasks', data: '...some data...',
    contentType: "whatever"});

  expect(
    xhr.requests[0].requestHeaders["Content-Type"]).contains("whatever");
});
```

To extend callService and make these tests pass, we only had to make minor changes—here's the modified function:

testdomjquery/todo/public/javascripts/src/tasks.js

```
var callService = function(options, callback) {
  var xhr = new XMLHttpRequest();

  xhr.open(options.method, options.url);

  xhr.onreadystatechange = function() {
    if(xhr.readyState === 4)
      callback(xhr.status, xhr.response);
  };

  xhr.setRequestHeader("Content-Type", options.contentType);

  xhr.send(options.data);
};
```

It was pretty easy to extend the function to send data to the server. Let's write tests for a few remaining pieces of work.

Design the Helper Functions

The correct operation of the addTask function relies on a few functions to be in place. We need to verify that updateMessage updates the message and also calls getTasks. Also, we need to check that initpage registers addTask as a handler for the create submit button's onclick event. Finally, we need to ensure that addTask returns false, for reasons we discussed during the analysis.

Let's start with the test to verify updateMessage's behavior.

testdomjquery/todo/test/client/tasks-test.js

```
it('addTask callback should update message', function() {
  updateMessage(200, 'added');

  expect(domElements.message.innerHTML).to.be.eql('added (status: 200)');
});
```

The test invokes updateMessage with a success status code and a message. It then verifies that the function updated the appropriate DOM element with the proper message. To make this test pass, we have to change the currently empty updateMessage function in tasks.js. We have to get the DOM element with id message and update its innerHTML property with the message that the test expects. After that, let's move on to the next test for updateMessage.

testdomjquery/todo/test/client/tasks-test.js

```
it('addTask callback should call getTasks', function() {
  var getTasksMock = sandbox.mock(window, 'getTasks');

  updateMessage(200, 'task added');
  getTasksMock.verify();
});
```

In this test we verify that the updateMessage function called the getTasks function, with the help of a mock for the latter method. Here's the updateMessage function that satisfies both tests.

testdomjquery/todo/public/javascripts/src/tasks.js
```
var updateMessage = function(status, response) {
  document.getElementById('message').innerHTML =
    response + ' (status: ' + status + ')';
  getTasks();
};
```

The next test, to move us forward with the design, should test that the initpage function registers addTask as the click event handler.

testdomjquery/todo/test/client/tasks-test.js
```
it('initpage should register add task click event', function() {
  initpage();
  expect(domElements.submit.onclick).to.be.eql(addTask);
});
```

The change to the initpage function to pass this test is simple:

testdomjquery/todo/public/javascripts/src/tasks.js
```
var initpage = function() {
  getTasks();
  document.getElementById('submit').onclick = addTask;
};
```

Next we need to test that addTask returns false.

testdomjquery/todo/test/client/tasks-test.js
```
it('addTask should return false', function() {
  expect(addTask()).to.be.false;
});
```

This test will introduce a trivial return at the end of the addTask function. Let's write one final test. For verifying a new task on the client side, addTask should call verifyTask. Furthermore, if that function returns false, then addTask should not invoke callService. Instead, it should call updateMessage. Let's write a test to verify these interactions:

testdomjquery/todo/test/client/tasks-test.js
```
it(
 'addTask for invalid task: should skip callServiceMock call updateMessage',
  function() {
  var updateMessageMock =
    sandbox.mock(window)
           .expects('updateMessage')
           .withArgs(0, 'invalid task');

  var callServiceMock = sandbox.spy(window, 'callService');
```

```
  sandbox.stub(window, 'validateTask')
         .returns(false);

  addTask();
  updateMessageMock.verify();
  expect(callServiceMock).to.not.be.called;
});
```

The test creates a stub for the validateTask function and instructs it to return false. The earlier tests will result in a call to the real validateTask function, but that's OK since the new tasks we used in those tests are all valid. In this test, even though the new task is the same as in previous tests, the stub for validateTask will simulate a failure. The mock for updateMessage and the spy for callService confirm that addTask dealt with the validation failure properly.

Let's take a look at the code for addTask to make the tests written so far pass.

testdomjquery/todo/public/javascripts/src/tasks.js

```
var addTask = function(fooback) {
  var date = new Date(document.getElementById('date').value);
  var newTask = {
    name: document.getElementById('name').value,
    month: date.getMonth() + 1,
    day: date.getDate(),
    year: date.getFullYear()
  };

  if(validateTask(newTask)) {
    callService({method: 'POST', url: '/tasks',
      contentType: 'application/json',
        data: JSON.stringify(newTask)}, updateMessage);
  } else {
    updateMessage(0, 'invalid task');
  }

  return false;
};
```

All the tests should be passing at this time. That completes the addTask feature.

See the Add Feature in Action

Let's quickly see the add task feature in action before moving on to implement the delete features. Start the back end, point the browser to the URL like before, and give the create button a try.

Once a task is added, the message returned by the server is displayed in the view and the new task appears in the task list.

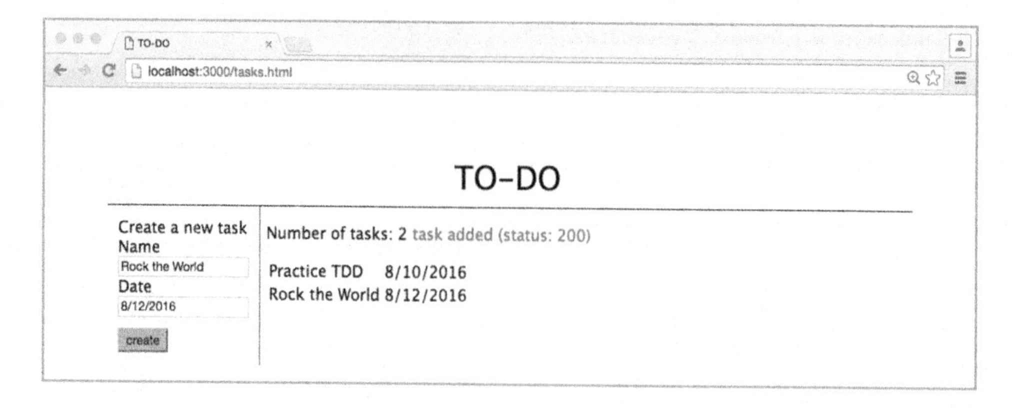

Design deleteTask

The final feature we'd like to provide on the client side is the ability to delete a task. For this we need a link next to the task in the view. When the link is clicked, deleteTask should send a call to the server, using callService of course, and update the message using updateMessage. That should be relatively easy, but we'll first update the test list.

- …
- ✓ addTask returns false
- ✓ addTask for invalid task should skip callServiceMock, call updateMessage
- updateTasks adds a link for delete
- deleteTask calls callService
- deleteTask registers updateMessage

Let's write the tests related to deleteTask. Here's the first test to verify the additional behavior of updateTasks:

testdomjquery/todo/test/client/tasks-test.js

```
it('updateTasks should add a link for delete', function() {
  updateTasks(200, responseStub);

  var expected = '<td>8/1/2016</td>' +
    '<td><A onclick="deleteTask(\'123412341201\');">delete</A></td>';
  expect(domElements.tasks.innerHTML).contains(expected);
});
```

The test says that updateTasks should provide a link to delete a task. Let's change that function to satisfy that test; here's the excerpt of code that changed:

testdomjquery/todo/public/javascripts/src/tasks.js

```
var row = function(task) {
  return '<tr><td>' + task.name + '</td>' +
    '<td>' + task.month + '/' + task.day + '/' +task.year + '</td>' +
    '<td><A onclick="deleteTask(\'' + task._id + '\');">delete</A></td>' +
    '</tr>';
};
```

The next test verifies that deleteTask calls callService.

testdomjquery/todo/test/client/tasks-test.js

```
it('deleteTask should call callService', function(done) {
  sandbox.stub(window, 'callService', function(params) {
    expect(params.method).to.be.eql('DELETE');
    expect(params.url).to.be.eql('/tasks/123412341203');
    done();
  });

  deleteTask('123412341203');
});
```

To pass this test, add the deleteTask function, in tasks.js, and invoke the callService function with the appropriate data. After that, let's write the third and last test for the deleteTask function:

testdomjquery/todo/test/client/tasks-test.js

```
it('deleteTask should register updateMessage', function() {
  var callServiceMock = sandbox.mock(window).
    expects('callService')
    .withArgs(sinon.match.any, updateMessage);

  deleteTask('123412341203');
  callServiceMock.verify();
});
```

This test verifies that updateMessage is passed as a handler to callService by the deleteTask function. Let's take a look at the necessary, but short, implementation for deleteTask.

testdomjquery/todo/public/javascripts/src/tasks.js

```
var deleteTask = function(taskId) {
  callService({method: 'DELETE', url: '/tasks/' + taskId}, updateMessage);
};
```

Karma should report all the tests passing. Once again, let's see the code in action. Start the back end and point the browser to the URL for the application to try the delete feature.

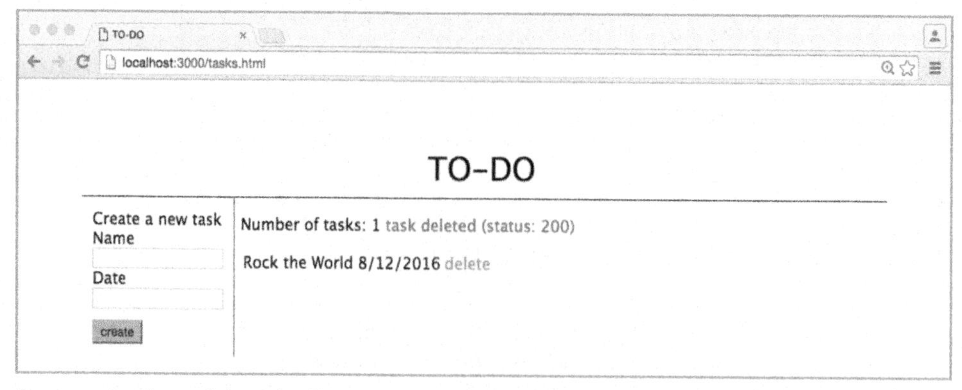

Once a task is deleted, the message from the server is displayed on the view and the task list refreshes as well to reflect the change.

You've seen how all the JavaScript code, both front end (in this chapter) and back end (in the previous chapter), can be designed in a way to run automated tests to get quick feedback.

Test with jQuery

We have a working client for the TO-DO application. But the client-side code we wrote is manipulating the DOM and accessing the web service directly using the functions available in browsers. Manipulating the DOM with the built-in functions can get tiring and the code can turn noisy. The jQuery library provides a number of convenience functions to select DOM elements, to navigate the DOM, and to update the DOM. Code using jQuery is far less noisy than code that directly interacts with the DOM. That's one of the reasons for the popularity of this library. It's highly likely that you may prefer to use jQuery to program the client side. To get a good feel for how to automate the tests for code that uses jQuery, we'll reimplement the client-side code, with tests, using jQuery.

Instead of walking through each test step-by-step, we'll discuss the main differences between testing code that uses jQuery and the code that directly interacts with the DOM. After going through the differences, you may want to reimplement the client-side code, with tests, using jQuery. When done, you can compare your solution to the one given in this book.

Get Ready to Test with jQuery

We need to verify that a few things are in place before we can write the test. First, we need the jQuery library. The uncompressed development version of the library file has already been downloaded[2] to the directory todo/public/javascripts

2. https://jquery.com/download

in the workspace. Also, the karma.conf.js in the current project already includes a reference to the jQuery file, as we see here:

testdomjquery/todo/karma.conf.js
```
frameworks: ['mocha', 'chai', 'sinon', 'sinon-chai'],

// list of files / patterns to load in the browser

files: [
  'public/javascripts/jquery-2.1.4.js',
  './test/client/**/*.js',
  './public/javascripts/**/*.js',
],
```

We wrote the client-side code that directly manipulated the DOM in todo/public/javascripts/src/tasks.js. We will place the version that uses jQuery in todo/public/javascripts/src/tasksj.js and the corresponding tests in todo/test/client/tasksj-test.js. For our easy identification, the filenames end with the letter j to convey jQuery-related implementation. Likewise, name the functions with a j prefix—for example, getTasks will become jGetTasks—this will help us keep both versions of code in place without the functions colliding and overwriting one another.

Let's explore how jQuery changes the way we'd test the client-side code.

Working with jQuery Selectors

In the DOM API, to access an element by its id, we'd write code like the following example:

```
document.getElementById('message').innerHTML = message;
```

You can drop characters by switching to jQuery selector syntax, like so:

```
$('#message').html(message);
```

When we used the document's getElementById, the test to stub the function looked like this:

```
var domElements;

beforeEach(function() {
  sandbox = sinon.sandbox.create();

  domElements = {
    name: {value: 'a new task'},
    date: {value: '12/11/2016'},
  };

  sandbox.stub(document, 'getElementById', function(id) {
    if(!domElements[id]) domElements[id] = {};
    return domElements[id];
  });
});
```

The stub for getElementById initialized an empty JSON object if the element did not exist. JavaScript has no issues setting a value for a nonexistent property. However, it can't survive calls to nonexistent functions. As a result, for the jQuery version, we'd have to set up the stub with a few more details for the functions that will be invoked—for example:

```
var domElements;

beforeEach(function() {
  sandbox = sinon.sandbox.create();

  domElements = {};

  sandbox.stub(window, '$', function(selector) {
    return {
      html: function(value) { domElements[selector] = value; },
      click: function(value) { domElements[selector] = value; },
      val: function() {
        if(selector === '#name') return 'a new task';
        return '12/11/2016';
      }
    };
  });
});
```

The stub for the $ function takes in a selector and returns a JSON object with various stubs for functions like html, click, and val—specifically the functions that will be used in the code.

Now to verify the behavior of the code and ensure it sets the proper DOM element, we'll change from

```
expect(domElements.message.innerHTML).to.be.eql('..err.. (status: 404)');
```

to

```
expect(domElements['#message']).to.be.eql('..err.. (status: 404)');
```

Next, let's see how to test the call to the back-end service.

Verifying Calls Using $.ajax

Sinon's FakeXMLHttpRequest was very helpful to verify the behavior of code that used the rudimentary XMLHttpRequest. With jQuery, you'd use $.ajax or one of its variations instead of XMLHttpRequest. That's a fundamental change in the API, but surprisingly it doesn't make much difference in the tests.

The function $.ajax is a wrapper around XMLHttpRequest, so the technique to intercept XMLHttpRequest using FakeXMLHttpRequest works really well for code that uses the jQuery wrapper functions. All the tests we wrote for the callService function are readily usable for the jCallService function as well.

The callback provided to XMLHttpRequest handled both success and error cases. When implementing with the $.ajax call, however, we need to write code to handle success and error separately; this is due to the nature of the API.

We need one extra test due to a small gotcha. The jQuery wrapper by default tries to guess the response format, like XML, JSON, and so on. The conversion from plain text to JSON format, for example, is done by the wrapper after the response arrives. The code we designed explicitly handles the conversion, so we don't really need this guesswork by jQuery. But that requires an explicit dataType option, in addition to setting the Content-Type header, to tell jQuery not to convert the response format.

Here's the test to verify this option is set, along with one other test for jCallService. The first test is pretty much the same as the one we wrote earlier for the non-jQuery version, except that the name of the function under test has been changed to refer to the jQuery-related version.

```
it('jCallService should make call to service', function() {
  jCallService({method: 'GET', url: '/tasks'}, sinon.spy());

  expect(xhr.requests[0].method).to.be.eql('GET');
  expect(xhr.requests[0].url).to.be.eql('/tasks');
  expect(xhr.requests[0].sendFlag).to.be.true;
});

it('ajax should set dataType to text', function() {
  var ajaxMock = sandbox.mock($, 'ajax', function(options) {
    expect(options.dataType).to.be.eql('text');
  });

  jCallService({method: 'POST', url: '/tasks', data: '...some data...'});
  ajaxMock.verify();
});
```

So, testing for the behavior of code that uses $.ajax is mostly the same as testing for code that uses XMLHttpRequest. There's one last thing: testing the last onload line in the code. Let's discuss that next.

Testing for document ready

If the HTML loads the script at the bottom, we may be able to directly call the jGetTasks function in the script to fetch the tasks from the server upon page load. However, let's still look at how to write tests for the document ready—it brings up some interesting challenges that are fun to tackle, and that technique may help you with other situations that may require similar tricks.

In the non-jQuery version, at the end of the client-side file tasks.js, the call

```
window.onload = initpage;
```

registered the initpage function to the window onload event. This results in the getTasks function running automatically when the view is loaded into a browser. In jQuery, you'd use a document ready function—which is much better—like so:

```
$(document).ready(jInitpage);
```

The jQuery version has a few benefits. It can fire the event as soon as the DOM is ready while the onload waits much longer for other things like images to complete loading. Also, the jQuery version gracefully deals with browser differences and falls back to alternate implementations depending on the browser. Overall, ready is much better than the raw onload. But how do we test for that? How do we verify that the code actually did register a handler with the document ready event?

In the non-jQuery version we simply checked the window's onload property to see if it had been set to the handler function—that was pretty straightforward. jQuery does not provide a way to pass the handler to ready—no way to query if the function was ever called. Sorry, it seems like that little one-line call can't be tested—darn it.

That's not a satisfying answer; you didn't pick up this book for us to give up so easily—that inner voice is saying "there's gotta be a way." Well, of course, but it involves a little trick.

Let's take another quick look at the file karma.conf.js:

testdomjquery/todo/karma.conf.js

```
frameworks: ['mocha', 'chai', 'sinon', 'sinon-chai'],

// list of files / patterns to load in the browser

files: [
  'public/javascripts/jquery-2.1.4.js',
  './test/client/**/*.js',
  './public/javascripts/**/*.js',
],
```

There's a reason for that load sequence—why jquery is first, the tests are next, and the files being tested come in last. Before the files with the source code being tested load up, we'll step in and spy the jQuery ready function—yes that's wicked…cool.

In the top of the test file, create a spy to the ready function.

testdomjquery/todo/test/client/tasksj-test.js

```
var readySpy = sinon.spy($.fn, 'ready');
```

Then write a test to verify that the handler was registered. For this, simply ask the spy if it saw the right handler being passed to the ready function.

testdomjquery/todo/test/client/tasksj-test.js

```
it('should register jInitpage handler with document ready', function() {
  expect(readySpy.firstCall.args[0]).to.be.eql(jInitpage);
});
```

A little trick of organizing the files loading in a specific order—one line to set up the spy and one to verify that the function was actually called—was all it took to accomplish what appeared so elusive at first.

The Complete Test and the Implementation Using jQuery

We discussed the differences in testing code written using the built-in functions versus using jQuery. You may want to take a break from reading and create the jQuery version from the ground up, as an exercise, with full automated tests. Practicing the example will help you hone in on the concepts and give you a much better insight than seeing the code examples. Once you're done with your exercise, take a look at the tests for the jQuery version in the media link[3] for this book. The client-side code[4] that corresponds to the tests in that file is also located in the media link.

We've written about 240 lines of test for about 80 lines of code. The code-to-test-ratio on the client side is close to the ratio we saw on the server side.

To use the jQuery version of code, we'll use the tasksj.html file, provided in your workspace. This file is similar to the tasks.html we saw earlier, except it includes a reference to the jQuery library and to the jQuery version of the client-side code instead of the version that directly manipulates the DOM.

Start the back end, like you did before, but this time point the browser to the new HTML file by visiting http://localhost:3000/tasksj.html. From the user's point of view, this should be no different from the feature seen at http://localhost:3000/tasks.html. Next, let's see how we did on code coverage.

Measure Code Coverage

Both the version with built-in functions and the jQuery one were created test first—not a single line of code was written without a test failing first. Then

3. https://media.pragprog.com/titles/vsjavas/code/testdomjquery/todo/test/client/tasksj-test.js
4. https://media.pragprog.com/titles/vsjavas/code/testdomjquery/todo/public/javascripts/src/tasksj.js

the minimum code was written to make the tests pass. You already know what the coverage for this code will be, but let's confirm.

The package.json file has a script to run the client-side coverage report—the cover-client command. It invokes Karma with the coverage option. The karma.conf.js file under the current project in your workspace includes the coverage-related preprocessor and reporters:

testdomjquery/todo/karma.conf.js

```
preprocessors: {
  './public/javascripts/src/*.js': 'coverage'
},
reporters: ['progress', 'coverage'],
```

That's asking all source code in the public/javascripts/src directory to be instrumented—since the jQuery file is in the parent of this directory, it will not be instrumented. To create the code coverage report, let's run the command

```
npm run-script cover-client
```

Once the test run completes, view the coverage report by opening the index.html file from the coverage/Chrome... subdirectory.

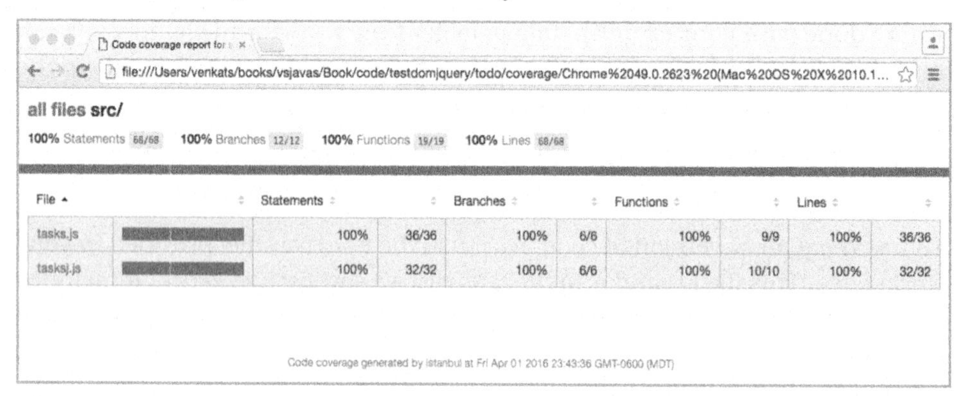

The report shows coverage for both tasks.js and tasksj.js. Click the filename links to view the line-by-line coverage. In case we entered some code without tests, this report will gently expose that urge.

The client-side JavaScript was thoroughly tested in this chapter. The link between HTML and the code, however, was not. While we manually verified that part worked, we'd certainly want automated quick feedback for that as well. Be assured, we'll explore that in Chapter 10, *Integrate and Test End-to-End*, on page 285.

Wrapping Up

The client-side JavaScript for two fully functional front-end views were test driven in this chapter. The knowledge from previous chapters on how to cope with dependencies played a vital role time and again throughout the exercise.

The chapter started with a sketch for the front-end views, followed by an initial test list. Soon upon analysis, the number of tests grew in size. The code to talk to the sever was modularized and reused among the different functions that needed to interact with the server. Also, the task validation code created in the previous chapter was reused on the client side.

In this chapter you learned how to approach testing the client side. We tested code that manipulated the DOM and also code that interacted with the server side. We tested both code that used built-in functions and code that relied on the jQuery library. You're all set to readily apply these techniques for the client side of your own applications.

While jQuery has been popular for years, AngularJS is gaining traction. It provides greater convenience for programming the client side, due to its ability to synthesize code to manipulate the DOM. In the next chapter we'll explore test-driving code that uses AngularJS.

CHAPTER 8

Using AngularJS

If manipulating the DOM is like driving a stick shift, then using jQuery is like driving an automatic. That would make using AngularJS like taking a cab—it's declarative: you tell it what to do and the framework synthesizes code to manipulate the DOM. The benefit is you write a lot less code to interact with the users and call services. But that doesn't diminish the need for automated testing. You still want to verify that your code does what's intended.

AngularJS is an opinionated framework—good automated testing is one of its opinions. Unlike tools that suggest testing is good, AngularJS goes the extra mile to make code actually testable. This is largely achieved by how AngularJS weaves different parts of the application code together—with dependency injection. Almost anything your controller needs is given to it as a parameter; as a result, you can easily stub or mock the dependencies for testing purposes.

In this chapter we'll test-drive an AngularJS implementation of the front end created in the previous chapter. We'll add a requirement to sort the task list in this implementation. This chapter uses AngularJS 1.5.8, which is the stable release as of this writing.

With the techniques you learn from this chapter, you'll soon be on your way to fully automate and verify the behavior of your own AngularJS applications.

Testing the AngularJS Way

Our approach to testing AngularJS code is different than the approach we used when testing jQuery code. The main reason is that AngularJS is a framework whereas jQuery is a library. Your code typically calls into a library, which, in turn, does things for you. On the other hand, a framework grows around your code, to take control, and do things *automagically* without explicit calls; that needs some extra effort and changes how you test.

An example will help refresh the AngularJS way and put things in context before we start writing tests. Here's a small controller that merely sets a greet variable's value after converting a string to lowercase.

angularsample/controller.js

```
var SampleController = function($filter) {
  var controller = this;

  alert('processing');
  controller.greet = $filter('lowercase')('HELLO');
};

angular.module('sample', [])
       .controller('SampleController', SampleController);
```

Here's an HTML file that refers to angular.min.js and the controller file.

angularsample/sample.html

```
<!DOCTYPE html>
<html data-ng-app="sample">
  <head>
    <title>Greet</title>
  </head>
  <body>
    <div data-ng-controller="SampleController as controller">
      <span>{{ controller.greet }}</span>
    </div>
    <script src=
 "https://ajax.googleapis.com/ajax/libs/angularjs/1.5.0-rc.0/angular.min.js">
    </script>
    <script src="controller.js"></script>
  </body>
</html>
```

The ng-app directive is where the magic begins; its presence signals AngularJS to process the DOM. Once the DOM is ready, the functions in the angular.min.js file trigger a systematic walk through the DOM, examining various attributes and expressions. When AngularJS comes across the ng-controller directive, it creates an instance of the given controller. Once that's over, AngularJS visits the children elements to further process any directives and expressions.

To try this example, you don't need any web servers. Just open the sample.html file in your favorite browser and watch AngularJS perform its show. While AngularJS creates an instance of the controller, it will stop for you to respond to the alert we placed in the constructor. Once you click OK, AngularJS will continue its processing and replace the expression on the page with the value.

The top part of the next figure illustrates the view of the page before the dialog is closed. The bottom part shows the view after the OK button is clicked.

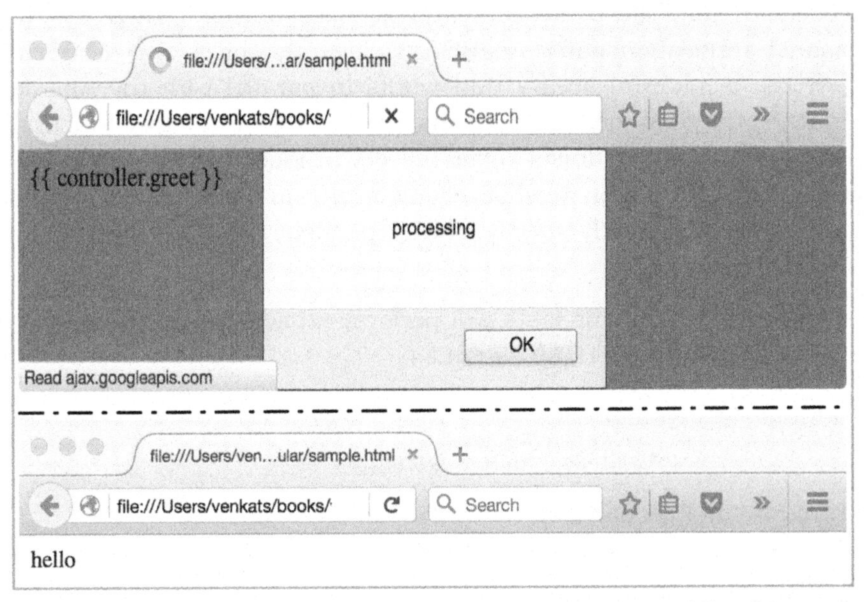

In the top part of the figure you caught AngularJS in the middle of processing. The raw expression appears on the page since AngularJS is not done with its walk through the DOM. If a failure happens midway, the users will be left to view a butchered view like this. A popular airline once showed such a spectacle on their reservation system—all the more reason to do automated testing to avoid such embarrassment.

Let's think about how to approach testing the code we put into controllers. We did not call any functions to load AngularJS or to create the controller instance—it just happened declaratively. We did not configure or pass a `$filter`, yet we used it in the controller to apply the `lowercase` function. AngularJS did so much auto-wiring when the browser loaded the HTML page.

During automated testing of the AngularJS code, we will not create or load any HTML files. That's because our focus is on verifying the code's behavior and we should not be forced to create an HTML file for that. But without one, how on earth will we create a controller, deal with the filter, and start testing? Dependency injection and mocking are the answers.

Automated Testing Is a First-Class Citizen in AngularJS

AngularJS was designed to make automated testing highly approachable. Dependency injection is used extensively for that reason.

During normal execution AngularJS does all the wiring when it sees the declarations for the dependencies. As you know, bringing in those real dependencies into the controllers and services during testing will make automated verification hard. AngularJS elegantly solves this issue using angular-mocks, a powerful library that works in parallel with the AngularJS dependency injection mechanism. This library provides factory functions to create test doubles and inject those objects in place of real dependencies. Thus, during test runs, instead of relying on the auto wiring that AngularJS provides, we will explicitly specify what dependency we want to pass to the code under test.

Let's get a feel for how the tests will perform explicit dependency injection. The declarative forms in HTML, such as

```
<html ng-app="sample">
...
<div ng-controller="SampleController as controller">
```

will turn into an injection request in the test suite, like so:

```
beforeEach(module('sample'));

beforeEach(inject(function($controller) {
  controller = $controller('SampleController');
}));
```

A call to module('sample') during the test run is the equivalent of the declaration ng-app='sample' during normal execution. Likewise, the call to inject returns an injector function that is passed to the beforeEach setup function. The injector then provides a controller factory function that can be used to instantiate a controller instance. This controller instance can then be used in each test.

That approach will take care of directives on the HTML page, but what about the dependencies in the controllers, like a call to web services? angular-mocks.js is the answer. By including this library, we can automatically replace the normal runtime environment with mocks. For example, we can make an Ajax call to a service. In short, AngularJS and angular-mocks provide an elegant way to test. Let's explore this further by building an AngularJS front end for the TO-DO application.

Start with an Initial Design

We sketched a design for the UI in the previous chapter, shown in the figure on page 199 again for your convenience. We'll implement the same look and feel for the AngularJS version as well.

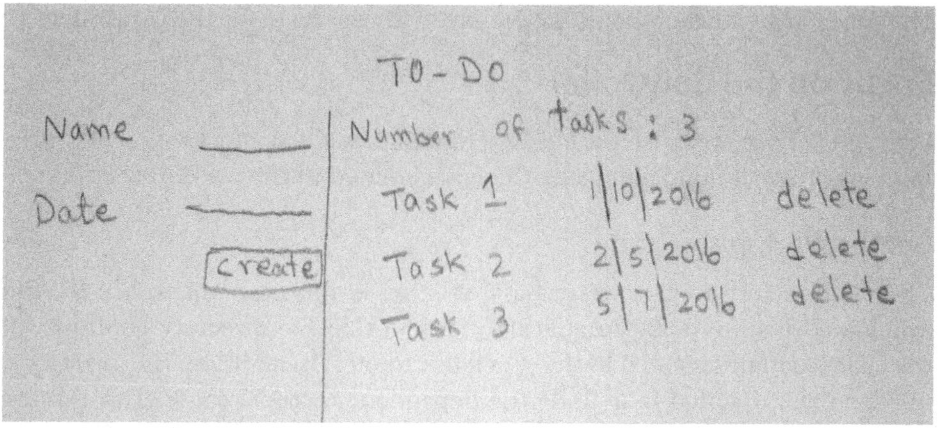

In addition, the task list in this version will appear in sorted order of the properties `year`, `month`, `day`, and `name`.

The HTML page will link to a `tasks-controller.js` file that will contain the AngularJS controller. This controller will contain the code for client-side computing and will interact with a service class in a `tasks-service.js` file. The service will act as a glue between the view in the browser and the data from the server. The HTML file will also declare an instance of the controller and refer to a couple of models.

We'll use two models: `tasks` to hold the transient state of the tasks fetched from the server and `newTask` to temporarily hold a task being created by the user on the front end. To list tasks we'll use an `ng-repeat` directive to loop through each item in the collection. To handle a button click by the user, we'll use the `ng-click` directive.

We need three functions in the controller. `getTasks` will fetch the tasks from the server through the service and sort it in the desired order. `addTask` will post a new task through the service. Finally, `deleteTask` will request the service to remove a task with a given `id` from the server.

We don't need the HTML file at this time. We are going to design the code using tests, and then we'll take it for a drive with the help of an HTML file. Let's get started with tests.

Let's think through some initial tests for the front end. We don't have to be perfect or complete—jot down what comes to mind. Here's an initial test list:

- `getTasks` should populate the `tasks` model with data from the service
- `getTasks` sorts `tasks`
- call `getTasks` on document ready
- `addTask` sends the data to the service
- `deleteTask` sends a delete request to the service

That gives us a starting point. Let's start with the tests for the controller.

Focus on the Controller

For this exercise, we'll use Karma, Mocha, Chai, angular-mocks, and of course AngularJS. We'll build alongside the code created in the previous chapter.

Get the Workspace Ready

Change directory to tdjsa/testangularjs/todo—this is the new workspace for the automated testing using AngularJS. This workspace directory contains all the code examples created in the previous chapter. In addition, the package.json file has been updated to include the dependency angular-mocks.js. The angular.js file has also been downloaded to the public/javascripts directory from the AngularJS download[1] page. Note that it's imperative for the version of angular-mocks.js to match the version of AngularJS, in case you plan to play with a different version of AngularJS than the one we use.

Finally, the karma.conf.js file has been updated to include the two new files. Here's part of the karma.conf.js that shows the new AngularJS-related references:

testangularjs/todo/karma.conf.js

```
frameworks: ['mocha', 'chai', 'sinon', 'sinon-chai'],

// list of files / patterns to load in the browser

files: [
'public/javascripts/jquery-2.1.4.js',
'public/javascripts/angular.js',
'node_modules/angular-mocks/angular-mocks.js',
'./test/client/**/*.js',
'./public/javascripts/src/todoapp.js',
'./public/javascripts/src/services/tasks-service.js',
'./public/javascripts/src/controllers/tasks-controller.js',
'./public/javascripts/**/*.js',
],
```

Also notice the order in which the files from the public/javascripts/src directory are loaded. This order is necessary to ensure the service is in place before the controller that needs it is loaded.

To install the necessary packages for this project, including angular-mocks.js, run npm install in the current workspace. Now we're all set to write our first AngularJS-related test for the project.

1. https://angularjs.org

Write the First Test

Open the pre-created empty test file test/client/tasks-controller-test.js. Write a canary test to verify that Karma is able to load all the necessary files, including angular-mocks.js:

testangularjs/todo/test/client/tasks-controller-test.js
```
describe('tasks controller tests', function() {
  // write canary test only if this is the first test
  //for the front-end in this project
  it('should pass this canary test', function() {
    expect(true).to.be.true;
  });
});
```

To run the test and confirm all is well, execute the following command:

```
npm run-script test-client
```

This will instruct Karma to load up all the necessary files and execute the tests it finds under the test/client directory.

The canary test should pass. Let's turn our attention to writing tests for listing tasks.

Design the Controller

The initial test list we jotted down has five tests. The first three relate to getting the task list from the service and displaying it on the view. Let's analyze the first test, "getTasks should populate the tasks model with data from the service," in the context of AngularJS.

In the controller, let's create a model, say tasks, which is a mere array of JSON objects that will hold the list of tasks that comes from the back end. On start, while we wait for data to arrive from the service, we need to initialize tasks. The getTasks function should focus on a single responsibility and not take on things that can be delegated to other functions—modular is better. As a good design, getTasks will only call the service and register handlers for success and error cases. Let's call these handlers updateTasks and updateError.

The first function, when called after a response arrives, should update the tasks model. The second function should update a message model with error details. We better initialize this model with an empty string in the beginning. That's a lot of detail already; we can think about other actions like sorting later. Let's update the test list with these fine-grained details.

- ~~getTasks should populate the tasks model with data from the service~~
- tasks is empty on create
- message is empty on create
- getTasks interacts with the service successfully
- getTasks handles error from the service
- updateTasks updates tasks
- updateError updates message
- getTasks sorts tasks
- call getTasks on document ready
- ...

The first two tests are simple; they will help us get started with the controller.

In the test file tasks-controller-test.js, create a test to verify that tasks is empty when the controller is created.

testangularjs/todo/test/client/tasks-controller-test.js

```
it('tasks should be empty on create', function() {
  expect(controller.tasks).to.be.eql([]);
});
```

That's probably one of the simplest tests ever, but it raises a question—where does the controller come from?

While AngularJS does everything for us during a normal run, we have to do some work to wire the dependencies during test runs. First, we need to bring in the module for the application, then inject the controller factory function, and finally create a controller for use in tests. In the test file, let's insert the following piece of code right above the new test:

```
var controller;

beforeEach(module('todoapp'));

beforeEach(inject(function($controller) {
  controller = $controller('TasksController');
}));
```

We first declared a variable named controller—this will be the reference to the controller instance we're looking for and will be used in each of the tests. Then, we called the beforeEach setup function twice. The first call initializes an AngularJS module named todoapp. The second call brings in the context factory function through dependency injection. Within the function passed to inject, we use the context to create an instance of TasksController and assign it to the controller variable. These series of steps in the test suite explicitly perform the steps that AngularJS automatically does during normal execution.

We're all set to run the test that verifies that the controller initialized the tasks model properly, but first we have to implement the minimum necessary code, in two files.

Open the file public/javascripts/src/todoapp.js and initialize the module for the application, like so:

testangularjs/todo/public/javascripts/src/todoapp.js
```
angular.module('todoapp', []);
```

This file with just one line defines the module that this AngularJS application will use. The other files will refer to this module. Recollect that this file was loaded first among the source files in the karma.conf.js file.

Add the following code to the public/javascripts/src/controllers/tasks-controller.js file:

```
var TasksController = function() {
  var controller = this;

  controller.tasks = [];
};

angular.module('todoapp')
       .controller('TasksController', [TasksController]);
```

At the bottom of the file is the standard AngularJS boilerplate code to define a controller. The name of the module and the controller in the code correspond to the respective names we gave for them in the test file. Within the controller constructor function we initialized tasks to an empty array. That's enough code to satisfy the test. Karma, which is currently running in the watch mode, may complain. If it does, restart the test run so AngularJS can load the module we just created. Once the test passes, move forward to the next test on the test list.

testangularjs/todo/test/client/tasks-controller-test.js
```
it('message should be empty on create', function() {
  expect(controller.message).to.be.eql('');
});
```

This is very similar to the previous test, but we need only one line of code to make it pass. Add the following line to the controller:

```
controller.message = '';
```

That one line of code will go right below the initialization of the tasks model. That was easy. The next test will need some work to deal with dependencies. Let's role up our sleeves to meet that challenge.

> **Joe asks:**
> ### Where's $scope?
>
> You may wonder about the $scope variable, or the absence of it, in our code so far. Most AngularJS tutorials misuse a variable with that name. This variable gives an implicit scope and removes the need to explicitly name the controller in HTML pages. Unfortunately, it pollutes the design—the code lacks clarity and it's easy to introduce errors.
>
> Define a controller object and use it with an explicit name for a cleaner design. With this approach, the scope of variables and state is crystal clear. Designing and calling functions on the controller is also a lot cleaner, not to mention the ease of testing.

Design Service Interaction

The details of interaction with the back end—the GET, POST, and DELETE requests—will be put away in a separate service object. The controller's getTasks function need not worry about them. It only has to make a call to the service and pass one callback for success and another for the error situation. These callbacks will be responsible for appropriately updating the models in the controllers.

From the design point of view, this approach makes the code modular and keeps the concerns apart in the code. From the testing point of view we don't want the controller to interact with the real service for two reasons. One, we haven't written the service yet. Two, interacting with the real service would make the test brittle and potentially slow. For these reasons, we'll mock out the service in the tests for the controller's getTasks function.

We'll design the getTasks function to call a get function of the service and pass two callbacks. All we need to verify is that the two callbacks are passed to the get function by the getTasks function. Initially we thought of two separate tests for getTasks, but we can cover both of those details with one test. Here's the test, in tasks-controller-test.js:

testangularjs/todo/test/client/tasks-controller-test.js

```
it('getTasks should interact with the service', function(done) {
  controller.updateTasks = function() {};
  controller.updateError = function() {};

  tasksServiceMock.get = function(success, error) {
    expect(success).to.be.eql(controller.updateTasks);
    expect(error).to.be.eql(controller.updateError);
    done();
  };

  controller.getTasks();
});
```

That's one simple interaction test. It verifies that the controller's getTasks calls the service's get function with the proper callback. Before we can run this test, we need to take a few steps. First, we need to create the mock for the service. Second, we have to somehow connect the service to the controller. Third, and finally, we have to implement the getTasks function.

Let's take care of the first step and part of the second step, here in the test. Modify the setup code we wrote earlier in the test file tasks-controller-test.js as follows:

```
var controller;
var tasksServiceMock;

beforeEach(module('todoapp'));

beforeEach(inject(function($controller) {
  tasksServiceMock = {};

  controller = $controller('TasksController', {
    TasksService: tasksServiceMock
  });
}));
```

We introduced a new variable tasksServiceMock and initialized it to an empty JSON object. Then, in the second beforeEach call, we modified the call to the factory function that created the controller. We're now passing the mock as a reference TasksService to the factory function. Let's understand how this is going to help.

When AngularJS bootstraps, it will wire the necessary dependencies between various components—controllers, services, directives, etc. Since we're in the test mode, we need to aid this wiring just a bit. In the setup part, within beforeEach we tell AngularJS to wire the mock service as the service that the controller will use.

We now need to modify the controller code so it can expect and accept a service. Let's change the bottom of the tasks-controller.js file as follows:

```
angular.module('todoapp')
       .controller('TasksController', ['TasksService', TasksController]);
```

We tell AngularJS to wire a TasksService into the controller during its creation. We also need to change the controller's constructor function to now accept the service:

```
var TasksController = function(tasksService) {
```

As a last step implement the getTasks function.

```
controller.getTasks = function() {
  tasksService.get(controller.updateTasks, controller.updateError);
};
```

Once you save the file, Karma should report all tests passing.

Step back and take a look at the current content of the tasks-controller.js file:

```
var TasksController = function(tasksService) {
  var controller = this;

  controller.tasks = [];

  controller.message = '';

  controller.getTasks = function() {
    tasksService.get(controller.updateTasks, controller.updateError);
  };
};

angular.module('todoapp')
       .controller('TasksController', ['TasksService', TasksController]);
```

The getTasks function is highly cohesive; it's concerned only about sending a request and registering the right callbacks. As a good citizen it delegates other responsibilities to the service and to the two callbacks. Let's work on those callbacks. We'll write tests for and design the function updateTasks first:

testangularjs/todo/test/client/tasks-controller-test.js

```
it('updateTasks should update tasks', function() {
  var tasksStub = [{sample: 1}];
  controller.updateTasks(tasksStub);
  expect(controller.tasks).to.be.eql(tasksStub);
});
```

The job of updateTasks is quite simple, at least for now. It should receive a list of tasks and set that into the model. The test sends a stub for the list of tasks and expects updateTasks to set that into the model. Let's implement updateTasks to make the test pass. Edit the tasks-controller.js to add this function to the controller:

```
controller.updateTasks = function(tasks) {
  controller.tasks = tasks;
};
```

Let's write the test to verify the behavior of the updateError function. This function should receive an error message and status code and update the message model in the controller. Here's the test:

testangularjs/todo/test/client/tasks-controller-test.js
```
it('updateError should update message', function() {
  controller.updateError('Not Found', 404);
  expect(controller.message).to.be.eql('Not Found (status: 404)');
});
```

Implement the updateError function in the tasks-controller.js file, within the controller, to make the test pass:

testangularjs/todo/public/javascripts/src/controllers/tasks-controller.js
```
controller.updateError = function(error, status) {
  controller.message = error + ' (status: ' + status + ')';
};
```

That was short and simple. Let's take a look at the test list.

- ...
- ✓ updateTasks updates tasks
- ✓ updateError updates message
- getTasks sorts tasks
- Call getTasks on document ready
- ...

We're done with the functions necessary to talk to the service and update the appropriate models. The next item on the list calls for sorting the data.

Separate Concerns, Reduce Mocking

We want the list of tasks to appear in the ascending order of year, month, day, and name. That calls for a sort operation, but where to put that? We need to make a careful decision about this—keep modularity and the single responsibility principle in mind.

Find the Right Place

AngularJS makes it very easy to sort data, right in the HTML page. Here's one possible solution that could go into the HTML page we'll design eventually:

```
<tr ng-repeat="task in controller.tasks | orderBy: year">...</tr>
```

That's sleek, or...is it sick?

At first sight that looks sleek—concise, declarative, elegant. But then, the sorting logic would be in the HTML page. We want to sort based on a particular precedence now and may want to change the criteria later. How do we verify that the sorting is done right? If the sorting code is in the HTML file, we can't test it using the tests on the controller. We'll have to rely on UI level testing and that won't be fun. It will be slow and brittle.

Avoid Features That Make Testing Hard

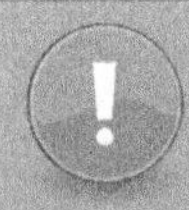

Avoid using features of libraries or frameworks that make testing hard. Find alternative ways that favor automated verification.

The controller is a better place for sorting. Also, testing the behavior of sort at this level is easier and faster as well.

In the controller, getTasks is responsible for getting the data from the back end. We could change getTasks to perform a sort on the list that's received, but that would lead to a few problems. First, getTasks is cohesive and focused on a single responsibility right now. We don't want to affect that good design. Second, adding more responsibility on this function would require more tests on it. More tests on getTasks will require more mocking, but it's better to minimize the use of mocks and use them only when unavoidable. All these issues tell us that we need to separate the concern of sorting away from getTasks.

getTasks is nicely delegating the response handling; a good place for sorting may be within the handler updateTasks. Let's think of the testing effort again. If updateTasks took on that responsibility, then each test to verify the sort operation would have to pass a list and then verify if controller.tasks is set to correctly sorted data. That's not as bad as having to write tests to verify the sorting on getTasks, but we can do a lot better by further separating the concern.

We could create a separate function sortTasks, which would take a list of tasks and return a sorted list. Since the sorting has to be based on various precedences, we'd have to write a few tests on sortTasks but that should be straightforward. Finally we'd need just one test to ensure that the sortTasks function is called at the right place.

Combine Empirical and Interaction Tests

Let's add the design idea that just emerged to the test list.

- ...
- ~~getTasks sorts tasks~~
- sortTasks sorts based on year
- sortTasks sorts on year, then month
- sortTasks sorts on year, month, then day
- sortTasks sorts on year, month, day, then name
- updateTasks calls sortTasks

Except for the last one, all the other tests related to sorting are empirical tests. The last one, however, is an interaction test. There are many ways to sort, but at the level of updateTasks we're not interested in those details. The sortTasks can be tested and designed separately. All we should care about at the level of updateTasks is that it calls sortTasks at the right place. Let's write those tests, one at a time.

First, let's verify that the sortTasks function sorts the given tasks in the ascending order of year:

testangularjs/todo/test/client/tasks-controller-test.js

```
it('sortTasks should sort based on year', function() {
  var task1 = { name: 'task a', month: 1, day: 10, year: 2017};
  var task2 = { name: 'task b', month: 1, day: 10, year: 2016};

  var sorted = controller.sortTasks([task1, task2]);
  expect(sorted).to.be.eql([task2, task1]);
});
```

To sort the tasks, we can make use of the AngularJS library of functions. The orderBy function alluded to in the HTML view can be exercised programmatically using the $filter dependency injection. To make use of this, the constructor function for the controller, in tasks-controller.js, has to change once again, like so:

```
var TasksController = function(tasksService, $filter) {
```

Also, we need to modify the controller configuration at the bottom of tasks-controller.js to inject the $filter dependency:

```
angular.module('todoapp')
       .controller('TasksController',
         ['TasksService', '$filter', TasksController]);
```

Now, we're all set to implement the sortTasks function within the controller:

```
controller.sortTasks = function(tasks) {
  var orderBy = $filter('orderBy');
  return orderBy(tasks, 'year');
};
```

The function gets a reference to the orderBy function from the injected $filter and asks it to transform the given task list to a sorted list.

Save the files and ensure the tests are passing.

Next, let's verify that the sortTasks function sorts based on the month if the year values are equal:

testangularjs/todo/test/client/tasks-controller-test.js
```
it('sortTasks should sort on year, then month', function() {
  var task1 = { name: 'task a', month: 2, day: 10, year: 2017};
  var task2 = { name: 'task c', month: 1, day: 10, year: 2016};
  var task3 = { name: 'task b', month: 1, day: 10, year: 2017};

  var sorted = controller.sortTasks([task1, task2, task3]);
  expect(sorted).to.be.eql([task2, task3, task1]);
});
```

We need to make a small change to the sortTasks function to make this pass:

```
return orderBy(tasks, ['year', 'month']);
```

We changed the second argument of orderBy from year to an array with two properties, year and month.

Next, test to verify that the sorting uses the day property:

testangularjs/todo/test/client/tasks-controller-test.js
```
it('sortTasks should sort on year, month, then day', function() {
  var task1 = { name: 'task a', month: 1, day: 20, year: 2017};
  var task2 = { name: 'task c', month: 1, day: 14, year: 2017};
  var task3 = { name: 'task b', month: 1, day: 9, year: 2017};

  var sorted = controller.sortTasks([task1, task2, task3]);
  expect(sorted).to.be.eql([task3, task2, task1]);
});
```

We need to change the sortTasks function once again to make this test pass. The final test for sortTasks will verify that the sorting is based on name if all other properties are equal:

testangularjs/todo/test/client/tasks-controller-test.js
```
it('sortTasks should sort on year, month, day, then name', function() {
  var task1 = { name: 'task a', month: 1, day: 14, year: 2017};
  var task2 = { name: 'task c', month: 1, day: 14, year: 2017};
  var task3 = { name: 'task b', month: 1, day: 14, year: 2017};

  var sorted = controller.sortTasks([task1, task2, task3]);
  expect(sorted).to.be.eql([task1, task3, task2]);
});
```

Here's the final implementation of the sortTasks function to pass all the tests:

testangularjs/todo/public/javascripts/src/controllers/tasks-controller.js
```
controller.sortTasks = function(tasks) {
  var orderBy = $filter('orderBy');
  return orderBy(tasks, ['year', 'month', 'day', 'name']);
};
```

The properties year, month, day, and name are passed in the descending order of priority to the orderBy function.

We have a function to sort the tasks, but we need one more test and a small change to the code to update the model with tasks in sorted order. We decided a good place to perform the sorting is in the updateTasks function. We already implemented this function, so let's add another test to verify it calls the sortTasks function. This is an interaction test—we don't need the real sortTasks function, so we'll mock it in the test for updateTasks.

testangularjs/todo/test/client/tasks-controller-test.js
```
it('updateTasks should call sortTasks', function() {
  var tasksStub = [{sample: 1}];

  controller.sortTasks = function(tasks) {
    expect(tasks).to.be.eql(tasksStub);
    return '..sorted..';
  };

  controller.updateTasks(tasksStub);
  expect(controller.tasks).to.be.eql('..sorted..');
});
```

For this test to pass we have to make one final change to the updateTasks function:

testangularjs/todo/public/javascripts/src/controllers/tasks-controller.js
```
controller.updateTasks = function(tasks) {
  controller.tasks = controller.sortTasks(tasks);
};
```

The updateTasks function now calls the sortTasks function and sets the result into the tasks model of the controller.

That completes the overall functionality for getting the tasks from the service and updating the models. There's one last step to complete the feature of listing tasks—invoke the getTasks function on document loading.

Test Loading Sequence

Upon loading the page, the getTasks function should be called as soon as the DOM is ready. In the jQuery implementation, in the previous chapter, there was no easy way to test for this and we had to employ some tricks. AngularJS makes this testing trivial.

At the end of the controller function we want to call the ready function on document. The document can be injected into the controller, using $document much like the way the service and the $filter were passed in. Then, in the test, the document can be stubbed out. There's one catch, however.

The controller instance is created within the beforeEach function. At that time, before any tests are run, the ready function will be exercised in code. The stubbing of the document has to precede the controller creation. Let's take the necessary step to achieve this.

In the test suite, we need a variable, a placeholder, to store the handler that will be registered with the ready function. Now let's create a variable named documentReadyHandler in the tasks-controller-test.js file:

```
//...
var controller;
var tasksServiceMock = {};
var documentReadyHandler;
//...
```

Then, the inject call should change once more, but this time to bring in the $document, like so:

```
beforeEach(inject(function($controller, $document) {
  $document.ready = function(handler) { documentReadyHandler = handler; }

  controller = $controller('TasksController', {
    TasksService: tasksServiceMock
  });
}));
```

In addition to the second new parameter, the first line of this function stubs the ready function and also saves the handler passed to it in the variable documentReadyHandler. This stub is created before the controller creation on the following line. The stub will be called when the controller is created—before any of the tests run. We need a new test to verify that the code actually called the ready function.

Here's the test that checks that the documentReadyHandler reference is set to the controller's getTasks function:

testangularjs/todo/test/client/tasks-controller-test.js

```
it('should register getTasks as handler for document ready', function() {
  expect(documentReadyHandler).to.be.eql(controller.getTasks);
});
```

Since we have a new dependency, we have to change the controller initialization code in tasks-controller.js once more:

```
angular.module('todoapp')
       .controller('TasksController',
         ['TasksService', '$filter', '$document', TasksController]);
```

The $document is injected as a dependency much like the way we injected the $filter. This will result in a change to the controller's constructor function declaration:

```
var TasksController = function(tasksService, $filter, $document) {
```

Finally, make a call to the ready function within the controller, like so:

```
$document.ready(controller.getTasks);
```

Upon saving this change, Karma will report all tests for listing tasks to be passing. There are two remaining features for the controller: to add a task and to delete a task. Let's take care of those next.

Continue the Design

The initial test list identified one task for adding a task and one for deleting a task.

- ...
- addTask sends the data to the service
- deleteTask sends a delete request to the service

Let's now focus on the addTask function.

Design addTask

When we analyzed the getTasks function, a single test for that function transformed into multiple tests in the test list. We can expect a similar result for the addTask function as well. Let's analyze the addTask function.

First, we need the data for the new task. A new model newTask within the controller can store this data. We need to initialize this model to have a name property and a date property. We also need a function to convert the newTask to the JSON format expected by the server.

addTask should call the service, register a callback—let's call it updateMessage—to handle the response, and register updateError to handle any errors. The updateMessage can display the message received. Also, after the response arrives, the task list has to be refreshed to reflect the change. For this, updateMessage can reuse the getTasks function we already have.

In addition, we should disable the create button if the user-entered task is not valid. However, we already have a function, validateTask, to validate a task. The function to disable the button can simply reuse that function.

Let's jot those ideas in the test list:

- ~~addTask sends the data to the service~~
- Verify newTask has empty name and date on create
- Convert newTask with no data to JSON format

- Convert newTask with data to JSON format
- addTask calls the service
- updateMessage should update message and call getTasks
- disableAddTask makes good use of validateTask

The tests for this feature will be a lot like the tests for listing tasks, except for a few minor differences.

Start with the first test in the list. Add the test to the tasks-controller-test.js file:

testangularjs/todo/test/client/tasks-controller-test.js
```
it('newTask should have empty `name` and `date` on create', function() {
  expect(controller.newTask.name).to.be.eql('');
  expect(controller.newTask.date).to.be.eql('');
});
```

The test merely verifies that a model named newTask in the controller has been initialized properly. Though it appears trivial, this test clearly expresses and documents the need to properly initialize newTask. If this model is not initialized properly, the functions that depend on it would fail. By having this test, we minimize both the need for extra tests and extra code in controller functions to deal with improper initialization of newTask. To make this test pass, add the following line to the controller:

testangularjs/todo/public/javascripts/src/controllers/tasks-controller.js
```
controller.newTask = {name: '', date: ''};
```

Before a new task can be sent to the server, we have to convert the data to the JSON format expected by the server. We'll take baby steps to create the function for this conversion. Here's the first test:

testangularjs/todo/test/client/tasks-controller-test.js
```
it('should convert newTask with no data to JSON format', function() {
  var newTask = controller.convertNewTaskToJSON();

  expect(newTask.name).to.be.eql('');
  expect(newTask.month).to.be.NAN;
  expect(newTask.day).to.be.NAN;
  expect(newTask.year).to.be.NAN;
});
```

The test calls a yet-to-be-implemented convertNewTaskToJSON function. This function will convert the model newTask to the necessary format. Since we haven't set the newTask, this test verifies that the function gracefully handles conversion when no data is available. Write the minimum code in the controller for this new convertNewTaskToJSON function to make the test pass. Then move on to the next test:

testangularjs/todo/test/client/tasks-controller-test.js
```
it('should convert newTask with data to JSON format', function() {
  var newTask = {name: 'task a', date: '6/10/2016'};
  var newTaskJSON = {name: 'task a', month: 6, day: 10, year: 2016};

  controller.newTask = newTask;

  expect(controller.convertNewTaskToJSON()).to.be.eql(newTaskJSON);
});
```

This test sets a sample task into the controller's newTask variable and verifies that convertNewTaskToJSON returns the appropriate response.

Here's the implementation necessary to make the tests pass:

testangularjs/todo/public/javascripts/src/controllers/tasks-controller.js
```
controller.convertNewTaskToJSON = function() {
  var dateParts = controller.newTask.date.split('/');

  return {
    name: controller.newTask.name,
    month: parseInt(dateParts[0]),
    day: parseInt(dateParts[1]),
    year: parseInt(dateParts[2])
  };
};
```

The convertNewTaskToJSON function designed using the previous tests will be reused in a couple of functions that need to work with newTask.

Next, we need to verify that addTask calls the service, passing the properly converted task and the callback handlers.

testangularjs/todo/test/client/tasks-controller-test.js
```
it('addTask should call the service', function(done) {
  controller.updateMessage = function() {};
  controller.updateError = function() {};

  var convertedTask = controller.convertNewTaskToJSON(controller.newTask);

  tasksServiceMock.add = function(task, success, error) {
    expect(task).to.be.eql(convertedTask);
    expect(success).to.be.eql(controller.updateMessage);
    expect(error).to.be.eql(controller.updateError);
    done();
  };

  controller.addTask();
});
```

The implementation of addTask to satisfy this test is quite easy:

testangularjs/todo/public/javascripts/src/controllers/tasks-controller.js

```
controller.addTask = function() {
  tasksService.add(
    controller.convertNewTaskToJSON(controller.newTask),
    controller.updateMessage,
    controller.updateError);
};
```

The completion of this step leads us to the next: design updateMessage that is used by the addTask. updateMessage has to perform two tasks. It should update the model message with the given message and also call getTasks so it can refresh the task list with the newly added task. Let's write a test to verify that behavior. Since getTasks talks to the service, which has not been implemented yet, we can't let updateMessage call the real getTasks—not just yet. We will stub out the getTasks in the test for updateMessage:

testangularjs/todo/test/client/tasks-controller-test.js

```
it('updateMessage should update message and call getTasks', function(done) {
  controller.getTasks = function() { done(); };
  controller.updateMessage('good');
  expect(controller.message).to.be.eql('good');
});
```

The test for updateTasks is a mixture of an interaction test and an empirical test. It verifies the interaction of the function with getTasks, but it also verifies that the function updated the model.

Here's the implementation of updateTasks to make the test pass:

testangularjs/todo/public/javascripts/src/controllers/tasks-controller.js

```
controller.updateMessage = function(message) {
  controller.message = message;
  controller.getTasks();
};
```

There's one final task for the "add a new task" feature. The create button should be disabled if the task is invalid. For this we need to design a disableAddTask function that makes use of the previously designed validateTask function. Let's write a test to verify this behavior:

testangularjs/todo/test/client/tasks-controller-test.js

```
it('disableAddTask should make good use of validateTask', function() {
  var newTask = {name: 'task a', date: '6/10/2016'};

  var originalValidateTask = window.validateTask;

  window.validateTask = function(task) {
    expect(task.name).to.be.eql(newTask.name);
    expect(
      task.month + '/' + task.day + '/' + task.year).to.eql(newTask.date);
```

```
    return true;
  };

  controller.newTask = newTask;

  var resultOfDisableAddTask = controller.disableAddTask();

  window.validateTask = originalValidateTask;

  expect(resultOfDisableAddTask).to.be.eql(false);
});
```

The test temporarily replaces the original validateTask function with a mock function. The mock verifies that validateTask is called by disableAddTask with the proper parameters and returns a canned true response. The test finally verifies that the disableAddTask function returns a false, an opposite of the response by the validateTask, since the task is assumed to be valid in this test.

Implement the disableAddTask function in the controller:

testangularjs/todo/public/javascripts/src/controllers/tasks-controller.js

```
controller.disableAddTask = function() {
  return !validateTask(controller.convertNewTaskToJSON());
};
```

That concludes the necessary code for adding a task. The last set of tests for the controller should focus on the final feature—deleting a task.

Design deleteTask

Destroying just about anything is easy in life; deleting a task should be no exception to that rule. Most of the functions needed for this operation are already in place. Let's write the test to verify the behavior of deleteTask and then implement it.

Here's the test:

testangularjs/todo/test/client/tasks-controller-test.js

```
it('deleteTask should delete and register updateMessage', function(done) {
  controller.updateMessage = function() {};
  controller.updateError = function() {};

  var sampleTaskId = '1234123412341234';

  tasksServiceMock.delete = function(taskId, success, error) {
    expect(taskId).to.be.eql(sampleTaskId);
    expect(success).to.be.eql(controller.updateMessage);
    expect(error).to.be.eql(controller.updateError);
    done();
  };

  controller.deleteTask(sampleTaskId);
});
```

We merely have to confirm that the deleteTask function calls the service, requesting that it delete the task. The test verifies that proper callbacks are passed to the service.

The implementation of deleteTask should also pose no challenges and would need no extra dependencies. Let's implement the short function to make the tests pass.

testangularjs/todo/public/javascripts/src/controllers/tasks-controller.js

```
controller.deleteTask = function(taskId) {
  tasksService.delete(
    taskId, controller.updateMessage, controller.updateError);
};
```

The controller is in good shape. Let's take a look at the result of our test-driven effort. Here's the full controller code:

testangularjs/todo/public/javascripts/src/controllers/tasks-controller.js

```
var TasksController = function(tasksService, $filter, $document) {
  var controller = this;

  controller.tasks = [];
  controller.message = '';

  controller.newTask = {name: '', date: ''};

  controller.getTasks = function() {
    tasksService.get(controller.updateTasks, controller.updateError);
  };

  controller.updateTasks = function(tasks) {
    controller.tasks = controller.sortTasks(tasks);
  };

  controller.updateError = function(error, status) {
    controller.message = error + ' (status: ' + status + ')';
  };

  controller.sortTasks = function(tasks) {
    var orderBy = $filter('orderBy');
    return orderBy(tasks, ['year', 'month', 'day', 'name']);
  };

  $document.ready(controller.getTasks);

  controller.convertNewTaskToJSON = function() {
    var dateParts = controller.newTask.date.split('/');

    return {
      name: controller.newTask.name,
      month: parseInt(dateParts[0]),
      day: parseInt(dateParts[1]),
      year: parseInt(dateParts[2])
    };
  };
```

```
  controller.addTask = function() {
    tasksService.add(
      controller.convertNewTaskToJSON(controller.newTask),
      controller.updateMessage,
      controller.updateError);
  };

  controller.updateMessage = function(message) {
    controller.message = message;
    controller.getTasks();
  };

  controller.disableAddTask = function() {
    return !validateTask(controller.convertNewTaskToJSON());
  };

  controller.deleteTask = function(taskId) {
    tasksService.delete(
      taskId, controller.updateMessage, controller.updateError);
  };
};

angular.module('todoapp')
       .controller('TasksController',
         ['TasksService', '$filter', '$document', TasksController]);
```

It's time to complete the last piece that's necessary: the service.

Design the Service

The service sits between the controller and the back-end server. The controller functions depend on three functions of the service: get, add, and delete. Let's design these functions, one at a time. While designing the service, we have to keep in mind the needs of the controller and the expectations of the server. Let's get started with the get function.

Design the get Function

get should receive two callbacks as parameters and make a GET request to the /tasks endpoint of the server. If the server responded back successfully, the function should call the first callback given to it; otherwise, it should call the second callback.

We don't have the back end running right now. There's no need; depending on the real back end will make the tests brittle and nondeterministic. Thankfully, angular-mocks can simulate Ajax calls by injecting an httpBackend mock object.

Mock the Back End

We'll first set up a new test suite for testing the service. Open the test/client/tasks-service-test.js file and add the following setup code:

testangularjs/todo/test/client/tasks-service-test.js

```
describe('tasks service tests', function() {
  var service;
  var httpBackend;
  var notCalled = function() { throw 'not expected'; };

  var newTaskJSON = {name: 'task a', month: 6, day: 10, year: 2016};

  beforeEach(module('todoapp'));

  beforeEach(inject(function(TasksService, $httpBackend) {
    service = TasksService;
    httpBackend = $httpBackend;
  }));
});
```

In the new test suite we first created a notCalled function, which blows up if called. Use this to stand in as arguments for callbacks that are not expected to be called within a test sequence. Then we created a sample newTaskJSON that will be used as a sample task object in tests.

The function passed to inject has two parameters: TasksService and $httpBackend. The dependency injector is pretty smart about the names of the parameters. It will recognize that TasksService is the name of the service since we'll soon register that name as a service. Names like $controller and $httpBackend are sacred; that's how the dependency injector knows to inject a controller factory or an HTTP mock. Some developers like to add underscores to the variable names, like _$httpBackend_, so they could use a local variable like $httpBackend—the injector strips out the underscores decorations if it sees them. Since we're using httpBackend, and not $httpBackend, as the local variable, we don't need the underscores.

We stored the mock injected through the $httpBackend parameter into the httpBackend variable. We also saved a reference to the service object in the service variable. Let's now turn to writing the first test for the service.

Write the First Test for get

In the first test for the service's get function, we'll prepare the mock for the HTTP GET request, telling it to return a successful status code of 200 and a response sample data. We'll also stub the callback functions that get will receive as arguments. Here's the test:

testangularjs/todo/test/client/tasks-service-test.js

```
it('get should call service, register success function', function(done) {
  httpBackend.expectGET('tasks')
            .respond(200, '...some data...');

  var success = function(data, status) {
    expect(status).to.be.eql(200);
    expect(data).to.be.eql('...some data...');
    done();
  };

  service.get(success, notCalled);
  httpBackend.flush();
});
```

httpBackend is a mock and the expectGET call tells the mock what to accept for the URL. The respond call tells the mock what to return to the caller. flush simulates the asynchrony of Ajax calls on the mock. Within the get function, when the response arrives from the back end after an HTTP call, it should pass the result to the callback registered as the first argument. However, this will happen correctly only if get registers that callback properly with the HTTP request—we'll see this in code shortly. The stubbed-out success function, for the first argument, verifies that the response returned by the HTTP request is received by the callback. Since this is a happy path, the callback passed through the second argument should not be called; the stub passed in for the second argument confirms that.

In short, this test says that get should send a GET request to the tasks URL and register the first argument as the callback to handle the response.

To make this test pass, we'll write the minimum code for the service. Open the public/javascripts/src/services/tasks-service.js file and add the following code:

testangularjs/todo/public/javascripts/src/services/tasks-service.js

```
var TasksService = function($http) {
  var service = this;
};
angular.module('todoapp')
       .service('TasksService', ['$http', TasksService]);
```

At the bottom of the file we introduced our service to the AngularJS module. First, we provided the name of the service as TasksService—by reading this configuration the injector figures out what service to inject into our test environment. Second, within the array, we mentioned that the $http object should be injected into our service constructor named TasksService.

In the first line in the file, we created a constructor function with the $http parameter. During normal execution, AngularJS will inject the appropriate

HTTP request object into the $http variable, which can be used to make Ajax calls. During test runs, angular-mocks.js injects the mock that can be arranged to simulate a canned response.

Let's now write the minimum code for the get function to make the test pass. Within the constructor function, create the following code:

```
service.get = function(success, error) {
  $http.get('tasks')
       .success(success);
};
```

The function does what the test expected of it—calls the HTTP service, sends a GET request to the tasks URI, and registers the first parameter as the success callback. It currently ignores the second parameter.

Save the files and the tests should pass, confirming that our service is evolving.

Complete the Design of get

The next test will confirm that the error handler is registered properly:

testangularjs/todo/test/client/tasks-service-test.js

```
it('get should call service, register error function', function(done) {
  httpBackend.expectGET('tasks')
             .respond(404, 'Not Found');

  var error = function(data, status) {
    expect(status).to.be.eql(404);
    expect(data).to.be.eql('Not Found');
    done();
  };

  service.get(notCalled, error);
  httpBackend.flush();
});
```

This test is a lot like the previous one, except it's sending a failure code 404 and expecting the error handling callback to be called with the proper error message and status.

Using these error numbers in tests reminds me of a day at home. My son asked me if he could have something. Busy coding, I tersely blurted "302." He quickly turned around, asking "Mom?", to which—without missing a beat—she replied "404." It's a moment of harmony when an entire family can communicate using HTTP status codes.

This test verifies that proper error details are passed from the HTTP request to the error handler that was given as the second parameter. Since this is a negative test, the callback registered though the first argument should not be called. The test set this up as an expectation by passing the notCalled function as the first argument.

Let's make a small change to the get function to make this test pass:

testangularjs/todo/public/javascripts/src/services/tasks-service.js
```
service.get = function(success, error) {
  $http.get('tasks')
       .success(success)
       .error(error);
};
```

That pretty much completes the design of the get function. We were able to test it and ensure the callbacks are registered properly to interact with the back end, without actually running the back-end service. This shows the power and the benefits of angular-mocks—very cool.

Design the add Function

Let's write the first test for add, our next service function:

testangularjs/todo/test/client/tasks-service-test.js
```
it('add should call service, register success function', function(done) {
  httpBackend.expectPOST('tasks', newTaskJSON)
             .respond(200, 'added');

  var success = function(data) {
    expect(data).to.be.eql('added');
    done();
  };

  service.add(newTaskJSON, success, notCalled);
  httpBackend.flush();
});
```

Unlike the get function, which made a GET request, the add function should make a POST request. Furthermore, the task to be added should accompany the request sent to the server. To verify this, we arrange the $httpBackend mock with the expectPOST call, which will verify both the URI and the data to be passed. The rest of the test is much like the tests we wrote for get.

Implement the minimum code for the add function of the service class in public/javascripts/src/services/tasks-services.js and then move forward to the negative test.

testangularjs/todo/test/client/tasks-service-test.js

```
it('add should call service, register error function', function(done) {
  httpBackend.expectPOST('tasks', newTaskJSON)
             .respond(500, 'server error');

  var error = function(error, status) {
    expect(error).to.be.eql('server error');
    expect(status).to.be.eql(500);
    done();
  };

  service.add(newTaskJSON, notCalled, error);
  httpBackend.flush();
});
```

This test simulates a failure of the back-end service and verifies that the details of error are received by the callback passed as the last argument. Make the necessary change to the add function to make this test pass.

Here's the code for the add function that passes the two tests:

testangularjs/todo/public/javascripts/src/services/tasks-service.js

```
service.add = function(task, success, error) {
  $http.post('tasks', task)
       .success(success)
       .error(error);
};
```

The add function makes a POST request to the tasks URI and forwards the task it receives to the back-end service.

Design the delete Function

Let's now focus on the design of the last service function: delete. Here's the positive test for delete:

testangularjs/todo/test/client/tasks-service-test.js

```
it('delete should call service, register success function', function(done) {
  httpBackend.expectDELETE('tasks/1234123412341234')
             .respond(200, 'yup');

  var success = function(data) {
    expect(data).to.be.eql('yup');
    done();
  };

  service.delete('1234123412341234', success, notCalled);
  httpBackend.flush();
});
```

This test uses expectDELETE instead of expectPOST, and also the id of the task to delete is passed as part of the URI. Everything else looks familiar in this test. Implement the minimum code for the delete function of the service. Then move on to the negative test:

testangularjs/todo/test/client/tasks-service-test.js
```
it('delete should call service, register error function', function(done) {
  httpBackend.expectDELETE('tasks/1234123412341234')
             .respond(500, 'server error');

  var error = function(error, status) {
    expect(error).to.be.eql('server error');
    expect(status).to.be.eql(500);
    done();
  };

  service.delete('1234123412341234', notCalled, error);
  httpBackend.flush();
});
```

Like the negative tests for get and add, this test also verifies that the error was handled properly. Here's the code for delete to make the two tests pass:

testangularjs/todo/public/javascripts/src/services/tasks-service.js
```
service.delete = function(taskId, success, error) {
  $http.delete('tasks/' + taskId)
       .success(success)
       .error(error);
};
```

We have designed, with tests, the controller and the service. It's time for us to take this for a ride, but before that let's take a peek at the code coverage.

Measure Code Coverage

Looking at the tests and the code designed with them, the test-to-code ratio we discussed in the previous chapters has held here too—we have a 3:1 ratio of tests to the AngularJS controller and server code.

The package.json file already contains the script to create the coverage report. Simply run the command

```
npm run-script cover-client
```

and take a look at the generated coverage report by opening the file index.html under the subdirectory coverage.

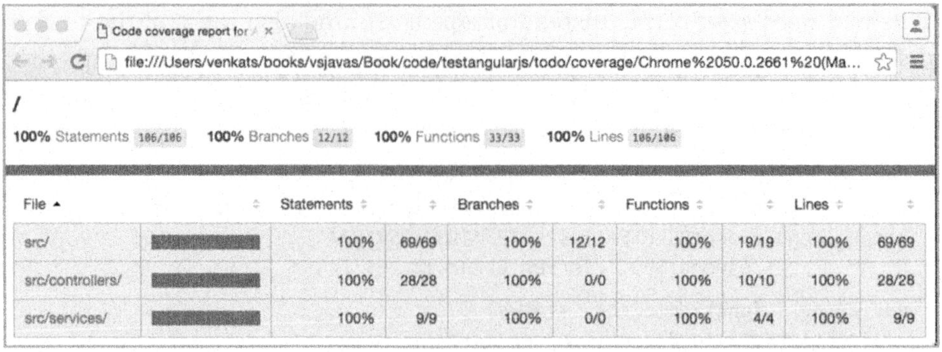

Code coverage report for /

file:///Users/venkats/books/vsjavas/Book/code/testangularjs/todo/coverage/Chrome%2050.0.2661%20(Ma...

/

100% Statements 106/106 100% Branches 12/12 100% Functions 33/33 100% Lines 106/106

File		Statements		Branches		Functions		Lines	
src/		100%	69/69	100%	12/12	100%	19/19	100%	69/69
src/controllers/		100%	28/28	100%	0/0	100%	10/10	100%	28/28
src/services/		100%	9/9	100%	0/0	100%	4/4	100%	9/9

The report shows coverage for the controller and the server we wrote in this chapter along with the files created in the previous chapter. Click on the links in the report to view the line-by-line coverage. If any code was written without tests, those will show up in red.

Take the UI for a Drive

The controller and service code are ready, but we need an HTML file for the view. Let's create a file, public/tasksa.html, that will integrate with the AngularJS controller we created.

testangularjs/todo/public/tasksa.html

```
<!DOCTYPE html>
<html data-ng-app="todoapp">
  <head>
    <title>TO-DO</title>
    <link rel="stylesheet" href="/stylesheets/style.css">
  </head>
  <body data-ng-controller="TasksController as controller">
    <div class="heading">TO-DO</div>
    <div id="newtask">
      <div>Create a new task</div>
      <label>Name</label>
      <input type="text" data-ng-model="controller.newTask.name"/>
      <label>Date</label>
      <input type="text" data-ng-model="controller.newTask.date"/>
      <input type="submit" id="submit" data-ng-click="controller.addTask();"
        data-ng-disabled="controller.disableAddTask();"
        value="create"/>
    </div>
  <div id="taskslist">
    <p>Number of tasks: <span>{{ controller.tasks.length }}</span>
    <span id="message">{{ controller.message }}</span>
    <table>
      <tr data-ng-repeat ="task in controller.tasks">
      <td>{{ task.name }}</td>
      <td>{{ task.month }}/{{ task.day }}/{{ task.year }}</td>
```

```
      <td>
        <A data-ng-click="controller.deleteTask(task._id);">delete
        </A></td>
    </table>
  </div>
  <script src="javascripts/angular.js"></script>
  <script src="javascripts/src/todoapp.js"></script>
  <script src="javascripts/src/controllers/tasks-controller.js"></script>
  <script src="javascripts/src/services/tasks-service.js"></script>
  <script src="javascripts/common/validate-task.js"></script>
  </body>
</html>
```

The HTML file references angular.js and the AngularJS-related JavaScript code we created. It has the necessary ng directives to tie the UI parts to the models and the functions in the controller. You can download[2] the stylesheet referenced from the media link for the book.

To see the UI in action, first start the mongodb daemon and the Express server—see *Take the UI for a Short Drive*, on page 175 for the steps. Following that, direct your browser to the URL http://localhost:3000/tasksa.html. Watch the controller and the service, whose behavior has been fully verified using automated tests, come to life once again, but this time outside of the test environment.

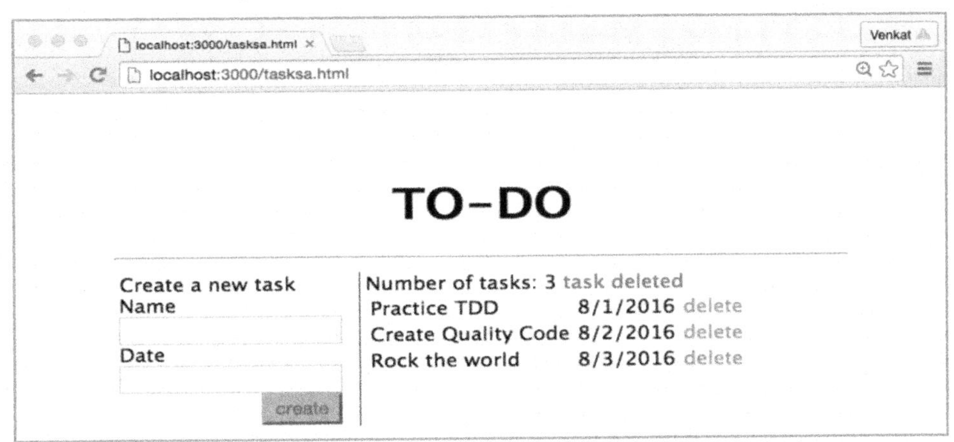

The view shows the list of tasks in the desired sorted order. Also, the create button is disabled when the new task details are not complete or valid.

Wrapping Up

AngularJS has been designed from the ground up for testability. AngularJS and angular-mocks interplay to facilitate the testing of client-side code written

2. https://media.pragprog.com/titles/vsjavas/code/testangularjs/todo/public/stylesheets/style.css

using AngularJS. The test suites can inject test doubles for the dependencies that the controllers need. Also, by tactfully mocking the back end, the behavior of the client-side JavaScript was fully verified using automated scripts. We did not have to bring up the server or create any HTML pages to get the code tested.

The AngularJS team has learned a great deal from the active use of the AngularJS 1.x framework. As a total rewrite, Angular 2 is vastly different from AngularJS 1.x. In projects where you currently use AngularJS 1.x you can use the techniques presented in this chapter. For new projects in which you plan to use Angular 2, however, you'll need a totally different approach. We explore that in the next chapter.

CHAPTER 9

Test-Drive Angular 2

Angular 2—we'll refer to it from here on as Angular—is a total rewrite of the AngularJS framework. The complete revamp was based on feedback and learnings from the extensive use of AngularJS 1.x in the industry. Angular is written using TypeScript. It was created with speed and performance improvements in mind. This chapter uses Angular 2 release candidate 4 (rc-4).

Creating Angular applications is quite different from creating AngularJS 1.x applications. So, testing Angular applications is also different. Angular applications are built using components, services, and pipes, and all these are configured using annotations. Furthermore, the dependencies for components and services are injected more explicitly in Angular than in AngularJS 1.x. This makes automated testing of Angular code simpler and easier than testing AngularJS 1.x code.

Angular applications may be developed using TypeScript, Dart, or JavaScript. This book is focused on test-driving JavaScript applications, so we will not focus on TypeScript or Dart. To develop with JavaScript, you may use either ECMAScript 5—the good old JavaScript—or ECMAScript 2015. Currently the commonly used browsers support ECMAScript 5. To use ECMAScript 2015 you'd have to invest significant time to configure tools that polyfill features.

Since we're keen on learning about test-driving applications, we'll keep the distractions low by using ECMAScript 5 in this chapter. That will help keep our focus on learning about test automation, and we won't be dragged into the myriad of tools we'd need to use ECMAScript 2015. If you decide to transition from ECMAScript 5 to ECMAScript 2015, it will be relatively easy since you will already know how to write tests and the code in ECMAScript 5.

In this chapter you'll learn how to test-drive Angular applications by creating an Angular version of the client side for the TO-DO application. But first, since it's impossible to test-drive code when it's not clear how to implement it, we'll start with a short spike and create a fully working program in Angular. Then, we'll apply that knowledge to test-drive an Angular front end for the TO-DO application we created in the earlier chapters.

Spike to Learn Angular

Your end goal is to learn about test-driving Angular applications so you can reap the benefits of automated verification on Angular projects. You will use the TO-DO app as a vehicle to learn that, but first you need to get comfortable with writing Angular code. To achieve that, let's create a spike that has the parts that any typical Angular application will have.

The spike we'll create will fetch a list of language names from the server and display them in sorted order. We want to keep our focus on Angular and don't want to get dragged into any server-side code when creating this spike. With that in mind, we'll keep the language names list in a plain-text file and fetch it using an Ajax call from Angular code. Let's get started.

Pipes, Services, and Components

Angular nicely separates the various concerns we have to deal with into separate classes. Let's take a minute to get familiar with the major parts of an Angular application.

- Pipes: These are transformation functions. They take in a piece or a collection of data and return a transformed result. For example, given a sentence, we may want to replace any foul word with asterisks but keep the good words as is. A custom `FoulWordFilterPipe` would serve that purpose.
- Service: These are the classes that will talk to the back-end services. They make HTTP calls and know how to extract the data from the services. These also gracefully deal with any error communicating with the services.
- Components: These are the glue between the data that we obtain from the services and the view of the data. They work with services to get or send data and with pipes to transform the data. They also tell us where or how the data will be rendered.

We will create each of these types of Angular classes in our spike. Let's get a project ready so we can write some code.

Set Up the Project

In your workspace, change to the tdjsa/angularspike directory. Take a quick look at the package.json file. It includes the dependencies for Angular and other necessary modules. The start script launches the lightweight HTTP server that readily serves files. Using this server removes the need to create any server-side code to serve files. Run npm install to get the dependencies downloaded and installed on your system.

The client side of this sample program will display names of languages obtained from the server. We need a list of languages for this purpose.

Edit the file languages and add a few languages of your choice, like so:

angularspike/languages
```
JavaScript
TypeScript
Haskell
Java
C#
F#
Clojure
Scala
Ruby
Elixir
```

When we visit the page index.html, the application should display the language names served from the languages file, but in sorted order. For this we need a pipe, a service, a component, and a couple of HTML files. Let's get started by creating them, in that order.

Create a Pipe

We want the language names to appear in sorted order. In AngularJS 1.x we may use the orderBy filter for this purpose. Angular does not have any built-in function for sorting. Furthermore, filters have been replaced by pipes in Angular.

Pipes follow the idea of Unix pipe transformations. For example, in the Unix command-sequence ls | grep js | wc -l, the standard output from one command flows into the standard input of the following command. In the example, the output of ls flows into the input of grep. The output of grep, in turn, flows into the input of the wc command. Angular pipes are similar. For example, name | uppercase | lowercase will transform the value in the name variable to uppercase and then the result of that is further transformed to lowercase. That example is not a very useful series of transformations but it illustrates the point. In this example, uppercase and lowercase are pipes—in fact, they're among the few built-in pipes in Angular.

There are currently only a few built-in pipes in Angular; more may be provided later by the authors of the framework and by third parties. To create our own pipe in Angular, we have to decorate a class with a Pipe attribute and provide a name and a transform function. A pipe's transform function is called automatically when the data flows through a pipe sequence in which the pipe is involved.

We're ready to create our first Angular client-side code. We will follow the Angular filenaming convention where filenames will include the words like pipe, component, or service depending on what they contain.

Let's create a pipe to sort a collection of names, using the good old JavaScript syntax. Edit the empty file src/app/langs/sort.pipe.js in the current workspace and enter the following code:

angularspike/src/app/langs/sort.pipe.js

```
(function(app) {
  app.SortPipe = ng.core
    .Pipe({ name: 'sort' })
    .Class({
    constructor: function() {},
    transform: function (languages) {
        return languages.slice().sort();
    }});
})(window.app || (window.app = {}));
```

Let's first read the last line of the file. We're calling the function created in this file with window.app as an argument, if that variable exists. If it does not exist, we create the window.app variable, initialize it to an empty JSON object, and pass it as the argument. The purpose of window.app is so that all of our stuff—pipes, services, and components—will be created as members of this JSON object. That way we do not pollute a global namespace and accidentally collide or replace any existing classes or functions.

Within the function, we define the pipe class SortPipe. It's Angular convention to suffix pipe names with the word Pipe, services with the word Service, and components with the word Component. We use the builder pattern to create and annotate classes in Angular, using a chain of function calls. We first annotate the class with the Pipe annotation, using the ng.core.Pipe function. It takes on an attribute name, which is set to the value sort in this example. Then we define the details of the class, using the ng.core.Class function, and provide it with the constructor and the necessary transform function.

The constructor is merely an empty function in the pipe. In the transform function we make a copy of the given languages array, sort, and return the sorted list of names.

We gave the name sort for our pipe. That's the name users of our pipe will use, much like the name uppercase used to refer to Angular's built-in pipe class UpperCasePipe.

Our pipe is ready to transform a collection of names. Next let's fetch the collection of language names from the server. We need a service class for that.

Create a Service

Much like in AngularJS 1.x, a service class takes on the responsibility in Angular of talking to the back-end services. The service will know and encapsulate what URL it needs to talk to on the back end, what type of request to send, and how to process the response received.

The service will need an HTTP object to make Ajax calls. Directly depending on an HTTP object will make testing rather hard. Dependency injection is the way of life in Angular and so the HTTP object will be injected into the service. During normal execution, it will be a real instance of the ng.http.Http object. During test runs, as we'll see later, a mock for the object will be used.

A service is a class in Angular with a constructor annotated to inject the necessary dependencies. Let's first define the service class named LangsService with the necessary constructor. Open and edit the src/app/langs/langs.service.js file in the current workspace and enter the following code:

angularspike/src/app/langs/langs.service.js

```
(function(app) {
  app.LangsService = ng.core
    .Class({
      constructor: [ng.http.Http, function(_http) {
        this.http = _http;
      }],
    });
})(window.app || (window.app = {}));
```

We used the ng.core.Class function to create the class and provide the constructor. The constructor property receives an array with the dependency to be injected as the first value and the constructor function as the second value. Within the constructor, we store the injected _http object into the http field.

Our service needs to make a request to the back end, to the URL /languages, and then extract the text from the response and make it available to the caller.

It also needs to gracefully deal with errors. We'll split these actions into a few modular functions.

First, let's write a function that sends out an HTTP GET request. Let's add a get function to the service class. Define this function using a property named get. Place this right after the ending comma of the definition of the constructor property in src/app/langs/langs.service.js:

angularspike/src/app/langs/langs.service.js

```
get: function() {
  return this.http.get('/languages')
                  .map(this.extractData)
                  .catch(this.returnError);
},
```

The get function uses the new Angular HTTP module. This module's HTTP-related functions like get, post, and delete return an Rx.Observable from the RxJS reactive extensions library. An Observable is like a collection, except, rather than a bounded list, it is an asynchronous stream of data flowing through from the service to a subscriber.

The map function is quite useful to transform the Observable<Response> to Observable<Data>, where Data is whatever data we would like to return. Generally, it would be the content we extract from the response, either as JSON data or a plain text. Instead of dealing with that detail here, we'll delegate that responsibility to a separate extractData function. If something goes wrong, the catch function will have to transform the error details into an Observable object. We will design it so that the catch function delegates that responsibility to a returnError function.

The get function returns an instance of Rx.Observable to the caller. The caller may subscribe to this Observable and asynchronously receive either the data sent by the back end or error details if the request fails.

Let's now implement the extractData function; place this right below the get function in the service:

angularspike/src/app/langs/langs.service.js

```
extractData: function(response) {
  if(response.status !== 200)
    throw new Error("error getting data, status: " + response.status);
  return response.text();
},
```

If the response received has a status code other than 200, then the function throws an exception. Since this function is called from the map function in the Observable call chain, the RxJS library will catch the exception and automatically route the error details to the failure handler of the subscriber. We'll discuss this further when we write the component where we'll subscribe to the Observable returned by the get function. If the status code is 200, then the function extracts and returns the body of the response, using the text() function.

Next, let's write the returnError function:

angularspike/src/app/langs/langs.service.js

```
returnError: function(error) {
  return Rx.Observable.throw(
    error.message || "error, status: " + error.status);
}
```

This function will be called if something goes wrong with the HTTP request. In this function we invoke the throw function of Observable so that the error details will be propagated up the chain, asynchronously, through the Observable call chain to the subscriber.

We've completed the implementation of the service class. Let's step back and take a look at the complete code for the service:

angularspike/src/app/langs/langs.service.js

```
(function(app) {
  app.LangsService = ng.core
    .Class({
      constructor: [ng.http.Http, function(_http) {
        this.http = _http;
      }],

      get: function() {
        return this.http.get('/languages')
                        .map(this.extractData)
                        .catch(this.returnError);
      },

      extractData: function(response) {
        if(response.status !== 200)
          throw new Error("error getting data, status: " + response.status);
        return response.text();
      },

      returnError: function(error) {
        return Rx.Observable.throw(
          error.message || "error, status: " + error.status);
      }
    });
})(window.app || (window.app = {}));
```

We have the pipe and the service in place. We need the component to request the data from the service and tie that to the view.

Create a Component

A component in Angular is the glue between one or more services, pipes, and views. In our example, the component has to receive the data from the service and render it on a view, with the language names sorted. Angular expects several pieces of information from our component:

- Which tag in the view should it replace with the content from the component? The selector annotation attribute will convey that.
- Which HTML page should it render? The templateUrl annotation attribute will give that detail. Angular also allows a template attribute instead of templateUrl. The template will directly refer to the HTML whereas templateUrl refers to a file with the HTML content. We will not use template since placing HTML in JavaScript is rather unwieldy, error prone, and the easiest way to turn amiable colleagues into arch enemies.
- What services should be injected into the component or be made available for the parts the components depend on? The providers annotation attribute is used for this purpose.
- What transformation pipes does the component need? As you may guess, the pipes annotation attribute is used for that.

Let's open the src/app/langs/langs.component.js file and create the component with the attributes we discussed.

angularspike/src/app/langs/langs.component.js

```
(function(app) {
  app.LangsComponent = ng.core
    .Component({
      selector: 'lang-names',
      templateUrl: 'langs.component.html',
      providers: [ng.http.HTTP_PROVIDERS, app.LangsService],
      pipes: [app.SortPipe]
    })
})(window.app || (window.app = {}));
```

The component is defined using the ng.core.Component function. In the definition, we have placed the four annotation attributes we discussed. The selector is referring to a lang-names, which will be a tag in an HTML file that will be replaced by the view rendered by this component. Speaking of the view, the templateUrl refers to the file that will be rendered by this component. The providers attribute lists the dependencies to be injected. The ng.http.HTTP_PROVIDERS refers to the providers that will create the appropriate HTTP object that will be used by the service class to talk to the back end. The second value given to the providers attribute is the constructor or class of the service we created earlier. Finally, the pipes attribute refers to the pipe, the first class we created for this spike.

The component class will house the model or data that it fetches from the service that the view can display. It also needs to hold on to the injected service so the functions of the component can access them. For this, we'll write the constructor for our component class. Place the following code right at the end of the Component section in the src/app/langs/langs.component.js file:

angularspike/src/app/langs/langs.component.js

```
.Class({
  constructor: [ app.LangsService, function(_langsService) {
    this.langsService = _langsService;
    this.langs = [];
    this.message = '';
  }],
});
```

The .Class call chains right at the end of the .Component() function call. The constructor attribute takes in an array. The first value refers to the service class or constructor that will be injected into the constructor function. The second value refers to the constructor function. The constructor saves the injected service into a field named langsService. In addition, it initializes two fields—langs and message—to an empty array and an empty string, respectively. These fields of the components are viewed as models by Angular.

The HTML file that the component renders—langs.component.html in this example—will have bindings to the fields of the components we initialized in the constructor. We'll see this part when we put all the things together, once we complete the implementation of the component.

We have the necessary fields or models in the component. Next we need a function, getLangs, that will fetch the data from the service and set the appropriate models. If all goes well we need to update the langs model. If the service falters, we need to update the message model. But that's too much work for the getLangs to do. We'll modularize. Here's the getLangs function; write it within the Class({}) declaration but after the constructor[...] code:

angularspike/src/app/langs/langs.component.js

```
getLangs: function() {
  this.langsService.get()
                  .subscribe(
                    this.updateLangs.bind(this),
                    this.updateError.bind(this));
},
```

The getLangs function calls the get function of the service that was injected into the component. Recall that the get returns an Observable. The Observable may send us the data or an error, as we discussed during the implementation of the service.

In the getLangs function, we subscribe to the response from the Observable using the subscribe function. This function may take up to three arguments:

- A function that's invoked when the Observable sends a piece of data
- A function that's invoked when the Observable wants to provide an error message
- A function that the Observable may call to tell us it has completed and there will be no further data or error

We provide only the first two arguments and ignore the completed message. If data arrives, we pass that to an updateLangs function. If an error arrives instead, we pass that to an updateError message.

Let's now implement the updateLangs function in the component, right after the getLangs function:

angularspike/src/app/langs/langs.component.js

```
updateLangs: function(langs) {
  this.message = '';
  this.langs = langs.split('\n');
},
```

The function clears any values in the message field; splits the given data into an array, with each language name as a separate value; and assigns the array to the langs field.

Let's move on to the next function. The updateError function is quite simple too:

angularspike/src/app/langs/langs.component.js

```
updateError: function(error) {
  this.message = error;
  this.langs = [];
},
```

This function clears the langs field and sets error details in the message field.

There's one final step we need. Right after the component is ready, we want the getLangs function to be exercised automatically without any user intervention. To perform such actions, Angular provides a special ngOnInit function. If this function is present on a component, it's invoked once the document is loaded and the DOM is ready. This is much like the traditional onLoad function. Let's implement the ngOnInit function next, right after the updateError function:

angularspike/src/app/langs/langs.component.js

```
ngOnInit: function() {
  this.getLangs();
}
```

In the ngOnInit function we merely call the getLangs function.

We created the component step-by-step. It will help to step back and take a look at the entire component we created. Here it is:

angularspike/src/app/langs/langs.component.js

```
(function(app) {
  app.LangsComponent = ng.core
    .Component({
      selector: 'lang-names',
      templateUrl: 'langs.component.html',
      providers: [ng.http.HTTP_PROVIDERS, app.LangsService],
      pipes: [app.SortPipe]
    })
    .Class({
      constructor: [ app.LangsService, function(_langsService) {
        this.langsService = _langsService;
        this.langs = [];
        this.message = '';
      }],

      getLangs: function() {
        this.langsService.get()
                         .subscribe(
                           this.updateLangs.bind(this),
                           this.updateError.bind(this));
      },

      updateLangs: function(langs) {
        this.message = '';
        this.langs = langs.split('\n');
      },

      updateError: function(error) {
        this.message = error;
        this.langs = [];
      },

      ngOnInit: function() {
        this.getLangs();
      }
    });
})(window.app || (window.app = {}));
```

From the listing, we get a good view of the two parts of the component—the Component annotation and the Class with its fields and functions. We're almost done with the essential parts. We need a small piece of code to bootstrap the component: an HTML file to display the language names, and one to load the JavaScript source files.

Put It All Together

The component refers to the service and the pipe. It makes good use of the service, but we haven't seen the pipe being used yet. We'll get to that soon. We need something to introduce the component to Angular and load all the relevant files. Let's take care of those last few steps.

A small piece of code in an src/main.js file will tell Angular to load up the component and start watching for the changes to the models/fields to update the DOM. Open the src/main.js file and add the following code to it:

angularspike/src/main.js

```
(function(app) {
 document.addEventListener('DOMContentLoaded', function() {
   ng.platformBrowserDynamic.bootstrap(app.LangsComponent);
 });
})(window.app || (window.app = {}));
```

The function in src/main.js registers our component by calling the bootstrap function when the DOMContentLoaded event is fired on the document. This sets off the chain reaction within Angular and it asynchronously starts watching the component fields for any change.

We need the langs.component.html file mentioned in the templateUrl attribute of the component. Let's create that next. Edit the file langs.component.html present right in the current workspace directory and add the following to it:

angularspike/langs.component.html

```
{{ message}}

<li *ngFor ="let lang of langs | sort">
        {{ lang }}
</li>
```

That's a short snippet. The first line binds an expression to the message model, the field with that name in the component. In the second line we use the new ngFor directive to loop over the values in the langs array. The directive iterates over the array and binds the values in the array, one at a time, to the lang variable. Before iterating through the array, however, the array will be transformed to a sorted array thanks to the pipe operation. The sort pipe is the name we assigned to the name property when we created the pipe. The component refers to the pipe class in the pipes attribute and so the template knows where the name sort comes from. Finally, the expression placed as the child element of the li element will be evaluated once for each value in the langs array.

We have just one final step to complete—implement the starting page index.html. Open this file, which is under the current workspace directory, and place the following content in it:

angularspike/index.html
```
<!DOCTYPE html>
<html>
  <head>
    <title>Languages</title>

    <script src="node_modules/zone.js/dist/zone.js"></script>
    <script src="node_modules/reflect-metadata/Reflect.js"></script>
    <script src="node_modules/rxjs/bundles/Rx.umd.js"></script>
    <script src="node_modules/@angular/core/bundles/core.umd.js"></script>
    <script src="node_modules/@angular/common/bundles/common.umd.js">
                    </script>
    <script
      src="node_modules/@angular/compiler/bundles/compiler.umd.js">
                </script>
    <script src="node_modules/@angular\
/platform-browser/bundles/platform-browser.umd.js">
    </script>
    <script src="node_modules/@angular\
/platform-browser-dynamic/bundles/platform-browser-dynamic.umd.js">
    </script>
    <script src="node_modules/@angular/http/bundles/http.umd.js"></script>

    <script src="src/app/langs/sort.pipe.js"></script>
    <script src="src/app/langs/langs.service.js"></script>
    <script src="src/app/langs/langs.component.js"></script>
    <script src="src/main.js"></script>
  </head>
  <body>
    <div>
      <lang-names>loading...</lang-names>
    </div>
  </body>
</html>
```

The first several script tags load up the Angular- and RxJS-related files. The last four script tags load up the source files for the pipe, the service, the component, and the bootstrap code.

The order in which these files are loaded is important; place what's needed by a file ahead of it in the load sequence.

Within the body tag, we have a lang-names tag—that's the once referenced by the selector annotation attribute in the component—with a temporary loading... message. Angular will replace this tag with the evaluated content of the langs.component.html file when it sees a change to the models in the component.

Our spiking effort is complete. We're ready to see the code in action. Make sure all the files are saved. On the command prompt, in the current project's workspace, type the command npm install and then the command

```
npm start
```

This will start the http-server server. Now open your favorite browser and point it at the URL http://localhost:8080. The index.html page should load up in the browser and that, in turn, should activate Angular, which will go through the bootstrap sequence. Once that completes, instead of seeing the loading... message we should see the language names listed, in sorted order. Let's take a quick look at a browser instance viewing the spike application:

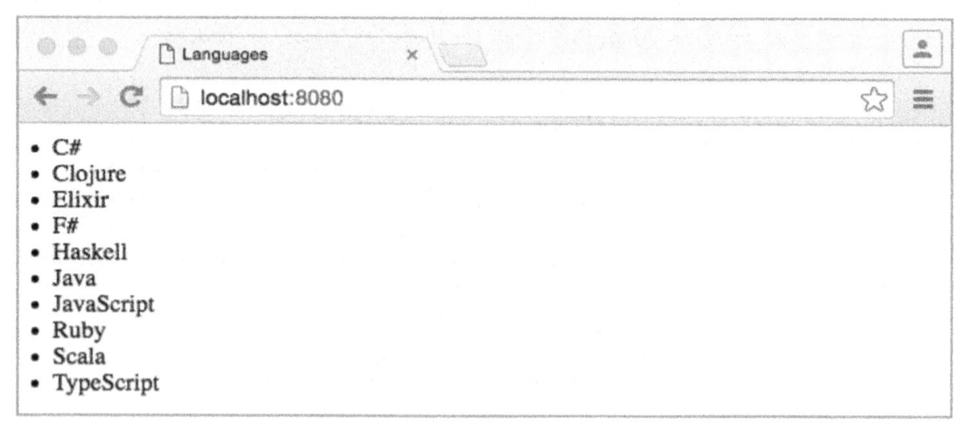

Take a few minutes to review the code created in this spiking exercise. Along the way, we'll think about how we may test-drive the creation of such code.

The pipe is the easiest to test. We only need to create an instance of the class, call the transform function on it, and verify it's returning the expected result. In addition, we need to ensure the name annotation attribute is set.

The service relies on the HTTP object being injected. Since this is a constructor parameter, we can easily pass in a mock during testing. We then have to verify that the functions in the service behave properly. For this we will have to mock out the Observable—though that sounds complicated, it's quite easy, as you'll see soon.

Finally, to test the behavior of the component, we can mock out its dependency—the service. In addition, we have to verify that all the annotation properties are set as expected.

The way Angular organizes and configures different parts together makes testing simple and easy. You must be eager to get started with testing. Enough kicking the tires—let's wait no longer.

Design Angular Apps with Tests

Let's test-drive an Angular version of the front end for the TO-DO app we created in Chapter 6, *Test-Drive Express Apps*, on page 121.

Most programmers are new to Angular and it's hard to write tests for a piece of code when the implementation is not clear in our minds. When unsure, you can refer back to the spike we just created. It gives you a fairly good idea of the shape and structure of any Angular application. Any time you're not sure about what test to write next, glance at the spike code to think through a possible implementation.

The client side we'll create will look the same as the previous versions we created using jQuery and AngularJS 1.x. The sketch is shown here again for your convenience:

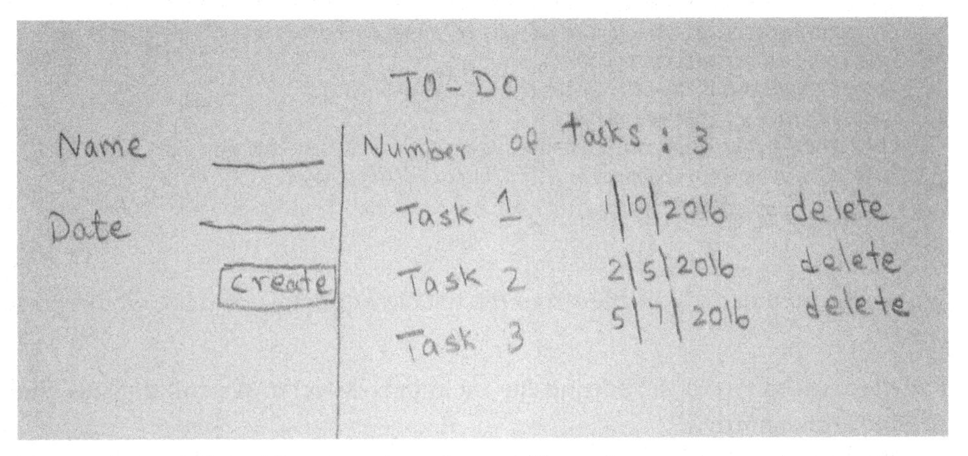

To implement this UI using Angular, we'll need a component, a service, a pipe, a bootstrap code, and two HTML files. We'll test-drive the design of all the classes and functions for this application.

We will build the application in increments. First, we'll test-drive the feature to get the list of tasks. Once that's complete, we'll then take on the feature to add a new task. Finally, we'll work on deleting a task.

Let's start with the necessary project files.

Set Up the Project

The directory tdjsa/testangular2/todo in your workspace contains a copy of the server-side code created in Chapter 6, *Test-Drive Express Apps*, on page 121, along with some changes necessary to work with Angular and client-side tests. We'll create the Angular-related code in this project. Change to this directory.

Take a look at the package.json file. It contains the dependencies for Angular-, RxJS-, and Karma-related modules. It also contains scripts to run the client-side tests in addition to the server-side tests. Run npm install to get the necessary packages installed for this project.

A karma.conf.js file is also provided in this project. Take a look at the files section of this file and notice that the Angular- and RxJs-related files are included:

testangular2/todo/karma.conf.js

```
files: [
  "./public/javascripts/zone.js/dist/zone.js",
  "./public/javascripts/reflect-metadata/Reflect.js",
  "./public/javascripts/rxjs/bundles/Rx.umd.js",
  "./public/javascripts/@angular/core/bundles/core.umd.js",
  "./public/javascripts/@angular/common/bundles/common.umd.js",
  "./public/javascripts/@angular/compiler/bundles/compiler.umd.js",
  "./public/javascripts/@angular/" +
    "platform-browser/bundles/platform-browser.umd.js",
  "./public/javascripts/@angular/" +
    "platform-browser-dynamic/bundles/platform-browser-dynamic.umd.js",
  "./public/javascripts/@angular/http/bundles/http.umd.js",

  './test/client/**/*.js',
],
```

We've also included all the files from the test/client directory and its subdirectories.

Pay close attention to the second file included—Reflect.js. We will discuss the need for this shortly.

In addition to the changes mentioned so far, empty files for various Angular code we'll write and the corresponding tests are provided in the project workspace. Let's get started with our journey to test-drive Angular code.

Create the Test List

Looking at the sketch and based on our previous efforts to create the different versions of the front end for the TO-DO app, we have a fairly good idea of things that we need to create for the Angular front end.

Let's jot down some of the tests that come to mind; we can refine these later as we proceed. Let's focus on the component-related tests first for the feature that lists the tasks.

- The component should set the selector attribute
- The component should set the templateUrl attribute
- The constructor should initialize tasks to an empty array
- The constructor should initialize message to an empty string
- getTasks should register handlers with service
- updateTasks should update tasks
- updateError should update message
- Tasks displayed should be in sorted order
- getTasks should be called on init

These tests are just for designing the component. We can look at the service and the rest of the details after we get through this pile. Let's get started with the component design.

Test-Drive the Component

The component glues together the view and the model that holds data obtained from the service. As a first step, we need to get a few necessary annotation attributes created in the component. The first two tests we have listed lead us exactly there. Let's start with the first test.

Verify That Component Attributes Are Set

To define the component we will use the ng.core.Component function call and set the annotation property selector in it. If it's not clear how this will look for our new component, take a quick look at the LangsComponent in the spike.

Writing the component is easy. We have seen an example of that already in the spike. The hard question is, how do we test for it? In other words, we want to write a failing test before we write the selector attribute.

For this we have to do some research and learn how Angular deals with annotations and attributes. Annotations and the related attributes are metadata. They are not kept within the class or its instances, but reside separately in a meta-class that stores these details. The Reflect[1] class, included through the script tag for Reflect.js file, is a gateway to create and obtain metadata. That's what we'll use to verify that our component has set the necessary annotation attributes.

The getMetadataKeys function of Reflect will give us a list of keys available for a class. We can then use the getMetadata function to get specific attributes from any of the keys.

To understand the metadata better, let's play again for a moment with the spike to explore the metadata for the app.LangsComponent. With the spike program running, open the browser to the URL http://localhost:8080. Then, in the console window of the browser, enter the commands shown in the following figure and see the response you get:

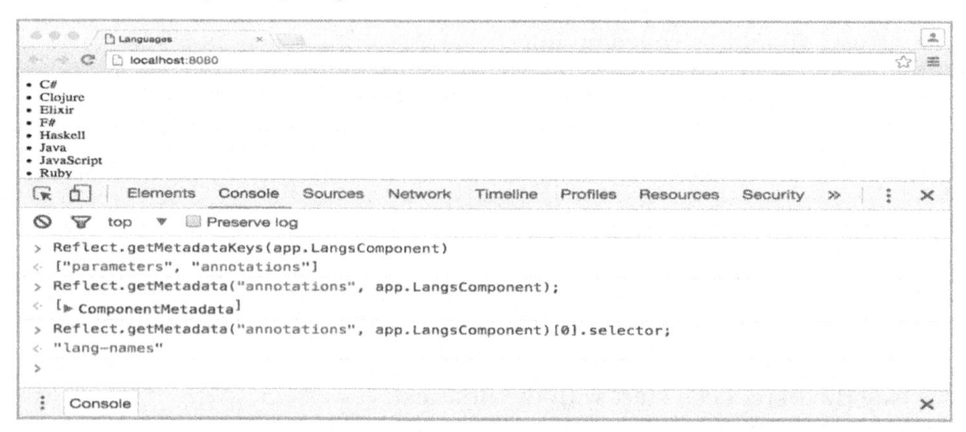

We see that for the command Reflect.getMetadataKeys(app.LangsComponent), we got the response ["parameters", "annotations"]. This tells us that we have two meta-keys available. We'll make use of those during testing. Then, with the command Reflect.getMetadata("annotations", app.LangsComponent)[0].selector; we were able to get the attribute's value of lang-names. This gives us a good idea of how we can test for the existence and the values of the attributes in our components.

Let's switch back to the tdjsa/testangular2/todo workspace. Open the empty test file test/client/app/tasks/tasks.component-test.js in the current project and enter the following first test for the component:

1. http://www.ecma-international.org/ecma-262/6.0/#sec-reflection

testangular2/todo/test/client/app/tasks/tasks.component-test.js

```
describe('tasks component tests', function() {
  it('should set the selector attribute', function() {
    var componentAnnotations =
      Reflect.getMetadata('annotations', app.TasksComponent)[0];

    expect(componentAnnotations.selector).to.be.eql('tasks-list');
  });
});
```

The test examines the annotations metadata for the component app.TasksComponent that we'll write shortly. We use the getMetadata function of Reflect to get the metadata. Then we verify that the selector attribute is set to the desired value.

Before we write the necessary code in the component, we want to see the test fail. Currently the karma.conf.js file does not include any source file; it includes only Angular-related files and the test files. To include the source files, we can't use the wildcard (**)—recall from the spiking exercise that the Angular-related files have to be loaded in specific order. Let's change the files section in the karma.conf.js file to include the component's source file:

```
//...
'./test/client/**/*.js',
'./public/src/app/tasks/tasks.component.js',
```

Now we're ready to fire up Karma and run the client-side test we wrote. Run the following command and watch the test fail in Mocha:

```
npm run-script test-client
```

Let's implement the minimum code to make the test pass. Open the public/src/app/tasks/tasks.component.js file and enter the following code:

```
(function(app) {
  app.TasksComponent = ng.core
    .Component({
      selector: 'tasks-list',
    })
    .Class({
      constructor: function() {}
    });
})(window.app || (window.app = {}));
```

Both the Component and the Class calls are necessary along with the empty constructor. Without those the Reflect API will complain that it could not get any metadata. The selector attribute of Component has been assigned to the desired value—this represents the tag name of the element we expect to replace in the index.html file we'll write eventually.

As soon as you save the file, Karma—which is watching for file changes—will trigger Mocha, which in turn will report the test as passing.

Let's move on to the next test in our test list. Here's the test to verify that the templateUrl attribute has been set to the desired value:

testangular2/todo/test/client/app/tasks/tasks.component-test.js

```
it('should set the templateUrl attribute', function() {
  var componentAnnotations =
    Reflect.getMetadata('annotations', app.TasksComponent)[0];

  expect(componentAnnotations.templateUrl).to.be.eql(
    'tasks.component.html');
});
```

To make this test pass, we only need a small change to our component; add the templateUrl attribute to the selector:

```
selector: 'tasks-list',
templateUrl: 'tasks.component.html'
```

You now know how to verify the component attributes. Next, let's verify that the necessary models, the fields in the component, are initialized properly.

Initialize the Models

The component needs to store into a model the list of tasks that it gets from the service. Also, it needs a model to store any messages it gets in response from the service. Since calls to the service are asynchronous and the response may take some time, we need to display safe initial values for these models. Let's write a test to verify that the tasks model is initialized properly—this test again goes into the test/client/app/tasks/tasks.component-test.js file.

testangular2/todo/test/client/app/tasks/tasks.component-test.js

```
it('should initialize tasks to an empty array', function() {
  expect(tasksComponent.tasks).to.be.eql([]);
});
```

This test is verifying that the tasks field on an instance of our component is set to the desired initial value. But we do not have the reference to an instance of the component yet. At the top of the test suite, add the following beforeEach setup code:

```
var tasksComponent;

beforeEach(function() {
  tasksComponent = new app.TasksComponent();
});
```

To make this pass, create and initialize a tasks field within the constructor of our TasksComponent. Edit the public/src/app/tasks/tasks.component.js file like so:

```
constructor: function() {
  this.tasks = [];
}
```

Likewise, here's a test to verify that the message model is initialized properly:

testangular2/todo/test/client/app/tasks/tasks.component-test.js

```
it('should initialize message to an empty string', function() {
  expect(tasksComponent.message).to.be.eql('');
});
```

Set the desired initial value for the message field in the component class's constructor:

```
constructor: function() {
  this.tasks = [];
  this.message = '';
}
```

We have the necessary attributes and the fields for the component. It's time to design the first function of the component.

Design getTasks

The getTasks function of the component should call a service to get the task list from the back-end server. When the data arrives, it will have to update the tasks model. We can delegate the update of the model to another function. The responsibility of the getTasks function is first to call the service. Recall from the spiking example that a service will return an Rx.Observable. The getTasks will then have to register the appropriate handlers with the subscribe function of the Observable.

The test we write for getTasks is going to be an interaction test. However, we have multiple interactions to verify and it's not easy to see through all of them. Let's get some help from the spike we created. The getTasks function is going to be a lot like the getLangs function. It will help to review that function. Let's take a look:

```
getLangs: function() {
  this.langsService.get()
                  .subscribe(
                    this.updateLangs.bind(this),
                    this.updateError.bind(this));
},
```

Looking at this code, we can form, in our mind, the steps we need to verify the behavior of the getTasks function we're about to write. First we need to stub the bind function of both the handlers that are passed to the subscribe function. We need to mock out the subscribe function and verify that the parameters passed to it are the functions returned by the 'bind' functions we stubbed out. That's going to take some effort—we'll use Sinon to create the stubs and the mocks.

Start by changing the test suite to add a few new variables, change the beforeEach function, and then add the afterEach function. In the test suite, test/client/app/tasks/tasks.component-test.js, we currently have this setup code:

```
var tasksComponent;

beforeEach(function() {
  tasksComponent = new app.TasksComponent();
});
```

Change it to the following:

```
var sandbox;
var tasksComponent;
var tasksService;
var observable = { subscribe: function() {} };
var updateTasksBindStub = function() {};
var updateErrorBindStub = function() {};

beforeEach(function() {
  tasksService = {
    get: function() {},
    add: function() {},
    delete: function() {}
  };

  tasksComponent = new app.TasksComponent(tasksService);

  sandbox = sinon.sandbox.create();

  sandbox.stub(tasksComponent.updateTasks, 'bind')
         .withArgs(tasksComponent)
         .returns(updateTasksBindStub);

  sandbox.stub(tasksComponent.updateError, 'bind')
         .withArgs(tasksComponent)
         .returns(updateErrorBindStub);

        sandbox.stub(tasksService, 'get')
               .withArgs()
               .returns(observable);
});

afterEach(function() {
  sandbox.restore();
});
```

Let's go over the change to understand all the different steps we took. Let's start with the fields/variables.

We have variables declared for the Sinon sandbox, component, and service. Since the service does not really exist at this time, the variable tasksService will refer to a stub. observable is a stub for Rx.Observable and so it has a no-op subscribe function. updateTasksBindStub and updateErrorBindStub are no-op stubs for the functions that will be returned by the bind function, as you'll see soon.

In the beforeEach function we first create a stub for the service and pass the service to the constructor of our component. Then we create a stub for the component's updateTasks function's bind function. In this stub, we verify that the given parameter is in fact a reference to our component and then return the stub we created to stand in as the result of the bind function. We implement the stub for the updateError function's bind function similarly. Finally, we stub out the get method of the service stub to return the fake observable that we created earlier.

In addition, in the afterEach function we restore all the changes that Sinon did while stubbing and mocking.

We're ready now to write our test to verify the behavior of the getTasks function. Add the following test to the test suite:

testangular2/todo/test/client/app/tasks/tasks.component-test.js

```
it('getTasks should register handlers with service', function() {
  var observableMock =
    sandbox.mock(observable)
           .expects('subscribe')
           .withArgs(updateTasksBindStub, updateErrorBindStub);

  tasksComponent.getTasks();

  observableMock.verify();
});
```

In the test we create a mock for the subscribe function of the Observable's stub. The mock expects the subscribe function to be called with the proper handlers—the stubs we created to stand in for the result of calls to bind on the two handlers. We then call the function under test getTasks and verify that the subscribe function on the Observable returned by the service was called correctly by the getTasks function.

The test needed significant effort—that's a downside. However, there's an upshot—we're able to verify the behavior of the getTasks function without needing the real service. That in turn tells us that we can get a quick and deterministic feedback of this code's behavior without needing the back-end service to be up and running.

Let's implement the getTasks function to make the test pass. We also need to modify the constructor to take in the service as a parameter and store it into a local variable. In addition, we need to initialize the handler functions—a no-op implementation will suffice for now. Open the component class, change the constructor, and add the new functions, as follows:

```
.Class({
  constructor: function(_tasksService) {
    this.tasks = [];
    this.message = '';
    this.service = _tasksService;
  },
  getTasks: function() {
    this.service.get()
                .subscribe(this.updateTasks.bind(this),
                           this.updateError.bind(this));
  },
  updateTasks: function() {},
  updateError: function() {},
});
```

Save the files and ensure the tests are passing.

If the effort in the previous test left you a bit worried, be assured that that was the most difficult test we will write for Angular. The rest of the tests ahead will be relatively easy, as you'll see.

Implementing the two handlers will hardly take any effort. Let's write a test for the updateTasks function. The function will receive a list of tasks from the service and should set that into the tasks model.

testangular2/todo/test/client/app/tasks/tasks.component-test.js

```
it('updateTasks should update tasks', function() {
  var tasksStub = [{sample: 1}];
  tasksComponent.updateTasks(tasksStub);
  expect(tasksComponent.tasks).to.be.eql(tasksStub);
});
```

This test is pretty straightforward; it sends as an argument a list or array of tasks to the function and verifies that the tasks model in the component has been updated with that value. We currently have a no-op function for updateTasks in our component. Modify it to make the test pass:

```
updateTasks: function(tasks) { this.tasks = tasks; },
```

The test to verify updateError will pose no challenges. It's as simple as the previous test:

testangular2/todo/test/client/app/tasks/tasks.component-test.js
```
it('updateError should update message', function() {
  tasksComponent.updateError('Not Found');
  expect(tasksComponent.message).to.be.eql('Not Found');
});
```

Replace the no-op function that's currently in place for the updateError function with the following code:

```
updateError: function(error) { this.message = error; },
```

The next test in our test list refers to sorting the tasks that are displayed. That's a big topic and it involves several steps. Let's postpone that and work on something relatively easier and fast to do. After that we will revisit what's needed for sorting.

When the document is loaded and the DOM is ready, the getTasks function should be called automatically without any user intervention. That way the user can readily see the list of tasks as soon as the page is loaded. For this, we'll use the ngOnInit function that Angular will call automatically at the right time, if present. There's one catch.

If we call getTasks from ngOnInit, that function in turn will make a get call on the service. We don't have a service at this time and even if we did, we wouldn't want to rely on it in this test. One solution would be to mock the service—but that would be a lot of work. Let's think through this a bit more. We want to verify that ngOnInit is calling getTasks. It's an interaction test. We can easily verify the interaction by mocking the getTasks function.

testangular2/todo/test/client/app/tasks/tasks.component-test.js
```
it('getTasks should be called on init', function() {
  var getTasksMock = sandbox.mock(tasksComponent)
                            .expects('getTasks');

  tasksComponent.ngOnInit();
  getTasksMock.verify();
});
```

One simple change to the component class should get us moving forward. Add the following code right after the updateError function in the component:

```
ngOnInit: function() { this.getTasks(); }
```

For the component, we have everything we need in place for the feature to get tasks and display—well, almost everything. We still need to sort the tasks. Let's focus on that job next.

Sort the Task List

The test in our test list related to sorting says "tasks displayed should be in sorted order." How and where should we do the sorting is the next question we need to tackle.

Let's revisit how we did the sorting in the spiking exercise. We added the pipes annotation to the component, but we let the view do the transformation using the declarative style expression let lang of langs | sort in the HTML file. This has exactly the same bad smell that orderBy in AngularJS 1.x did—see *Find the Right Place*, on page 207.

It's Not Good if It's Hard to Test

It does not matter how awesome and slick a piece of code looks; it's not good if it's hard to test.

Instead of placing the pipe in the HTML file, we'll do the sorting in code, within the component. We know that we can easily test and verify that sorting is done properly when we do this at the code level. But we don't want to put the entire code for sorting within our component.

We'll write the sorting operation as a pipe instead of implementing it within the component. That way, if the sort operation is needed somewhere else later on we have it available as a readily reusable class. By writing it as a pipe we can also use it from HTML during prototyping exercises. By naming it as a pipe, the intention becomes clear as well. In other words, we will write it as a pipe but will use it like a service.

Since we plan to use the pipe from within the component instead of using the pipes annotation attribute, we'll place it in providers. But we're jumping ahead; let's get to those details later on. Let's bring our focus back to sorting the tasks.

We're in the middle of implementing the component. We just made a design decision that the sorting transformation will happen in a pipe. Right now, all we need to verify is that updateTasks delegates the concern of sorting to a separate object's function. So, the test we identified earlier for the sorting function changes as follows:

- ~~tasks displayed should be in sorted order~~
- updateTasks calls the transform function of pipe

We'll think through the tests needed for the pipe later on when we get to the design of the pipe.

We have already designed and implemented the updateTasks function. Let's add another test for the changed behavior of this function. We need a couple of things in the test suite before we can write the test.

First, add the following variable declaration in the test suite, right after the definition of updateErrorBindStub:

```
var sortPipe = { transform: function(data) { return data; } }
```

Second, in the beforeEach function, change the arguments passed to the constructor of our component from

```
tasksComponent = new app.TasksComponent(tasksService);
```

to

```
tasksComponent = new app.TasksComponent(tasksService, sortPipe);
```

We have created a stub for the pipe—the transform function in this stub merely returns the given data. We then passed this stub to the constructor as the new second argument. The necessary things are in place to write the test. Here's the new test for updateTasks:

testangular2/todo/test/client/app/tasks/tasks.component-test.js

```
it('updateTasks should call transform on pipe', function() {
  var tasksStub = '...fake input...';

  var expectedSortedTasks = '...fake output...';

  sandbox.stub(sortPipe, 'transform')
         .withArgs(tasksStub)
         .returns(expectedSortedTasks);

  tasksComponent.updateTasks(tasksStub);
  expect(tasksComponent.tasks).to.be.eql(expectedSortedTasks);
});
```

The test creates a fake output for the transform function to return. Then it stubs out the transform function in the pipe's stub with a version that returns the fake output, when the expected input is given. Finally, it calls the updateTasks function on our component and verifies that the function returns the result that was returned by the transform function.

Before we make the small but necessary change to the updateTasks function, we have to change the constructor of our component to take in a new second parameter. Let's make that change now:

```
constructor: function(_tasksService, _sortPipe) {
  this.tasks = [];
  this.message = '';
  this.service = _tasksService;
  this.sortPipe = _sortPipe;
},
```

With that change, we're ready to change the updateTasks function:

```
updateTasks: function(tasks) {
  this.tasks = this.sortPipe.transform(tasks);
},
```

Save the files and ensure all tests are passing. Looking at the code we have so far in the component, there's some unfinished business related to getting the tasks. We need to set up dependency injection so that Angular will properly wire our component with the service and the pipe. Let's tend to that next.

Verify Dependency Injection

You learned from the spiking exercise the syntax necessary to perform dependency injection. We need two things: we have to set a new providers attribute and change the constructor attribute to specify the classes/constructors that will be used for injection. Let's take care of the first one.

Program Deliberately

It's easy to lose sight of why we write some boilerplate code when working with frameworks. Program deliberately—express your intentions through tests and then write the minimum code to fulfill those expectations.

Let's add the following test to the component's test suite:

testangular2/todo/test/client/app/tasks/tasks.component-test.js

```
it('should register necessary providers', function() {
  var componentAnnotations =
    Reflect.getMetadata('annotations', app.TasksComponent)[0];

  var expectedProviders =
    [ng.http.HTTP_PROVIDERS, app.TasksService, app.TasksSortPipe];

  expect(componentAnnotations.providers).to.be.eql(expectedProviders);
});
```

The test fetches the providers annotation attribute by using the Reflect class's getMetadata function—much like how we got the selector attribute earlier. Then it verifies that the value set for the attribute is the expected series of values.

To make this test pass, modify the component to include the providers attribute, right after the templateUrl attribute, like so:

```
templateUrl: 'tasks.component.html',
providers: [ng.http.HTTP_PROVIDERS, app.TasksService, app.TasksSortPipe]
```

Save the files and ensure the tests pass. The next test is to verify that the constructor attribute is configured properly for dependency injection.

testangular2/todo/test/client/app/tasks/tasks.component-test.js

```
it('TasksService should be injected into the component', function() {
  var injectedServices =
    Reflect.getMetadata('parameters', app.TasksComponent);

  expect(injectedServices[0]).to.be.eql([app.TasksService]);
  expect(injectedServices[1]).to.be.eql([app.TasksSortPipe]);
});
```

This test also uses the Reflect class's getMetadata function, but instead of fetching the annotations property, it's asking for parameters. While the attributes we put into Component goes into annotations, the attributes we placed into the constructor goes into the parameters property. We then verify that the two values in the array passed to the constructor attribute are as expected.

There's one small gotcha here. The classes app.TasksService and app.TasksSortPipe are currently undefined. That's OK; later on when we define these classes, these references will come to life to refer to the actual classes/constructors instead of being undefined.

Let's modify the constructor attribute of our component to inject the necessary classes/constructors:

```
constructor: [app.TasksService, app.TasksSortPipe,
  function(_tasksService, _sortPipe) {
    this.tasks = [];
    this.message = '';
    this.service = _tasksService;
    this.sortPipe = _sortPipe;
  }],
```

Save the files and make sure all the tests pass.

All the code necessary in the component to get the task list is done. While we may continue to work on the component for other features, it's more fun to get some coding done for the service and the pipe, put all the code together, and see in action the feature that gets all the tasks. Then we can come back to the component to complete the add feature and the delete feature.

Let's shift our attention to the design of the service class next.

Test-Drive the Service

The service class needs to provide a get function. This function will talk to the back end, fetch the data, extract the JSON response, and return an Observable to the caller. Let's design this function, test first.

As the first step, let's list the tests we need to implement the get function. Here again you can learn from the service you created during the spiking exercise.

- get should make GET request to /tasks
- extractData should return result from json()
- extractData should throw exception for invalid status
- returnError should return the error Observable

The first test is going to be an interaction test. The methods of HTTP return Rx.Observable. We will be calling the map and catch functions on the returned Observable. Since we do not want to talk to the real back-end service, we'll have to mock out the Observable.

Open the test/client/app/tasks/tasks.service-test.js file, create a new test suite for testing the service, and create a few variables that we'll need:

testangular2/todo/test/client/app/tasks/tasks.service-test.js

```
describe('tasks service tests', function() {
  var sandbox;
  var http;
  var observable;
  var tasksService;
});
```

In the new test suite we've created a few variables. We already know the purpose of sandbox. http will hold a reference to a stub for HTTP to emulate calls to the back end. observable will be a reference to a stub for the Rx.Observable that will be returned by the functions on HTTP. Finally, tasksService will be a reference to the service under test.

Next put these variables to use in the setup function of the test suite. First, create a lightweight stub to stand in for HTTP and pass it as constructor argument to the service instance we create. Then create a stub for Observable. We will then lay out a chain of stubs for the following sequence: The stub for HTTP's get will return the stub for the Observable if the passed in argument is the correct URL, /tasks. The stub for the Observable's map function will return the Observable if the argument given is the proper handler function. Likewise, the stub for the Observable's catch function will return the Observable if the given argument is the proper handler function that should be passed to catch.

Let's implement the beforeEach function and also the afterEach function to restore Sinon's sandbox. Add the following code, right under the variable declarations we just added, within the test suite in test/client/app/tasks/tasks.service-test.js:

testangular2/todo/test/client/app/tasks/tasks.service-test.js

```
beforeEach(function() {
  sandbox = sinon.sandbox.create();

  http = {
    get: function() {},
  };

  tasksService = new app.TasksService(http);

  observable = {
    map: function() {},
    catch: function() {}
  };

  sandbox.stub(http, 'get')
         .withArgs('/tasks')
         .returns(observable);

  sandbox.stub(observable, 'map')
         .withArgs(tasksService.extractData)
         .returns(observable);

  sandbox.stub(observable, 'catch')
         .withArgs(tasksService.returnError)
         .returns(observable);
});

afterEach(function() {
  sandbox.restore();
});
```

We have everything ready to write the interaction test for the service's get function. Here's the test:

testangular2/todo/test/client/app/tasks/tasks.service-test.js

```
it('get should make GET request to /tasks', function() {
  expect(tasksService.get()).to.be.eql(observable);
  expect(http.get.calledWith('/tasks')).to.be.true;
  expect(observable.map.calledWith(tasksService.extractData)).to.be.true;
  expect(observable.catch.calledWith(tasksService.returnError)).to.be.true;
});
```

The test calls the get function on our service and verifies that it returned the expected Observable. In addition, the test verifies that when get was called, the get method of HTTP was really called. Furthermore, it verifies that both the map and the catch functions were called correctly on the Observable returned by HTTP get. This last few checks ensure that the calls to map or catch were not skipped.

Before we run this test, we have to make a change to the karma.conf.js file. In the files section, add a reference to the now empty public/src/app/tasks/tasks.service.js file, right before the reference to the tasks.component.js file—remember that the order is important. The files section will look like this after the change:

```
files: [
  'node_modules/angular2/bundles/angular2-polyfills.js',
  'node_modules/rxjs/bundles/Rx.umd.js',
  'node_modules/angular2/bundles/angular2-all.umd.js',
  './test/client/**/*.js',
  './public/src/app/tasks/tasks.service.js',
  './public/src/app/tasks/tasks.component.js',
],
```

Restart Karma after saving the file and Mocha will complain that it has no clue what app.TasksService is. We're now ready to implement the minimum code for the service class to make the test pass. Open the public/src/app/tasks/tasks.service.js file and add the following code:

```
(function(app) {
  app.TasksService = ng.core.Class({
    constructor: function(_http) {
      this.http = _http;
    },
    get: function() {
      return this.http.get('/tasks')
                  .map(this.extractData)
                  .catch(this.returnError);
    },
  });
})(window.app || (window.app = {}));
```

The service is only a class, not a component. We used the ng.core.Class function to create the class. We assigned a function to the constructor property and in it we stored the reference to the given _http object in the http field. In the get function we called the get function of HTTP and provided the necessary function handlers to the map and the catch functions. We don't have these handler functions yet, but that's fine—they will fall in place soon.

Save the file and ensure that all the tests—those for the component and the one test for the service—are passing.

The get function relies on two handlers. Let's implement the next test from out test list: extractData should return result from json().

testangular2/todo/test/client/app/tasks/tasks.service-test.js
```
it('extractData should return result from json()', function() {
  var fakeJSON = {};
  var response = {status: 200, json: function() { return fakeJSON; } };

  expect(tasksService.extractData(response)).to.be.eql(fakeJSON);
});
```

The test sends a canned response object as an argument to the extractData function and expects the result of the function call to be the result returned by the json() function of the response object. To make this test pass, open the service class and implement the minimum code in it for a new extractData function, right below the get function:

```
extractData: function(response) {
    return response.json();
},
```

That was short—the function merely returned the result of the call to the json() function. Even though the test provided a value for status, that was not used here—true to the words of writing the minimum code, we added only what's essential to make the tests pass.

Let's now move on to write the next test that will force the function to make use of the status property:

testangular2/todo/test/client/app/tasks/tasks.service-test.js
```
it('extractData should throw exception for invalid status', function() {
  var response = {status: 404 };

  expect(function() {
    tasksService.extractData(response);
    }).to.throw('Request failed with status: 404');
});
```

This test sends a status of 404 and expects the function under test to blow up. It's an exception test—it will pass if the function throws the right exception. We need to change the function under test to make this test pass:

```
extractData: function(response) {
  if(response.status !== 200)
    throw new Error('Request failed with status: ' + response.status);

    return response.json();
},
```

Let's implement the last test on our test list. This one will drive the implementation of the returnError function.

testangular2/todo/test/client/app/tasks/tasks.service-test.js

```
it('returnError should return an error Observable', function() {
  var error = {message: 'oops'};
  var obervableThrowMock =
    sandbox.mock(Rx.Observable)
           .expects('throw')
           .withArgs(error.message);

    tasksService.returnError(error);
    obervableThrowMock.verify();
});
```

This test calls the returnError function with an error object and expects the function to return an Observable in response—not just any Observable but precisely the one created using the throw function. Let's now implement the returnError function in our service to make the test pass.

testangular2/todo/public/src/app/tasks/tasks.service.js

```
returnError: function(error) {
  return Rx.Observable.throw(error.message);
},
```

Oh, one more thing. The service needs an instance of HTTP to be injected. The constructor attribute needs to change for that, but let's write the test first:

testangular2/todo/test/client/app/tasks/tasks.service-test.js

```
it('should inject HTTP into the constructor', function() {
  var injectedServices =
    Reflect.getMetadata('parameters', app.TasksService);

  expect(injectedServices[0]).to.be.eql([ng.http.Http]);
});
```

Now change the constructor to make the test pass. In addition to seeing the change to the constructor, let's take a look at the entire service class, incrementally developed using the tests.

```
(function(app) {
  app.TasksService = ng.core.Class({
    constructor: [ng.http.Http, function(_http) {
      this.http = _http;
    }],
    get: function() {
      return this.http.get('/tasks')
                 .map(this.extractData)
                 .catch(this.returnError);
    },
    extractData: function(response) {
      if(response.status !== 200)
        throw new Error('Request failed with status: ' + response.status);

        return response.json();
```

```
    },
    returnError: function(error) {
      return Rx.Observable.throw(error.message);
    },
  });
})(window.app || (window.app = {}));
```

That completes the implementation of our service for returning a task list. We still don't have the pipe to sort the tasks. Let's take care of that next.

Test-Drive the Pipe

The pipe class and its transform function is the easiest to test. Our pipe should transform a given list into a sorted list. Let's list the tests we will need:

- Should have the pipe's name set to sort
- Should sort tasks based on year
- Should sort tasks based on year, then month
- Should sort tasks based on year, month, then day
- Should sort tasks based on year, month, day, then name

First, edit the files section in karma.conf.js to add a reference to the currently empty pipe file; place it before the reference to the service file, like so:

```
'./public/src/app/tasks/tasks-sort.pipe.js',
'./public/src/app/tasks/tasks.service.js',
'./public/src/app/tasks/tasks.component.js',
```

Restart Karma after saving the file. Then open the file test/client/app/tasks/tasks-sort.pipe-test.js and create a new test suite:

testangular2/todo/test/client/app/tasks/tasks-sort.pipe-test.js

```
describe('tasks-sort pipe test', function() {

  var sortPipe;

  beforeEach(function() {
    sortPipe = new app.TasksSortPipe();
  });
});
```

Within this test suite we'll implement out first test for the pipe, to verify that its name property is set to sort:

testangular2/todo/test/client/app/tasks/tasks-sort.pipe-test.js

```
it('should have the pipe`s name set to sort', function() {
  var annotations =
    Reflect.getMetadata('annotations', app.TasksSortPipe)[0];

  expect(annotations.name).to.be.eql('sort');
});
```

This test is very similar to the first test we wrote for the component. It gets the annotation metadata and confirms that the name attribute is set to the desired value.

Now let's implement the necessary code in the pipe class—go ahead and open the public/src/app/tasks/tasks-sort.pipe.js and enter the following code:

testangular2/todo/public/src/app/tasks/tasks-sort.pipe.js

```
(function(app) {
  app.TasksSortPipe = ng.core
    .Pipe({
      name: 'sort'
    })
    .Class({
      constructor: function() {},
    });
})(window.app || (window.app = {}));
```

The class has been configured to be a pipe, it has a name, and it is eagerly waiting for us to write the transform function. Let's write the first test for the transform function:

testangular2/todo/test/client/app/tasks/tasks-sort.pipe-test.js

```
it('should sort tasks based on year', function() {
  var task1 = { name: 'task a', month: 1, day: 10, year: 2017};
  var task2 = { name: 'task b', month: 1, day: 10, year: 2016};

  var sorted = sortPipe.transform([task1, task2]);
  expect(sorted).to.be.eql([task2, task1]);
});
```

The test sends a sample list of tasks and expects the returned result to appear in sorted order. Implement the transform function in the pipe to return a sorted collection of the tasks based on the year property. The function will go right next to the constructor property, like so:

```
//...
constructor: function() {},
transform: function(tasks) {
  var compareTwoTasks = function(task1, task2) {
    return task1.year - task2.year;
  }

  return tasks.sort(compareTwoTasks);
}
```

The sort function of the JavaScript Array class is used in the implementation of the transform function. A local compareTwoTasks function returns a value of 0 if the year values are the same. It returns a negative value if the first task's year is smaller than the year of the second task. Otherwise, it returns a positive value. That's exactly the function that Array's sort expects. Save the files and ensure the tests are passing.

Let's now write a test to verify that the tasks are sorted based on both year and month:

testangular2/todo/test/client/app/tasks/tasks-sort.pipe-test.js

```
it('should sort tasks based on year, then month', function() {
  var task1 = { name: 'task a', month: 2, day: 10, year: 2017};
  var task2 = { name: 'task c', month: 1, day: 10, year: 2016};
  var task3 = { name: 'task b', month: 1, day: 10, year: 2017};

  var sorted = sortPipe.transform([task1, task2, task3]);
  expect(sorted).to.be.eql([task2, task3, task1]);
});
```

Modify the transform function to make the test pass—make the minimum change necessary. After confirming that the tests are passing, move on to write the next test to verify that sorting is based on year, month, and day.

testangular2/todo/test/client/app/tasks/tasks-sort.pipe-test.js

```
it('should sort tasks based on year, month, then day', function() {
  var task1 = { name: 'task a', month: 1, day: 20, year: 2017};
  var task2 = { name: 'task c', month: 1, day: 14, year: 2017};
  var task3 = { name: 'task b', month: 1, day: 9, year: 2017};

  var sorted = sortPipe.transform([task1, task2, task3]);
  expect(sorted).to.be.eql([task3, task2, task1]);
});
```

Once again, implement the minimum code to make the tests pass.

Now write the final test to verify that sorting is based on the name property:

testangular2/todo/test/client/app/tasks/tasks-sort.pipe-test.js

```
it('should sort tasks based on year, month, day, then name', function() {
  var task1 = { name: 'task a', month: 1, day: 14, year: 2017};
  var task2 = { name: 'task c', month: 1, day: 14, year: 2017};
  var task3 = { name: 'task b', month: 1, day: 14, year: 2017};

  var sorted = sortPipe.transform([task1, task2, task3]);
  expect(sorted).to.be.eql([task1, task3, task2]);
});
```

To make the test pass, once again change the transform function. Here's the code that passes all the tests written so far:

```
transform: function(tasks) {
  var compareTwoTasks = function(task1, task2) {
    return task1.year - task2.year ||
      task1.month - task2.month ||
      task1.day - task2.day ||
      task1.name.localeCompare(task2.name);
  };

  return tasks.sort(compareTwoTasks);
}
```

All the tests that we planned out are implemented and passing. However, there's one thing that's really ugly in our implementation, something that our elders will never approve of: *mutability*. We should prefer immutability whenever possible—fewer state changes make code easier to reason and easier to test, and also minimize the chances of errors.

Our current implementation is mutating the array given as input; *sshhh*, let's fix that before anyone sees it—after writing the test first, of course.

Here's the test to verify that transform is a good citizen and does not change the given input:

testangular2/todo/test/client/app/tasks/tasks-sort.pipe-test.js

```
it('should not mutate the given input', function() {
  var task1 = { name: 'task a', month: 1, day: 14, year: 2017};
  var task2 = { name: 'task b', month: 1, day: 14, year: 2017};

  var input = [task2, task1];

  sortPipe.transform(input);
  expect(input[0]).to.be.eql(task2);
});
```

As soon as you save the file, the test will fail since the given argument has been modified by the function. Change the last line in the transform function to sort a copy of the given array. Here's one possible way to achieve that:

```
return tasks.slice().sort(compareTwoTasks);
```

Let's step back and take a look at the entire pipe class that was created using the series of tests:

testangular2/todo/public/src/app/tasks/tasks-sort.pipe.js

```
(function(app) {
  app.TasksSortPipe = ng.core
    .Pipe({
      name: 'sort'
    })
    .Class({
      constructor: function() {},
      transform: function(tasks) {
        var compareTwoTasks = function(task1, task2) {
          return task1.year - task2.year ||
            task1.month - task2.month ||
            task1.day - task2.day ||
            task1.name.localeCompare(task2.name);
        };

        return tasks.slice().sort(compareTwoTasks);
      }
    });
})(window.app || (window.app = {}));
```

Ah, that's much better. We can proudly now show the code to others, and let them know that our transform function is *pure* and has no side effects; it does not modify any variables in its reach.

We're almost done with the feature that displays the tasks. We need to bootstrap the component in the DOMContentLoaded event handler. Let's do that next.

Test-Drive the BootStrap Code

The code we'll place in public/src/main.js will bootstrap the TasksComponent when the document's DOMContentLoaded event is fired. Following our tradition, we'll write a test for that before we implement the code.

As a first step, open the karma.conf.js file once more and add a reference to the ./public/src/main.js file, but add this as the last entry in the files section. We want the file main.js to be loaded after the component file has been loaded. Restart Karma after saving this file.

We need to intercept the addEventListener function and stub it out before it gets called in main.js. Since that file is loaded last, we have plenty of time to take care of it, provided we put the stub code in the right place.

We will discuss how to achieve this right after creating the test. Open the test/client/main-test.js file, and create a new test suite by entering this code:

testangular2/todo/test/client/main-test.js

```
describe('main tests', function() {
  var handler;

  document.addEventListener = function(event, eventHandler) {
    if(event === 'DOMContentLoaded')
      handler = eventHandler;
  };

  it('main registers TasksComponent with bootstrap', function(done) {
    ng.platformBrowserDynamic.bootstrap = function(component) {
      expect(component).to.be.eql(app.TasksComponent);
      done();
    };

    handler();
  });
});
```

Right within the test suite we stub out the addEventListener function. In the stub we verify that the parameter passed is the expected event name. If it is, then we save the provided event handler in the handler variable. Then within the test, we stub the bootstrap function and in it verify that the passed-in argument is the component we expect. Finally, we invoke the saved handler function, which refers to the registered event handler. When the event handler calls the bootstrap function, like it's supposed to, the verification will succeed and the test will pass.

Implement the necessary code in the public/src/main.js file:

testangular2/todo/public/src/main.js

```
(function(app) {
 document.addEventListener('DOMContentLoaded', function() {
   ng.platformBrowserDynamic.bootstrap(app.TasksComponent);
 });
})(window.app || (window.app = {}));
```

As soon as you save the file, all the tests should pass. All the JavaScript source files needed are in place. The last things we need are the HTML files. We'll create them next and see the application in action through a browser.

Take It for a Ride

We need to create two HTML files, one that is referenced by the component's templateUrl attribute and the other, which will load up Angular and get things in motion.

Let's edit the public/tasks.component.html file first.

```
<body>
  <div class="heading">TO-DO</div>

  <div id="taskslist">
    <p>Number of tasks: <span id="length">{{ tasks.length }}</span>
    <span id="message">{{ message }}</span>
    <table>
      <tr *ngFor ="let task of tasks">
      <td>{{ task.name }}</td>
      <td>{{ task.month }}/{{ task.day }}/{{ task.year }}</td>
    </table>
  </div>
</body>
```

The file displays the number of tasks using the expression that binds to the component's tasks model. It then uses the new *ngFor directive to iterate over each task in the tasks list to display the name and the date details.

Next we need the starting page public/index.html, so let's edit that file.

testangular2/todo/public/index.html

```
<!DOCTYPE html>
<html>
  <head>
    <title>TO-DO</title>
    <link rel="stylesheet" href="/stylesheets/style.css">

    <script src="javascripts/zone.js/dist/zone.js"></script>
    <script src="javascripts/reflect-metadata/Reflect.js"></script>
    <script src="javascripts/rxjs/bundles/Rx.umd.js"></script>
    <script src="javascripts/@angular/core/bundles/core.umd.js"></script>
    <script src="javascripts/@angular/common/bundles/common.umd.js"></script>
    <script src=
      "javascripts/@angular/compiler/bundles/compiler.umd.js"></script>
    <script src="javascripts/@angular\
/platform-browser/bundles/platform-browser.umd.js">
    </script>
    <script src="javascripts/@angular\
/platform-browser-dynamic/bundles/platform-browser-dynamic.umd.js">
    </script>
    <script src="javascripts/@angular/http/bundles/http.umd.js"></script>

    <script src="src/app/tasks/tasks-sort.pipe.js"></script>
    <script src="src/app/tasks/tasks.service.js"></script>
    <script src="src/app/tasks/tasks.component.js"></script>
    <script src="src/main.js"></script>
    <script src="javascripts/common/validate-task.js"></script>
  </head>
  <body>
    <tasks-list>loading...</tasks-list>
  </body>
</html>
```

The file does not have a whole lot other than script references. It first brings in the Angular- and RxJS-related files. Then it loads the client-side JavaScript files we created. Finally, the body holds an element with the name tasks-list, which matches with the value of the selector attribute we specified in our component.

When running the tests the file karma.conf.js referred to the Angular-related files from the node_modules directory. We can't directly reach into that directory from the running Express instance, but the running instance needs the Angular framework and RxJS library. Copy the directories node_modules/@angular, node_modules/reflect-metadata, node_modules/rxjs, node_modules/zone.js to public/javascripts.

We're now all set to run the application, but we need some sample data.

Before we can view any data, we need to start the database and populate it with sample data. The steps for this are the same we followed in *Take It for a Drive*, on page 156. Start the database daemon, run npm start to start the Express server, and populate the data into the database using either the Curl program or the Chrome Extensions. After that, fire up the browser and point to the URL http://localhost:3000 and watch the magic unfold—well, we wrote the code test driven, so there's really no magic, but it feels good to think so.

Here's a view of Chrome showing the list of tasks, through the eyes of the Angular front end.

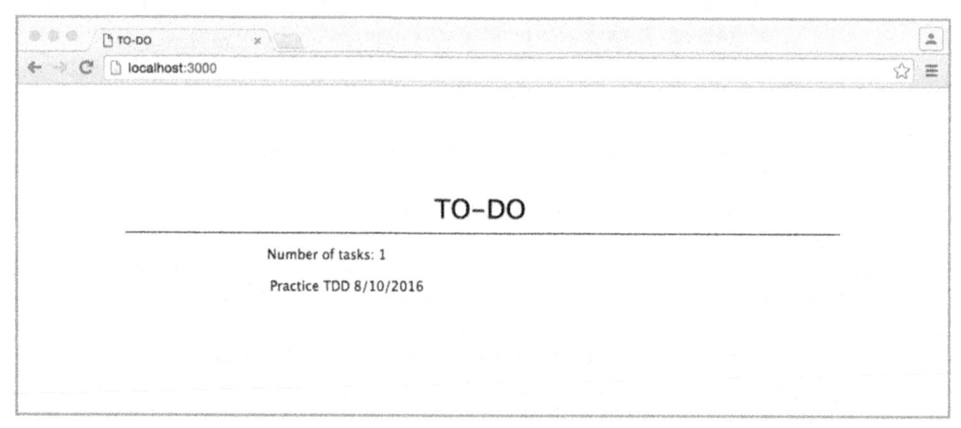

We've come a long way. Take a break, celebrate the occasion, call your friends, tweet about your learnings...and when you're done and well rested, we will get back to finish the remaining parts of the front end.

Complete the Design

We're able to list the tasks, but we also need the ability to add a new task and delete an existing task through the Angular UI. Let's implement the feature to add a task next.

Design the Add Task Feature

To implement the feature to add a new task, we will need some new code in our component and in our service. The pipe will not change. We will also have to change the tasks.component.html file. Let's start with the component-related work first.

Evolve the Component

To support the add task feature, the component should pass these tests:

- newTask should be initialized properly
- The component should properly convert newTask with no data to JSON
- The component should properly convert newTask with data to JSON
- addTask should register handlers with service
- updateMessage should update message and call getTasks
- disableAddTask should use validateTask

That looks like a fun exercise; let's jump in.

Open the test/client/app/tasks/tasks.component-test.js file and add the first test related to adding a task—verify that the newTask model is properly initialized.

testangular2/todo/test/client/app/tasks/tasks.component-test.js

```
it('newTask should be initialized properly', function() {
  expect(tasksComponent.newTask.name).to.be.eql('');
  expect(tasksComponent.newTask.date).to.be.eql('');
});
```

The test merely verifies that the model has been initialized to a safe default. To make this test pass we need a simple change in the constructor of the component. Open the file public/src/app/tasks/tasks.component.js and make the change:

```
this.newTask = {name: '', date: ''};
```

Let's move on to the next test. When we're ready to send data to the back end, we need to convert the new task into JSON format. Let's take one step at a time. Let's write a test to convert a new task with no valid data in it.

testangular2/todo/test/client/app/tasks/tasks.component-test.js

```
it('should properly convert newTask with no data to JSON', function() {
  var newTask = tasksComponent.convertNewTaskToJSON();

  expect(newTask.name).to.be.eql('');
  expect(newTask.month).to.be.NAN;
  expect(newTask.day).to.be.NAN;
  expect(newTask.year).to.be.NAN;
});
```

This test calls a new convertNewTaskToJSON function and verifies that it handled the new task model with no useful data in it. Implement the code for this new function in the component. We will see the code for this function after writing the next test. Let's move on to the next test.

testangular2/todo/test/client/app/tasks/tasks.component-test.js

```
it('should properly convert newTask with data to JSON', function() {
  var newTask = {name: 'task a', date: '6/10/2016'};
  var newTaskJSON = {name: 'task a', month: 6, day: 10, year: 2016};

  tasksComponent.newTask = newTask;

  expect(tasksComponent.convertNewTaskToJSON()).to.be.eql(newTaskJSON);
});
```

This test verifies the conversion went well when there is data in the new task model. Here's the implementation of the convertNewTaskToJSON that satisfies both tests.

testangular2/todo/public/src/app/tasks/tasks.component.js

```
convertNewTaskToJSON: function() {
  var dateParts = this.newTask.date.split('/');

  return {
    name: this.newTask.name,
    month: parseInt(dateParts[0]),
    day: parseInt(dateParts[1]),
    year: parseInt(dateParts[2])
  };
},
```

Once we have a new task and it's converted to the JSON format, we should send it off to the service, which will in turn communicate with the back-end server. Let's write a test to verify that addTask interacts properly with the service's add function—this latter function doesn't exist yet, but we'll get to that when we evolve the service. Here's the new test in test/client/app/tasks/tasks.component-test.js:

testangular2/todo/test/client/app/tasks/tasks.component-test.js

```
it('addTask should register handlers with service', function() {
  var observableMock =
    sandbox.mock(observable)
           .expects('subscribe')
           .withArgs(updateMessageBindStub, updateErrorBindStub);

  var taskStub = {};

  tasksComponent.convertNewTaskToJSON = function() { return taskStub; };

  sandbox.stub(tasksService, 'add')
         .withArgs(taskStub)
         .returns(observable);

  tasksComponent.addTask();

  observableMock.verify();
});
```

Let's read the test from the bottom. It verifies proper action was performed on a mock of the Observable. Right before that we invoke addTask, the function under test. When this function executes, it should call the add function on the service. To verify this, in the test, we stubbed out the add function on the service. We then set an expectation on the mock that it will be called with a sample task, taskStub, and ask that it return observable, which is a mock of Rx.Observable. Since addTask should send the result of convertNewTaskToJSON to the service, we mocked convertNewTaskToJSON to return a fake task, taskStub. Finally, in the top of the test we mocked the Observable and configured it to expect that proper handlers are passed in to the subscribe function.

For this test we need to make two changes to the test suite. First, we need to define a variable in the test suite:

```
var updateMessageBindStub = function() {};
```

Second, we need to stub the bind function of the new handler updateMessage to return the appropriate fake function. This change goes into the beforeEach function of the test suite:

```
sandbox.stub(tasksComponent.updateMessage, 'bind')
       .withArgs(tasksComponent)
       .returns(updateMessageBindStub);
```

We're ready to implement the addTasks function in the component. Open the public/src/app/tasks/tasks.component.js file and add the following to the class:

```
addTask: function() {
  this.service.add(this.convertNewTaskToJSON())
            .subscribe(this.updateMessage.bind(this),
                       this.updateError.bind(this));
},
updateMessage: function() {},
```

The addTask function calls the service, passes the converted new task object, receives an Observable, and registers the handlers with the subscribe function. For the error case we reuse the existing updateError function. For the success case we will use a new updateMessage function. This function is temporarily set to a no-op function for the test to pass.

Let's now design the updateMessage function. This function should update the message model with the received message and call the getTasks function to refresh any new task that was added. Here's the test to verify this behavior:

testangular2/todo/test/client/app/tasks/tasks.component-test.js

```
it('updateMessage should update message and call getTasks', function(done) {
  tasksComponent.getTasks = function() { done(); };
  tasksComponent.updateMessage('good');
  expect(tasksComponent.message).to.be.eql('good');
});
```

The test stubs out the getTasks function—after all, we don't want to call the real function, which will talk to the back-end server. It then calls the updateMessage with a fake message and verifies that the message model was updated and that the getTasks function was invoked.

Change the updateMessage function in the component to make this test pass:

```
updateMessage: function(message) {
  this.message = message;
  this.getTasks();
},
```

We have one final function to write in the component for the add task feature. If the task is not valid, the add button should be disabled. For this we need a function that converts the newTask model to JSON and sends it to the validateTask common validation function we already have in place. Let's write tests to verify this new function's behavior.

First we'll write a test to verify that the component's validateTask property refers to the common validateTask function. Introducing this property makes testing easier. Here's the test:

testangular2/todo/test/client/app/tasks/tasks.component-test.js
```
it('should set validateTask to common function', function() {
  expect(tasksComponent.validateTask).to.be.eql(validateTask);
});
```

To make this test pass, we need to add the following property to the component, in the constructor:

```
this.validateTask = validateTask;
```

Remember to change the files section of the karma.conf.js file to include a reference to the ./public/javascripts/common/validate-task.js file.

Next, we'll write a test to verify that disableAddTask returns the expected result and that it correctly made use of the validateTask function.

testangular2/todo/test/client/app/tasks/tasks.component-test.js
```
it('disableAddTask should use validateTask', function() {
  tasksComponent.newTask = {name: 'task a', date: '6/10/2016'};

  var validateTaskSpy = sinon.spy(tasksComponent, 'validateTask');
  expect(tasksComponent.disableAddTask()).to.be.false;
  expect(validateTaskSpy).to.have.been.calledWith(
    tasksComponent.convertNewTaskToJSON());
});
```

In the test we created a spy for the validateTask function and verified that it was invoked by the disableAddTask function as expected.

Modify the component to implement the disableAddTask function:

```
disableAddTask: function() {
  return !this.validateTask(this.convertNewTaskToJSON());
},
```

We have the necessary code in place in the component. We need to change the service to provide the new add function that the addTask function of the component expects.

Evolve the Service

The new add function that we need in the service should make an HTTP POST request to the back-end server. The data it should send must be in JSON format. We can reach out to the spiking example to understand the specifics of how the function will interact with the back end through the HTTP object. Based on that, we can write the test for the add function.

Open test/client/app/tasks/tasks.service-test.js and add a new post property for the http stub in the beforeEach function, next to the get property that's already there:

```
beforeEach(function() {
  sandbox = sinon.sandbox.create();

  http = {
    get: function() {},
    post: function() {}
  };

  tasksService = new app.TasksService(http);
  //...
```

To test the add function, we will stub out the post function of HTTP and verify that it's called with the correct URL, the appropriate POST data, and the proper content type settings. We will also verify that add registers the proper handlers for the map and the catch functions on the Observable returned by the post function of HTTP. Here's the test that does just that.

testangular2/todo/test/client/app/tasks/tasks.service-test.js

```
it('add should pass task to /tasks using POST', function() {
  var taskStub = {name: 'foo', month: 1, day: 1, year: 2017};

  var options =
    {headers: new ng.http.Headers({'Content-Type': 'application/json'})};

  sandbox.stub(http, 'post')
         .withArgs('/tasks', JSON.stringify(taskStub), options)
         .returns(observable);

  expect(tasksService.add(taskStub)).to.be.eql(observable);
  expect(observable.map.calledWith(tasksService.extractData)).to.be.true;
  expect(observable.catch.calledWith(tasksService.returnError)).to.be.true;

});
```

To make this test pass we have to create the add function in the service. Open the public/src/app/tasks/tasks.service.js file and add the function:

testangular2/todo/public/src/app/tasks/tasks.service.js

```
add: function(task) {
  var options =
    {headers: new ng.http.Headers({'Content-Type': 'application/json'})};

  return this.http.post('/tasks', JSON.stringify(task), options)
             .map(this.extractData)
             .catch(this.returnError);
},
```

The function creates the necessary content type header and invokes the post function on the HTTP object. It also registers the already defined extractData and returnError functions with the map and the catch functions, respectively.

There's one catch, however. We designed the extractData when we wrote the get function. The back-end service returns the data in JSON format when queried for the list of tasks. However, the back end returns a plain text, with a message like "added task," in response to an add request. We need to change the extractData function to handle either a JSON response or a plain-text response. Let's write a test first:

testangular2/todo/test/client/app/tasks/tasks.service-test.js

```
it('extractData should return text if not json()', function() {
  var fakeBody = 'somebody';
  var response = {status: 200, text: function() { return fakeBody; } };

  expect(tasksService.extractData(response)).to.be.eql(fakeBody);
});
```

The response object passed to the extractData function in this test does not have a json() function. Instead it has a text() function. The previous test for extractData had the json() function. We will modify the extractData function to make use of the json() function first. If that fails, it can switch over to the text() function. Here's the change in the service class:

testangular2/todo/public/src/app/tasks/tasks.service.js

```
extractData: function(response) {
  if(response.status !== 200)
    throw new Error('Request failed with status: ' + response.status);

    try {
      return response.json();
    } catch(ex) {
      return response.text();
    }
},
```

We have evolved the component and the service. Let's see the new feature we added in action.

View the Add Task Feature

Before we can add a new task through the UI we need to change the tasks.component.html file. It needs to have input fields for the user to enter the new task details. Let's change the HTML file like so:

```
<body>
  <div class="heading">TO-DO</div>

  <div id="newtask">
    <div>Create a new task</div>
    <label>Name</label>
    <input type="text" id="name" [(ngModel)]="newTask.name"/>
    <label>Date</label>
    <input type="text" id="date" [(ngModel)]="newTask.date"/>
    <input type="submit" id="submit" (click)="addTask();"
      [disabled]="disableAddTask()" value="create"/>
  </div>

  <div id="taskslist">
    <p>Number of tasks: <span id="length">{{ tasks.length }}</span>
    <span id="message">{{ message }}</span>
    <table>
      <tr *ngFor ="let task of tasks">
      <td>{{ task.name }}</td>
      <td>{{ task.month }}/{{ task.day }}/{{ task.year }}</td>
    </table>
  </div>
</body>
```

We added the newtask div part to the existing tasks.component.html file. This part contains a few labels and input fields to read in the name and the date values for the newTask model. Angular uses [(ngModel)] to specify that an attribute on the HTML page should be bound to a property within the component's model. Also, it uses (click) to bind a function in the component with a DOM event, the click event in this example. Finally, [disabled] ties the HTML input's disabled attribute to the desired function on the component.

We're ready to give the program a try using a browser. Start the database daemon. Then start Express by running npm start. Finally, point your browser to the URL http://localhost:3000. Here's a sample of interaction with the program through Chrome:

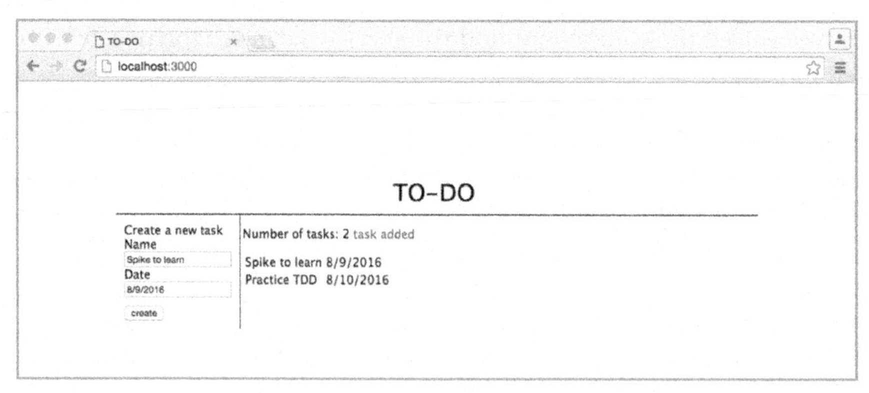

We have the get task list and the add a new task features working. Take a well-deserved break. When you return, we will continue with the example to implement the feature to delete an existing task.

Design the Delete Task Feature

To delete an existing task, we need to evolve once again the component and the service, and make a small change to the tasks.component.html file.

Let's start with the change to the component first.

Evolve the Component Again

The component needs a new function, deleteTask, which will pass the request to delete a task over to the service. The new function can reuse the response handlers we've already implemented in the component. As a result, we'll need only one test to verify the behavior of the deleteTask function.

Before we write that test, let's verify that the stub for the service in test/client/app/tasks/tasks.component-test.js includes the delete function:

```
beforeEach(function() {
  tasksService = {
    get: function() {},
    add: function() {},
    delete: function() {}
  };
  tasksComponent = new app.TasksComponent(tasksService, sortPipe);
       //...
```

Now we can add the following test for the component:

testangular2/todo/test/client/app/tasks/tasks.component-test.js

```
it('deleteTask should register handlers with service', function() {
  var sampleTaskId = '1234123412341234';

  var observableMock =
    sandbox.mock(observable)
           .expects('subscribe')
           .withArgs(updateMessageBindStub, updateErrorBindStub);

  sandbox.stub(tasksService, 'delete')
         .withArgs(sampleTaskId)
         .returns(observable);

  tasksComponent.deleteTask(sampleTaskId);

  observableMock.verify();
});
```

The test verifies that deleteTask invoked the delete function of HTTP and subscribed with the proper handlers by calling the subscribe function on the returned Observable.

Implementing the deleteTask function in the component is quite simple:

testangular2/todo/public/src/app/tasks/tasks.component.js

```
deleteTask: function(taskId) {
  this.service.delete(taskId)
              .subscribe(this.updateMessage.bind(this),
                         this.updateError.bind(this));
},
```

The component is ready, but we need to change the service.

Evolve the Service Again

The service now needs an additional function: delete. Before we write the test for that function, we need to make a small change to the stub for HTTP. Open the test/client/app/tasks/tasks.service-test.js file and add a new delete function to the stub in the beforeEach function, like so:

```
beforeEach(function() {
  sandbox = sinon.sandbox.create();

  http = {
    get: function() {},
    post: function() {},
    delete: function() {}
  };

  tasksService = new app.TasksService(http);
  //...
```

Now add the test for the delete function of the service:

testangular2/todo/test/client/app/tasks/tasks.service-test.js

```
it('delete should pass task to /tasks using DELETE', function() {
  var taskId = '1234';

  sandbox.stub(http, 'delete')
         .withArgs('/tasks/' + taskId)
         .returns(observable);

  expect(tasksService.delete(taskId)).to.be.eql(observable);
  expect(observable.map.calledWith(tasksService.extractData)).to.be.true;
  expect(observable.catch.calledWith(tasksService.returnError)).to.be.true;
});
```

The test is pretty straightforward; it verifies that the service's delete function called the delete function of HTTP with the proper URL. It also verifies that the function passed the required handlers to the map and the catch functions of the Observable returned by the HTTP's delete function.

Implement the delete function in the service:

testangular2/todo/public/src/app/tasks/tasks.service.js
```
delete: function(taskId) {
  return this.http.delete('/tasks/' + taskId)
             .map(this.extractData)
             .catch(this.returnError);
},
```

This function is very similar to the add function, except that the function it calls on the HTTP object and the URL it passes are different.

View the Delete Task Feature

The coding is almost complete. We need to change the tasks.component.html file to bring in a link to delete a task. Here's the complete file with the link to delete a task added toward the bottom:

testangular2/todo/public/tasks.component.html
```
<body>
  <div class="heading">TO-DO</div>

  <div id="newtask">
    <div>Create a new task</div>
    <label>Name</label>
    <input type="text" id="name" [(ngModel)]="newTask.name"/>
    <label>Date</label>
    <input type="text" id="date" [(ngModel)]="newTask.date"/>
    <input type="submit" id="submit" (click)="addTask();"
      [disabled]="disableAddTask()" value="create"/>
  </div>

  <div id="taskslist">
    <p>Number of tasks: <span id="length">{{ tasks.length }}</span>
    <span id="message">{{ message }}</span>
    <table>
      <tr *ngFor ="let task of tasks">
      <td>{{ task.name }}</td>
      <td>{{ task.month }}/{{ task.day }}/{{ task.year }}</td>
      <td>
        <A (click)="deleteTask(task._id);">delete</A>
      </td>
    </table>
  </div>
</body>
```

Once again start the database daemon, run npm start to run Express, and point your browser at the URL http://localhost:3000. Here's a sample of the view right after a delete operation:

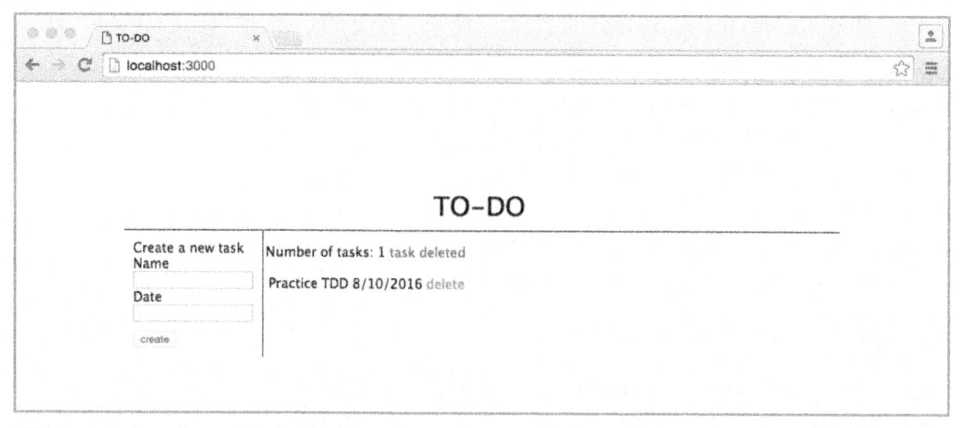

We have developed a fully functional Angular front end for the TO-DO application, test driven. The design of the JavaScript code we wrote was driven by tests. However, we only manually verified that the HTML files are wired properly to the code they call into. In the next chapter you'll learn how to automate the verification, all the way to the UI level.

Let's see how we did on the code coverage side.

Measure Code Coverage

The package.json file in the current project already contains a script to run Istanbul for the client-side code coverage. Also, in the karma.conf.js file, the preprocessors section already refers to all files under public/src and its subdirectories for coverage instrumentation.

Run the command

```
npm run-script cover-client
```

to run the test and measure the coverage at the same time.

Once the test run completes, open the index.html file under the subdirectory of the coverage directory to view the coverage report. You will see a 100 percent coverage, as shown in the figure on page 283.

The Angular front end for the TO-DO app was entirely test driven and the code coverage showed that we did fairly good on the promise to write tests before writing any code.

Code coverage report for ... ×

file:///Users/venkats/books/vsjavas/Book/code/testangular2/todo/coverage/Chrome%2050.0.2661%20(Mac%20O...

all files src/app/tasks/

100% Statements 37/37 83.33% Branches 10/12 100% Functions 22/22 100% Lines 37/37

File ▲		Statements		Branches		Functions		Lines	
tasks-sort.pipe.js		100%	5/5	100%	6/6	100%	4/4	100%	5/5
tasks.component.js		100%	19/19	50%	1/2	100%	11/11	100%	19/19
tasks.service.js		100%	13/13	75%	3/4	100%	7/7	100%	13/13

Wrapping Up

Angular 2.0 is a brand-new total rewrite of the AngularJS framework. In this chapter we covered a lot of ground with this new tool. You first learned to program in Angular using good old JavaScript—ECMAScript 5. Then we dug into the metadata to discover the annotations and properties that are needed to configure pipes, services, and components in Angular. Along the way we figured out how to use lightweight test doubles for the HTTP module and the Rx.Observable. These classes play a vital role in communicating with the back-end server. Finally we ran the code coverage tool to confirm that our effort was in fact test driven and that no code was written without a failing test that prompted its design.

The automated tests we wrote so far all test code, but in isolation. These tests are quite valuable, fast running, deterministic, and provide rapid feedback. However, we can't get too comfortable and overly confident that all is well. We need to ensure the different pieces of code also work when integrated with each other. We also want to verify that the events and the models in the HTML files are wired appropriately with the components. And we want to use automated tests to confirm that as well. We'll get to that in the next chapter.

CHAPTER 10

Integrate and Test End-to-End

If automated testing were a meal, integration testing would be the salt in it—highly essential, but it should be limited.

Integration or end-to-end testing is done with all parts of the application up and running. While these tests provides great value, they may also take longer to run and may be fragile.

Integration tests serve multiple purposes. First, they verify that the UI is wired properly. They confirm that other parts are connected together correctly as well. For example, it's imperative to check that the client side is talking to the correct URLs on the server side. Likewise, it's critical to verify that the server is tied properly to the database. Furthermore, we want to verify all things are correct in the future when we make changes to the database, the URL routes, or just about anything else.

To gain true confidence from automated tests, the efforts have to culminate with a focused but small set of end-to-end tests. That way we're not only sure that individual parts work well but that the whole application in the integrated form is in good shape as well.

We must take care that end-to-end testing doesn't get complex and out of hand. With a proper plan, design, structure, and limited use, it can serve us quite well.

In this chapter you'll first learn to set up the end-to-end testing tool Protractor. You'll quickly learn how to write and run tests using Protractor for a third-party website. With those basics under your belt, you'll then explore ways to launch the TO-DO application on a web server for integrated testing, seed the database with test data, and interact with the application through a browser, all from automated tests. You'll also see what Protractor offers specifically for testing apps that use AngularJS.

Get to Know Protractor

Protractor is one of many testing tools that automate browser-based user interactions. It can be used to script data entry into web forms, perform button clicks, and verify the details returned by a website. Selenium is the most popular among the tools. Protractor makes use of Selenium, runs on Node.js, and provides a fluent JavaScript API to interact with different parts of an HTML page. For programmers using JavaScript, the fluency and convenience of Protractor gives a far better automation experience than directly using Selenium.

To test the TO-DO application created in the previous chapters, we need to get a few things set up. While it's not much code to write, there's a lot of details to consider. Trying to figure those out before giving Protractor a try can get overwhelming and frustrating. Instead, let's first write a few Protractor tests to access the Google search page. Since this service is ubiquitous and already running, it will give you a direct exposure to the capabilities of Protractor with the least effort. After learning how to use Protractor, you can take on the task of testing the TO-DO app by setting up the server, seeding the database with sample data, and running the integration tests.

Let's first discuss why Protractor is a great tool for integrated end-to-end testing. Then we'll get the tool installed and run some tests with it.

Reasons to Use Protractor

Among the UI-level testing tools, Selenium arguably being the most popular, Protractor has a few benefits:

- It runs in Node.js. That means you can write UI-level tests much like the other tests you've written so far—using Mocha.
- Protractor can act as a proxy and a wrapper around the Selenium WebDriver. You get all the power of Selenium, plus some extensions, but with a more fluent and expressive API. Tests written to use Protractor are a lot more concise compared to tests that directly use the WebDriver.
- A direct connect feature of Protractor can bypass Selenium and interact directly with Chrome and Firefox. As a result, your direct connect tests can run faster than the ones running through the WebDriver. Also, with this feature, you'll have to deal with fewer moving parts. That, in turn, makes the test runs less brittle.

- Protractor has special functions for you to gain access to different AngularJS directives. While non-AngularJS applications can use and benefit from Protractor, projects using AngularJS can gain more from this tool.

Since Protractor runs within Node.js, you have the full power of a solid runtime on your hands when running the tests. The best way to appreciate the power of the tool is to use it. Let's set it up and move on to writing some tests.

Install Protractor

We'll use the usingprotractor workspace under tdjsa/usingprotractor for this exercise. The project has been set up with the Protractor dependency. Change to the workspace directory and run npm install to get Protractor installed for this project. Protractor is installed along with a webdriver-manager, but you have to update the necessary browser drivers. For that, run the command

```
npm run-script update-driver
```

which will execute webdriver-manager update to update the drivers.

We will use the direct connect feature of Protractor to connect with Chrome. That also works for Firefox. However, if you'd like to use some other browser, Protractor can interact with it through the WebDriver.

Test with Protractor

In this exercise, to help us familiarize with Protractor, we'll write tests to verify the Google search page is functioning well.

We'll write the following tests:

- Verify that http://www.google.co.uk has the "I'm Feeling Lucky" button
- Submit a search for a text and confirm the result has an expected value

Protractor can either take command-line arguments for various parameters or read those from a configuration file. It's easier to use the configuration file; then you don't have to mess around with command-line arguments each time to run the tool. When starting Protractor, you may specify a configuration file name. If you don't give one, it looks for and loads a file named protractor.conf.js. The workspace already contains this file with the necessary configuration for your convenience. Let's take a minute to examine this file and understand its contents:

usingprotractor/protractor.conf.js

```
exports.config = {
  directConnect: true,

  baseUrl: 'https://www.google.co.uk',

/*
  capabilities: {
    'browserName': ['firefox'] //default chrome
  },
*/

  framework: 'mocha',

  mochaOpts: {
    reporter: 'dot',
    timeout: 10000,
  },

  specs: ['test/integration/*.js'],
};
```

The directConnect parameter tells Protractor to directly interact with the browser without going through the WebDriver proxy. Keep this parameter to run the tests in Chrome or Firefox. To run the tests in other browsers, simply drop or comment out this line. Protractor will then launch an instance of the Selenium WebDriver and interact with the browser through that instance.

The baseUrl parameter is the URL of the application under test. Having this parameter in the configuration file removes the need to give the full path for each request in the tests. It reduces the noise in tests. Furthermore, it also makes it easy to run the same tests on different endpoints. This latter benefit can be very useful to test different versions or installations of an application.

The capabilities parameter is shown commented out. It's optional and by default Protractor uses the Chrome browser. To use other browsers, include this parameter with the appropriate browser name. Instead of capabilities, you may also provide a multiCapabilities parameter if you'd like to run the tests in two or more browsers at the same time.

The default testing tool that Protractor supports is Jasmine. However, using Mocha is real simple—provide the framework parameter. To specify runtime options for Mocha, use the mochaOpts parameter.

Finally, the file includes the location of the tests. You may list just one file or a comma-separated list of files, or use a wildcard like we did.

The configuration file should be in the directory from which Protractor will be run. Generally, a good place is the top-level directory of projects. Since we're running tests on a third-party site in this example, we've placed the configuration file in the workspace's top-level directory usingprotractor.

It's time for us to roll out our first UI-level test. Let's prepare the test file and make a GET request.

Prepare for UI-Level Tests

We'll place the tests in the file test/integration/google-search-test.js under the current workspace tdjsa/usingprotractor. Let's open this pre-created file and add the setup code for the test suite:

usingprotractor/test/integration/google-search-test.js

```
var expect = require('chai').expect;
require('chai').use(require('chai-as-promised'));

describe('Google search page tests', function() {
  beforeEach(function() {
    browser.ignoreSynchronization = true;
    browser.get('/');
  });

  afterEach(function() {
    browser.ignoreSynchronization = false;
  });
});
```

Protractor's functions constantly have to evaluate the DOM, send off request to services, and analyze results from web services. This will take some time, certainly more than fractions of a second. In JavaScript, any function that takes time is designed to be asynchronous. So, it's no surprise that most of the functions in Protractor are asynchronous—they return promises.

When writing Protractor tests, make use of the asynchronous testing techniques we learned earlier in the book. In the test file, once Chai is loaded, the convenience functions from chai-as-promised are also loaded using the use function.

In the test suite, the beforeEach function first accesses a global browser object. Much like how browsers provide a global window object, Protractor provides a few globals: browser, element, by, and so on. The availability of these globals make Protractor tests quite concise. The first line within beforeEach is rather unclear, but it's a way to tell Protractor not to wait for AngularJS to complete processing—use this setting for testing non-AngularJS sites. The afterEach is a good place to reset this flag.

The beforeEach function sends a request to the URL http://www.google.co.uk/—that URL is obtained by prefixing the baseUrl parameter's value, from the configuration file we saw earlier, with the argument given to the get function.

Everything we need to write the first test is ready—let's focus on the test next.

Write the First Test

When we visit http://www.google.co.uk the familiar Google search page appears with two buttons. The first test will show how to verify that the request landed on the right page and that the page has the expected content.

usingprotractor/test/integration/google-search-test.js

```
it('home page has the Feeling Lucky button', function() {
  var inputElement =
    element(by.xpath('//input[@value="I\'m Feeling Lucky"]'));

  expect(inputElement.isPresent()).to.eventually.be.true;
});
```

The test directly goes after what it's looking for. It calls the by.xpath function and asks for an HTML input element with "I'm Feeling Lucky" as the value for the attribute named value. Since most of the functions in Protractor are asynchronous, the element function returns a Promise. The function isPresent() in turn returns a Promise. The test uses the eventually facility of chai-as-promised to check that the Promise returned by isPresent resolves to the expected value of true.

The changes we made to the protractor.conf.js file and the setup code in the test file brought together everything this test needs. The protractor.conf.js file mentioned the baseUrl, the browser to use, the testing tool to use, and the location of the tests. The test issues a request to the desired URL and verifies that the page visited has the expected content.

Save the test file and run Protractor from the workspace directory using the command npm test. This command exercises the test command in package.json, which, in turn, runs the protractor command.

Protractor will read the protractor.conf.js file, launch the browser, and invoke Mocha. Once Mocha kicks in, it will load up the specified test file and run the test in it. Finally, Chai and chai-as-promised verify that the application—that is, Google Search—responds as expected. Here's the output from the run:

```
I/direct - Using ChromeDriver directly...
I/launcher - Running 1 instances of WebDriver

  ▯

  1 passing (893ms)

I/launcher - 0 instance(s) of WebDriver still running
I/launcher - chrome #01 passed
```

When you run the test, the console will report starting the driver and the progress of the tests. At the same time, you can notice the browser dancing around to the commands from the test. The tests mimic user interactions, except at machine speed instead of human pace. That is both good news and bad news. The speed of execution, compared to manually navigating pages to verify, is a big plus. The downside is that the interaction may be too fast and that may make some tests fail intermittently. Keep an eye on it and if needed adjust the speed of execution with a wait request, as appropriate; we'll encounter this situation soon.

The test first obtained the element using the xpath query. Protractor provides functions to get elements using different methods, like by.id, by.tagName, by.xpath, by.linkText, and the list goes on. See the Protractor API documentation[1] for a full listing.

Test for Posting Data

The search page has a input text field and two submit buttons. Let's write a test to verify that Google's search engine has not gone on a break.

The test should first obtain a reference to the input text field and then enter data into it. To get the field, we need to know something about it—for example, its id or its CSS class. Open http://www.google.co.uk and use your browser's facilities to inspect the elements in the document to figure out the id of the field. Then you can use the Protractor API to programmatically get access to it.

Let's add a test to verify that Google Search works. Add this second test to the test suite in test/integration/google-search-test.js:

usingprotractor/test/integration/google-search-test.js

```
it('search brings back an expected result', function() {
  var inputField = element(by.id('lst-ib'));

  inputField.sendKeys('agilelearner.com');
  inputField.sendKeys(protractor.Key.ENTER);

  var link =
    element(by.xpath("//a[@href='https://www.agilelearner.com/']"));

  browser.wait(function() {
    return link.isPresent();
  });

  expect(link.isDisplayed()).to.eventually.eql(true);
});
```

The test has a few quirks. Let's go over them thoroughly.

1. https://angular.github.io/protractor/#/api

The first line gets the element using the locator obtained from the id for the input text field. The sendKeys function emulates the user's keystrokes. The first call to the function enters a search text and the second call enters the return key. In response to the user hitting the return key, the Google search page will perform the search and get back the results page. There's a gotcha here, however.

Google Search usually appears instantaneous for users on fast networks. However, logically it takes a non-zero amount of time for the response to return from a remote server. That time most likely will be greater than the time for your test to execute the line after the call to sendKeys. We need to account for that time delay. This is an unfortunate burden and may make tests brittle.

When you perform a get or a refresh, Protractor knows to wait for that call to complete before running the next line of code. However, when you perform a click or a key press to post a request to the server, Protractor is not aware of what happened. You need to instruct Protractor to wait for the response to arrive in these cases.

In the test, after sending the request to the search page, we look for an A tag with a particular href using the xpath function. Then we ask Protractor to wait for the element to be available using the wait function. This function returns a Promise. That Promise internally waits for the expected response. Once this Promise is resolved, Protractor moves on to execute the next line, which checks if the link is displayed.

If the page takes well beyond the timeout to respond or if the page that comes back does not have that link, then the test will time out and fail.

Even though the test was relatively short, it exposed some unpleasant aspects of UI-level testing. First, we have to know which elements to access. If the id or other locators used to access the elements are changed, the related tests will be dead in the water. Second, we may have to put in a lot of effort to get the locators. For example, if you miss the trailing / in the XPATH, the A tag will not be located. Third, if you forget to put the wait, the test will fail even though the page has the content you're looking for.

Writing Protractor tests on Google Search was useful in a couple of ways. First, it gave you a chance to see tests in action and learn to use Protractor. The fact that you were able to do it without having to spin your own web server kept your focus on learning the essentials. Second, the tests cautioned you on where things can get out of hand. The tests serve as a good reminder why you need them, but at the same time, you will have to keep these kinds of tests to a minimum.

Having tried out the example, you're likely eager to create full end-to-end Protractor tests for your own application. Writing tests for the TO-DO app will give you a fairly good idea of how to approach that. In the previous chapters we created the server side and different versions of the client side of the TO-DO application. We're now ready to write integration tests for that application. We'll first write the integration tests through the jQuery-based view for the application and then through the view built using AngularJS.

Start the Server and Configure the Database

The TO-DO application server side was written using Express. There are three versions of the client: one that manipulates the DOM directly, one that uses jQuery instead, and a third that uses AngularJS. Each part of the application was tested separately, and now we're poised to do the end-to-end testing.

We must cross two hurdles before writing any integration tests for the app.

First, for the integration test to succeed we need the application's server running. To run the tests we wrote in previous chapters, we did not have to start the server to execute the server-side automated tests. However, to get a glimpse of the server in action, for a few moments we ran the server manually using `npm start`. While that step is an option during integration tests, it would be so much better if the server comes to life automatically when we start Protractor tests. That will remove the need for any extra manual step before running the tests. That would also make it easy to run these tests on a continuous integration server. We'd still need the database server running, but that can be turned on as a daemon.

Second, the application interacts with a MongoDB database. At the beginning there's no data in the database. To verify that the page is showing a list of tasks, we'd need some sample data. We could populate some data manually, but soon the tests for add and delete tasks will mess those up. To keep our sanity, we have to get a couple of things right:

- We need to use a test database to test the application. This has to be separate from a database used for development and certainly the one that will be used in production. The reason for this is inarguable—it's no fun overwriting test data during development, and vice versa. The application has to smoothly pick up the right database depending on the development run versus the test run.

- We need an automated way to seed the test database with sample data and clean it up at the end of the tests. This will keep the tests FAIR—see *Design with Positive, Negative, and Exception Tests*, on page 21.

All that sounds complicated and does have the potential to get overwhelming. Thankfully, since Protractor runs on Node.js, we can fire up the server very easily, locally and in an automated fashion. Also, seeding the MongoDB database with sample data is not a big deal. Let's take care of those two steps quickly after installing Protractor for this application.

Install Protractor for the TO-DO App

The workspace at tdjsa/testendtoend/todo has a project set up for your use. It has all the test and code for the TO-DO application from the previous chapters carried over. The package.json file in this workspace has been updated with the Protractor dependency.

Change to the tdjsa/testendtoend/todo workspace directory and run the npm install command to download and install Protractor for this project. Then run the command npm run-script update-driver to update the WebDriver that will be used in this project.

An empty protractor.conf.js file along with many empty files under tdjsa/testendtoend/todo/test/integration have also been pre-created for you to edit easily as you follow along the example. Let's move on to write the integration tests for the TO-DO app.

Start the Server in the before Setup

When Protractor starts up, more precisely, before any Mocha tests runs, we want the Express server to be started. That way the server will be ready to serve the requests that come from the integration tests, starting with the very first test. But any nontrivial project would have multiple integration test files. Writing the code to start up the server within any of the test suites won't cut it. At the very least this would lead to duplication of the setup code.

Mocha permits global before and after. These can go into any file that's included in the test run but outside of any test suite. Let's set that up first.

Both client-side and server-side tests already exist for the TO-DO application. We will add the integration tests to the project. Under the test directory the two subdirectories, server and client, house the tests from previous chapters. The new third subdirectory, named integration, will hold all the integration or end-to-end tests that touch both the client side and the server side.

Edit the pre-created empty file named global-setup.js in the test/integration directory and enter these few lines of code:

testendtoend/todo/test/integration/global-setup.js

```
var http = require('http');
var app = require('../../app');

before(function() {
  var port = process.env.PORT || 3030;

  http.createServer(app).listen(port);
});
```

The server startup code is within the function passed to before. This setup code is not part of any test suite. It's in a standalone function and will be run before any test is run.

It did not take much at all to start the server. Surprised? Let's take a closer look at the two lines in the function.

First, the port number for the server is set to the value of an environment variable, PORT, if present; otherwise, it's set to a default value of 3030. Express by default runs on port 3000 or whatever port value is set in the PORT environment variable. We'll run the test server on a different port than 3000. That way the test server can come to life even when the development server is up and running. Neither has to die for the other to live.

Let's move on to examine the next line in the setup function. This line mimics what's in Express's ./bin/www file. The manual run of the npm start command invokes node with the file ./bin/www as an argument. This file merely gets an app object from app.js, creates a server, and registers the app function as a handler. There are a couple more steps in that file, but we don't need to worry about them during testing. The short code in the global-setup.js file follows along with what's happening in the ./bin/www file and is adequate to start a test server. Pretty nice, eh?

There is one final step for auto-starting the server. When Express runs, it logs the details of requests and responses, and it can get noisy in the test console. Let's disable this during test runs.

Change the line

testendtoend/todo/app.js

```
app.use(logger('dev'));
```

in the file app.js to

testendtoend/todo/app.js
```
if (app.get('env') !== 'test') {
  app.use(logger('dev'));
}
```

to suppress logs during test runs.

Set Up the Databases for Use in Different Environments

By default, Express runs in the "development" environment while Protractor runs in the "test" environment. We'll use the settings in a new file, config.json, to change the database name used in the "development," "test," and "production" environments. Edit the empty file named conf.json under the todo directory in the current workspace and enter the following code:

testendtoend/todo/config.json
```
{
  "development": {
    "dburl": "mongodb://localhost/todo"
  },
  "test": {
    "dburl": "mongodb://localhost/todouitest"
  },
  "production": {
    "dburl": "..."
  }
}
```

The file defines the database URL for the three different environments. The missing piece of the puzzle is how the application uses the database URL. The database connection was set in the app.js file back in *Design the Database Connection*, on page 125. Here's the related code in that file:

testendtoend/todo/app.js
```
var db = require('./db');

db.connect('mongodb://localhost/todo', function(err) {
  if(err) {
    console.log("unable to connect to the database");
    throw(err);
  }
});
```

The database URL is hardcoded in that file at this time—yikes. Let's change it to refer to different databases for different environments.

testendtoend/todo/app.js
```
var config = require('./config.json');
var dburl = config[app.get('env')].dburl;

console.log("using database: " + dburl);

var db = require('./db');
db.connect(dburl, function(err) {
  if(err) {
    console.log("unable to connect to the database");
    throw(err);
  }
});
```

Since Express by default runs in the "development" environments, it will use the development database name. Since Protractor runs in the "test" environment, when it starts the server in the before setup in global-setup.js, the test database name referred in the config.json file will be used instead of the development database.

Seed Data in the beforeEach Setup

Good tests don't step on each other's toes. They stay isolated from one another. The benefit is that tests can be run in any order, and adding or removing tests will not affect existing tests. Databases can jeopardize that goal if we're not careful. An add operation may run into database uniqueness errors if the data already exists. Likewise, a delete operation may fail if the data is not present. Other operations may also fail when actions performed in one test violate the assumptions of other tests.

In order to keep the tests isolated, we should keep the test database local to the machine where the tests are run. Sharing a database with other developers for testing is like sending an urgent invitation to trouble. The config.json file specifies what database to use and that the database specified is local to your system.

Before each test runs the test database should be wiped out and a fresh set of test data should be created. That way, each test gets a stable view of the world it relies upon and then performs its action without fear of being affected by other tests.

If you like to keep different seed data per test suite, then put the setup code in that suite's beforeEach function. If you like to share the seed data across multiple test suites, then place it in the beforeEach outside of any code. A good place for this scenario is the global-setup.js function that has the before function.

testendtoend/todo/test/integration/global-setup.js
```
beforeEach(function(done) {
  var db = require('../../db');
  var config = require('../../config.json');
  var dburl = config[app.get('env')].dburl;

  var callback = function() {
    db.get().collection('tasks').remove(function() {
      var tasks = [
        {name: 'Test Models', month: 12, day: 1, year: 2016},
        {name: 'Test Routes', month: 12, day: 2, year: 2016},
        {name: 'Test AngularJS', month: 12, day: 3, year: 2016},
        {name: 'Test UI', month: 12, day: 4, year: 2016}
      ];
      db.get().collection('tasks').insert(tasks, done);
    });
  };

  db.connect(dburl, callback);
});
```

In this setup, which runs before each test, the function grabs the database name from the config.json file, opens a connection to it, cleans up the tasks collection—it's a test database, thankfully—and populates it with a handful of sample tasks. Once these steps are complete, it signals the beforeEach function that the asynchronous function used in the setup is complete.

We have completed the necessary setup to start the server automatically and populate the database with fresh data for tests to use. We're now all set to write our first test for the TO-DO application.

Test jQuery UI

In the previous chapters we created different versions of UI for the TO-DO application. One version directly manipulated the DOM and another used jQuery. The HTML files for these two versions were almost the same, except for the JavaScript files they included. Let's focus on the jQuery version and write integration tests by interacting with the tasksj.html file.

Set Up the Protractor Configuration File

Protractor needs a configuration file, so let's get that file ready. Edit the pre-created empty file protractor.conf.js in the current workspace and enter the following code:

testendtoend/todo/protractor.conf.js

```
var app = require('./app');
var config = require('./config.json');

exports.config = {
  directConnect: true,

  baseUrl: 'http://localhost:' + (process.env.PORT || 3030),

  framework: 'mocha',

  mochaOpts: {
    reporter: 'dot',
    timeout: 10000,
  },

  specs: ['test/integration/*.js'],
};
```

This file is similar to the configuration file used in the tests of the Google Search page, except for two things. The baseurl points to localhost instead of google.co.uk. Also, the port number is obtained from the PORT environment variable or is defaulted to 3030. This is the same environment variable we used earlier in the global-setup.js file to start the server.

Discover the Necessary Tests

Take a few minutes to think through the integration tests for the TO-DO application. To get the most out of the end-to-end tests, we want to selectively target only the integration points not touched by other tests. There's no need to redundantly verify things taken care by other tests.

Write Minimum and Targeted Integration Tests

Keep integration tests to a minimum. Only write tests to verify things that are not already covered by tests in other layers.

Let's step back and visualize the different parts of the application and identify parts that have been tested versus those that have been left out from tests.

Each box shown in the figure on page 300 represents code in each of the layers. The code within each layer, which is hidden inside the boxes, has all been thoroughly tested using tests in those layers. What's left are the interactions between the layers.

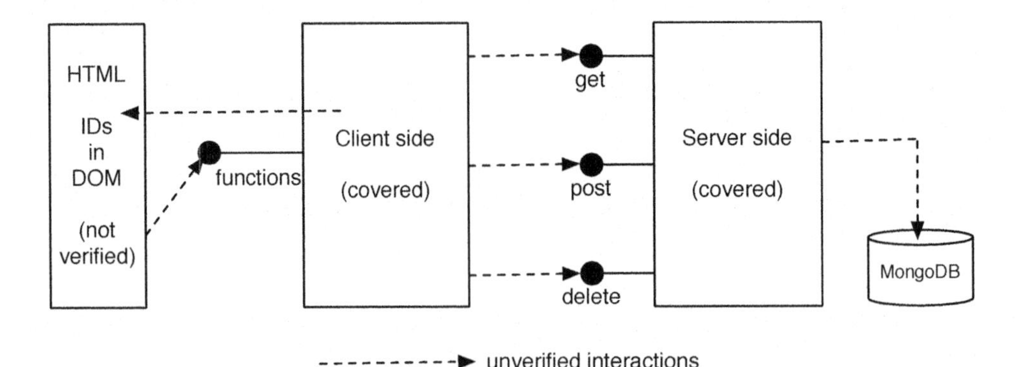

The integration tests should cover the unverified integration points in the application as shown in the figure. Also, the tests should ensure that the HTML file has the necessary DOM elements with the proper ids that the client-side scripts look for. Minimally, the following tests should take care of these needs:

- Verify task count shows correct value
- Verify tasks are displayed on the page
- Verify add task works
- Verify delete task works

These few tests will verify that the HTML is properly wired to the code below and also that the code below is properly connected to things it depends on, all the way down to the database.

Let's write one test at a time.

Implement the Integration Tests

Since the Protractor API returns Promises, we need to bring in both the Chai and Chai as Promised modules. Also, since the part being tested is non-AngularJS—it's jQuery—the ignoreSynchronization property of browser needs to be set. Once the page /tasksj.html is requested from the browser, the first test can verify the tasks count. Here's the first test along with the needed setup—enter this code into the testendtoend/todo/test/integration/tasksj-test.js file in your workspace:

testendtoend/todo/test/integration/tasksj-test.js

```
var expect = require('chai').expect;
require('chai').use(require('chai-as-promised'));

describe('tasks ui test', function() {
  beforeEach(function() {
    browser.ignoreSynchronization = true;
    browser.get('/tasksj.html');
  });
```

```
  afterEach(function() {
    browser.ignoreSynchronization = false;
  });

  it('should show correct task count', function() {
    expect(element(by.id('taskscount')).getText()).to.be.eventually.eql('4');
  });
});
```

From examining the HTML file, either directly or through View Page Source in the browser, we know that tasks count will be displayed in a span element with the id taskscount. The test first gets a locator for that id and then the DOM element with that id. A call to getText on the element returns a Promise, which will eventually be resolved. That will happen when the browser gets a chance to load the page and make the request for the tasks from the server.

Save the test and make sure the mongodb daemon is up and running. If it's not running, issue the command

```
mongod --dbpath db
```

to get it started. Leave this daemon running.

We don't have to start the back-end Express server—it starts automatically when we run our test. To run the test, execute the command npm run-script test-integration on the command prompt to start Protractor and see the test passing.

```
using database: mongodb://localhost/todouitest
Using ChromeDriver directly...
[launcher] Running 1 instances of WebDriver

  .

  1 passing (599ms)

[launcher] 0 instance(s) of WebDriver still running
[launcher] chrome #1 passed
```

The output shows that the name of the test database was used during the test run. It also shows one test passing and that the run is using Chrome, the default browser.

The test verified that the tasks count is showing up correctly. This one integration test confirmed several things from the figure on page 300.

1. At least one id is correct on the HTML page.
2. The correct script function was called when the page loaded.
3. The client-side code called the correct URL on the server side.
4. The server side is integrated properly with the database.

That's quite an accomplishment for just one test at the highest level. But there are a few more things that need to be verified. For example, the tasks should also show up in the task list. Let's write a test for that, in the testendtoend/todo/test/integration/tasksj-test.js file:

testendtoend/todo/test/integration/tasksj-test.js
```
it('should display tasks on the page', function() {
  expect(element(by.id('tasks')).getText())
    .to.eventually.contain('Test Models');
  expect(element(by.id('tasks')).getText())
    .to.eventually.contain('Test UI');
});
```

This test was not much different from the previous test in terms of the effort. It checks that the tasks div element has the text for at least two out of the four tasks in the task list. You may be tempted to add more tests to verify that the dates are showing up, but that's rather unnecessary at this level. That was more easily verified with lower-level tests. Likewise, here in the integration test, there's no need to verify that the task list is in sorted order of year, month, day, and name. That's also taken care by the lower-level tests.

The two tests so far only verified that some information appears as expected on the page when it's loaded. The next test to verify the add task operation needs to do more. Once the page is loaded, the user could enter data for a new task and click the submit button. The test has to emulate that. The sendKeys and click functions of the Protractor API that we saw in the earlier example will come in handy for that. Let's use those functions in the next test.

testendtoend/todo/test/integration/tasksj-test.js
```
it('should successfully add a task', function() {
  element(by.id('name')).sendKeys('Create Quality Code');
  element(by.id('date')).sendKeys('12/15/2016');
  element(by.id('submit')).click();

  expect(element(by.id('message')).getText())
    .to.eventually.contain('task added');
  expect(element(by.id('tasks')).getText())
    .to.eventually.contain('Create Quality Code');
});
```

This test isn't an innocent one- or two-liner. The first two lines set the text into the respective input text fields and the third emulates the click of the button. In the assertion phase the test verifies that the element with the message id has been updated and the task list has the new task. There's no need to verify the tasks count since lower-level tests verify that. The success of this test will confirm the proper wiring of the HTML page and the client-side scripts. It will also confirm that the client side is talking to the proper URL of the server side.

The final test to delete a task needs to perform a click of the delete link next to a task in the tasks table. Since there are multiple delete links, we should select one in the test. Let's choose the second link, index 1, so that the second task will be deleted. To get a locator using the text of the link, we use the by.linkText function of the Protractor API. Then to get all the elements that match that locator, we use the element.all function. Finally the get function returns the element at the given index.

testendtoend/todo/test/integration/tasksj-test.js
```
it('should successfully delete a task', function() {
  element.all(by.linkText('delete')).get(1).click();

  expect(element(by.id('message')).getText())
    .to.eventually.contain('task deleted');
  expect(element(by.id('tasks')).getText())
    .to.eventually.not.contain('Test Routes');
});
```

Save and make sure all the four tests pass. That completes the integration tests needed for the application through the jQuery implementation.

The content of tasks.html, which is tied to the scripts that manipulated the DOM using the built-in functions, is very similar to the taskj.html file. You may practice writing integration tests through that file. We still need to verify that the AngularJS implementation is integrated well with the tasksa.html file, but before that we'll make an effort to reduce the noise, coupling, and duplication in the integration tests.

Let's Use a Page Object

The integration tests were not really that complicated, but they can get cumbersome if we're not careful. There are four major problems in the integration tests we wrote:

1. *Noisy*: The code to access the elements and to verify the contents is noisy. Less noise would result in easier-to-maintain tests.

2. *Duplication*: The code to get an element, like tasks or message, for example, is duplicated throughout the tests. Less duplication would mean fewer errors and make it easier to deal with changes to the pages.

3. *Tight coupling on page implementation*: Suppose, for whatever reason, the span element that displays the tasks count is changed to have a class instead of an id. All the tests that use this element will have to change—this is a direct consequence of both tight coupling and duplication. The same issue exists for each one of the DOM elements accessed from the tests.

4. *Tight coupling on the API*: Each of the tests directly depends on the Protractor API. If we decide to use a different API or if Protractor changes the API in a future version, we're out of luck.

These problems can become severe with growing tests, but they're quite easy to fix if addressed early on. We'll use a *page* object for that.

A page object abstracts the contents of a page. The tests, instead of directly interacting with the browser object and the functions to access the parts of an HTML page, can use a page object. This object in turn will perform the interactions with the browser. The benefits are reduced noise, less duplication, and loose coupling.

Let's get a feel for using a page object before we create one.

A test like:

testendtoend/todo/test/integration/tasksj-test.js

```
it('should successfully add a task', function() {
  element(by.id('name')).sendKeys('Create Quality Code');
  element(by.id('date')).sendKeys('12/15/2016');
  element(by.id('submit')).click();

  expect(element(by.id('message')).getText())
    .to.eventually.contain('task added');
  expect(element(by.id('tasks')).getText())
    .to.eventually.contain('Create Quality Code');
});
```

will change to look like the following, with the use of a page object, to become concise, expressive, and easier to maintain:

testendtoend/todo/test/integration/tasksj-usepage-test.js

```
it('should successfully add a task', function() {
  page.name = 'Create Quality Code';
  page.date = '12/15/2016';
  page.submit();

  eventually(page.message).contain('task added');
  eventually(page.tasksAsText).contain('Create Quality Code');
});
```

There's so much more clarity and less clutter in the modified version compared to the one that directly uses the Protractor API.

Now that we know the benefit of page objects, let's create one. We need two files: a page class and a convenience function.

Each page in the application that's used in any of the tests will have a page object. Any part of the page that's accessed from a test, be it a simple read, send keys, or clicks, is abstracted using properties or functions in the page object. Let's create a page object named TasksJPage for the tasksj.html page.

testendtoend/todo/test/integration/tasksj-page.js

```
var fetchById = function(id) {
  return element(by.id(id));
};

var sendKey = function(element, text) {
  element.sendKeys(text);
};

var TasksJPage = function() {
  browser.get('/tasksj.html');
};

TasksJPage.prototype = {
  get tasksCount() { return  fetchById('taskscount').getText(); },
  get tasksAsText() { return fetchById('tasks').getText(); },
  get message() { return fetchById('message').getText(); },

  deleteAt: function(index) {
    return element.all(by.linkText('delete')).get(index);
  },

  set name(text) { sendKey(fetchById('name'), text); },
  set date(text) { sendKey(fetchById('date'), text); },

  submit: function() { fetchById('submit').click(); }
};

module.exports = TasksJPage;
```

The fetchById and sendKey functions are helper functions. The first gets an element when given an id, and the second emulates keystrokes into a given text field. The constructor for the page object TasksJPage fetches the page using the get function of the browser object. The prototype holds a number of properties, which are defined using getters or setters, and functions. Since the page has accessible elements that hold tasks count, the tasks, a new task, and so on, those manifest as properties or functions in the page object.

We can aim for more fluency and less noise beyond what's possible with the use of page objects. We can also reduce the noise of using expect...eventually in the tests with a convenience function. Edit the file testendtoend/todo/test/integration/eventually.js like so:

testendtoend/todo/test/integration/eventually.js

```
var expect = require('chai').expect;
require('chai').use(require('chai-as-promised'));

module.exports = function(object) {
  return expect(object).to.be.eventually;
};
```

The eventually function takes an object and a property, and returns a Promise using the chai-as-promised library. The tests now do not have to repeatedly call expect and instead can use a more concise syntax to verify.

Let's rewrite the tests in test/integrations/tasksj-test.js using the page object and the convenience function. Place the modified tests from that file in the file testendtoend/todo/test/integration/tasksj-usepage-test.js for easy comparison:

testendtoend/todo/test/integration/tasksj-usepage-test.js

```
var eventually = require('./eventually');
var TasksPage = require('./tasksj-page');

describe('tasks ui test', function() {
  var page;

  beforeEach(function() {
    browser.ignoreSynchronization = true;
    page = new TasksPage();
  });

  afterEach(function() {
    browser.ignoreSynchronization = false;
  });

  it('page should show correct task count', function() {
    eventually(page.tasksCount).eql('4');
  });

  it('page should display tasks', function() {
    eventually(page.tasksAsText).contain('Test Models');
    eventually(page.tasksAsText).contain('Test UI');
  });

  it('should successfully add a task', function() {
    page.name = 'Create Quality Code';
    page.date = '12/15/2016';
    page.submit();

    eventually(page.message).contain('task added');
    eventually(page.tasksAsText).contain('Create Quality Code');
  });

  it('should successfully delete a task', function() {
    page.deleteAt(1).click();

    eventually(page.message).contain('task deleted');
    eventually(page.tasksAsText).not.contain('Test Routes');
  });
});
```

The benefit is far beyond the number of lines saved. We only reduced 5 lines of code in the new modified version. However, every single line of test is less noisy and loosely coupled to the Promise API and to the parts on the page, and has no duplicated code to access the elements. Page objects are an invaluable part of integration tests. Make good use of them.

So far you've seen how to use Protractor to run tests for both the Google page and for the TO-DO app through the jQuery-based UI. Protractor has some special things in store for AngularJS apps, and we'll explore that next.

Test AngularJS UI

Protractor has special features for AngularJS. You saw calls like element(by.id(...)) to get elements on a page. Since pages that use AngularJS often use directives like ng-model and ng-repeat, Protractor provides convenience functions to access those. When your tests interact with the web pages, Protractor waits for AngularJS to complete its processing and updating of the DOM elements and bindings.

In the TO-DO app, the page tasksa.html is AngularJS specific and makes use of the TasksController in the taskscontroller.js file. One major difference between the files tasksj.html and tasksa.html is the former uses ids whereas the latter has no ids at all. It uses a few AngularJS models, bindings, and a repeater. As a result, there's no way to get the elements in the test using the by.id function. That's where the AngularJS-specific Protractor functions come in.

Let's explore some convenience functions to get locators for different directives:

AngularJS Directives	Example	Call to Get the Locator
ng-model	ng-model='...'	by.model('...')
bindings	{{ controller.message }}	by.binding('controller.message')
ng-click	ng-click='...'	by.css('[ng-click="..."]')
ng-repeat	ng-repeat="task in..."	by.repeater('task in...')
ng-repeat—a row	ng-repeat="task in..."	by.repeater('task in...') .row(index)
ng-repeat—columns	ng-repeat="..."	by.repeater('task in...') .column('task.name')

To obtain an element that holds an ng-model, use the by.model function. To get access to the elements that hold an expression, use the by.binding function. Getting an element with ng-click is tricky. For this, get access using the by.css function by providing the full ng-click attribute along with its value. The by.repeater along with row and column functions can get either a single child row of the expanded ng-repeat element or a particular expression used within the repeater.

Before we write tests to verify interactions through the tasksa.html file, let's write a page object that abstracts the HTML page's contents for access from tests. The purpose of this page object is the same as the page object we created earlier, except this one is customized for the tasksa.html page and uses the Protractor API that's geared toward AngularJS. Edit testendtoend/todo/test/integration/tasksa-page.js and enter the following code for the page object:

testendtoend/todo/test/integration/tasksa-page.js

```
var fetchByModel = function(model) {
  return element(by.model(model));
};

var fetchByBinding = function(binding) {
  return element(by.binding(binding));
};

var fetchByNgClick = function(clickFunction) {
  return element(by.css('[data-ng-click="' + clickFunction + '"]'));
};

var sendKey = function(element, text) {
  element.sendKeys(text);
};

var TasksAPage = function() {
  browser.get('/tasksa.html');
};

TasksAPage.prototype = {
  get tasksCount() {
    return  fetchByBinding('controller.tasks.length').getText();
  },
  get tasksAsText() {
    return element.all(by.repeater('task in controller.tasks')
           .column('task.name')).getText();
  },
  get message() { return fetchByBinding('controller.message').getText(); },

  deleteAt: function(index) {
    return element(by.repeater('task in controller.tasks').row(index))
           .element(by.tagName('A'));
  },

  set name(text) { sendKey(fetchByModel('controller.newTask.name'), text); },
  set date(text) { sendKey(fetchByModel('controller.newTask.date'), text); },

  submit: function() {
    fetchByNgClick('controller.addTask();').click();
  },

  get submitDisabled() {
    return fetchByNgClick('controller.addTask();').getAttribute('disabled');
  }
};

module.exports = TasksAPage;
```

The helper functions use the functions we discussed earlier to get elements based on ng-model, ng-click, or a binding. The function to get the tasks uses the function to access ng-repeater's column and returns an array of task names only. The rest of the code is pretty straightforward interaction with the page.

The tests for the AngularJS version HTML page tasksa.html are not very different from the tests for the tasksj.html page. The two respective page objects took on the most impact—that proves the benefit of page objects. Here's the tasksa-test.js file. It was copied over from tasksj-usepage-test.js and only three things were changed. We'll discuss the changes after the code listing.

testendtoend/todo/test/integration/tasksa-test.js

```
var eventually = require('./eventually');
var TasksPage = require('./tasksa-page');

describe('tasks ui test', function() {
  var page;

  beforeEach(function() {
    page = new TasksPage();
  });

  it('page should show correct task count', function() {
    eventually(page.tasksCount).eql('4');
  });

  it('page should display tasks', function() {
    eventually(page.tasksAsText).contain('Test Models');
    eventually(page.tasksAsText).contain('Test UI');
  });

  it('should successfully add a task', function() {
    page.name = 'Create Quality Code';
    page.date = '12/15/2016';
    page.submit();

    eventually(page.message).contain('task added');
    eventually(page.tasksAsText).contain('Create Quality Code');
  });

  it('should successfully delete a task', function() {
    page.deleteAt(1).click();

    eventually(page.message).contain('task deleted');
    eventually(page.tasksAsText).not.contain('Test Routes');
  });
});
```

The first change is that instead of requiring tasksj.page.js, this test file brought in the new tasjsa-page.js file. Second, since this test suite is for an AngularJS page, it doesn't have the ignoreSynchronization setting in beforeEach. For the same reason, there's no afterEach function. That's it—the rest of the code in the test suite—the four tests—are intact after the copy over from the tasksj-usepage-test.js file. Now, save the file and run Protractor. It should report a total of 12 tests running, four from tasksj-test.js, four from tasksj-usepage-test.js, and four from the newly created tasksa-test.js.

In addition to using AngularJS, the tasksa.html file had one other difference from the taskj.html file. It disabled the submit button if the new task's name or date input field was empty. The disableAddTask function exists in the client-side code, but its integration with the HTML file hasn't been tested. Let's write a test in tasksa-test.js to verify the button is disabled when the page loads up.

testendtoend/todo/test/integration/tasksa-test.js

```
it('should disable submit button on page load', function() {
  eventually(page.submitDisabled).eql('true');
});
```

The page object used in this test suite already has a property named submitDisabled. This property gets the element with the appropriate ng-click attribute and then gets that element's disabled attribute. The test merely verifies that this attribute's value is true to indicate the button is disabled on load.

Once the values are entered for a new task, the button should be enabled so the user can perform the submit action. Let's write a final test to verify this behavior works in the integrated code.

testendtoend/todo/test/integration/tasksa-test.js

```
it('should enable submit button on data entry', function() {
  page.name = 'Create Quality Code';
  page.date = '12/15/2016';

  eventually(page.submitDisabled).not.eql('true');
});
```

This test readily uses the page object to set the name and the date values. This actually emulates the user's keystrokes into the input text fields. Then the test verifies that the disabled attribute's value is not true.

Let's run the protractor command and see the test results:

```
using database: mongodb://localhost/todouitest
Using ChromeDriver directly...
[launcher] Running 1 instances of WebDriver


  ..............

  14 passing (4s)

[launcher] 0 instance(s) of WebDriver still running
[launcher] chrome #1 passed
```

While the tests run, you'll see Chrome simulate the user interactions for different actions, albeit at a far greater speed than capable even by any highly caffeinated users. Overall a total of fourteen tests passed. That includes six integration tests through the tasksa.html view.

Test Angular 2 UI

Now that you know how to test AngularJS 1.x UI, let's explore how to use Protractor to test the integration of the Angular UI that we developed in Chapter 9, *Test-Drive Angular 2*, on page 229.

Angular 2 is in beta at the time of this writing. Angular-specific capabilities of Protractor, like accessing elements with the attribute ngFor, are still in development. But, that shouldn't stop us from using Protractor to test Angular UI.

Change to the tdjsa/testangular2/todo directory in your workspace—this is the directory where you created the Angular UI for the TO-DO application. We will write integration tests using Protractor in this workspace.

The app.js and config.json files in this project are the same as the ones we used in the project for the AngularJS 1.x version. Also the script section of the package.json file has been updated to run Protractor. The protractor.conf.js file in this project is a copy of the same file from the AngularJS 1.x project, with one difference. Angular requires the following line to be added to the config:

```
useAllAngular2AppRoots: true,
```

This new setting is needed since Angular now uses a new Testability interface to access the applications under test. This configuration goes right below the baseUrl as in the following listing:

testangular2/todo/protractor.conf.js

```
var app = require('./app');
var config = require('./config.json');

exports.config = {
  directConnect: true,

  baseUrl: 'http://localhost:' + (process.env.PORT || 3030),
  useAllAngular2AppRoots: true,

  framework: 'mocha',

  mochaOpts: {
    reporter: 'dot',
    timeout: 10000,
  },

  specs: ['test/integration/*.js'],
};
```

The files test/integration/eventually.js and test/integration/global-setup.js are exact copies of the files we created in the AngularJs 1.x integration test project.

Since the look and feel of the Angular version is the same as that of the AngularJs 1.x version, the tests have to be the same as well. But the way these tests will interact with the HTML page will be different—that means the same tests, but a different page object. Thus, the file code/testangular2/todo/test/integration/tasksa-test.js is the exact copy of the file code/testendtoend/todo/test/integration/tasksa-test.js we created for integration testing of the AngularJs 1.x version.

In short, all the files except protractor.conf.js and test/integration/tasksa-page.js are the same between the AngularJS 1.x integration testing and integration testing of the Angular version. We already saw the one-line change to the protractor.conf.js file. The biggest change is to the test/integration/tasksa-page.js file, as listed here:

testangular2/todo/test/integration/tasksa-page.js

```
var fetchModelById = function(modelId) {
  return element(by.id(modelId));
};

var fetchBindingById = function(bindingID) {
  return element(by.id(bindingID));
};

var fetchClickById = function(clickId) {
  return element(by.id(clickId));
};

var sendKey = function(element, text) {
  text.split('').forEach(function(ch) {
    element.sendKeys(ch);
  });
};

var TasksAPage = function() {
  browser.get('/');
};

TasksAPage.prototype = {
  get tasksCount() {
    return fetchBindingById('length').getText();
  },

  get tasksAsText() {
    return element(by.css('table')).getText();
  },

  get message() { return fetchBindingById('message').getText(); },

  deleteAt: function(index) {
    return element.all(by.css('table tr')).get(index)
           .element(by.tagName('A'));
  },
```

```
  set name(text) { sendKey(fetchModelById('name'), text); },

  set date(text) {
    var textSplit = text.split('/');
    var dateElement = fetchModelById('date');
    sendKey(dateElement, textSplit[0]);
    sendKey(dateElement, '/' + textSplit[1]);
    sendKey(dateElement, '/' + textSplit[2]);
  },

  submit: function() {
    fetchClickById('submit').click();
  },

  get submitDisabled() {
    return fetchClickById('submit').getAttribute('disabled');
  }
};

module.exports = TasksAPage;
```

Instead of relying on any special Angular-specific facilities to get the elements, we get the necessary elements using the by.id or the by.css function, as appropriate. Since in the Angular version we are using the index.html as the starting page, the constructor of TasksAPage in this version sets the URL as / instead of tasks.html. The only other difference between this page class and the one used for integration testing the AngularJS 1.x version is in the way we set the input for the date input field. The sendKey in this version does not handle the / in the date value properly. As a workaround, the set date(text) function enters each part of the date separately.

To perform integration testing of your Angular version of the UI, first run npm install. Then run

```
npm run-script update-driver
```

to update the WebDriver. Then remember to start the database daemon by running the command

```
mongod --dbpath db
```

Finally, run

```
npm run-script test-integration
```

to launch Protractor. Here's the output from the integration test run of the Angular version:

```
> protractor

using database: mongodb://localhost/todouitest
[11:57:53] I/direct - Using ChromeDriver directly...
[11:57:53] I/launcher - Running 1 instances of WebDriver

  ......

  6 passing (4s)

[11:57:58] I/launcher - 0 instance(s) of WebDriver still running
[11:57:58] I/launcher - chrome #01 passed
```

The output shows that the six integration tests running on the Angular version of the UI as passing.

Wrapping Up

End-to-end testing is a critical part of automated testing. We need to use integration tests to gain confidence that the entire application continues to work well when integrated. Since these tests are often more complex to write and slower to run, and tend to be brittle, we have to keep them to a minimum. Also, we should avoid writing tests at this level that could be written at a lower level.

In this chapter you learned how to use Protractor to write end-to-end integration tests. The tool is a nice wrapper around the Selenium WebDriver and brings fluency to tests that verify application behavior through the web UI. Protractor also provides special functions to work with AngularJS directives and bindings.

In addition to using Protractor, we looked at how to launch the server automatically at the start of the test run and seed the database with test data. These steps facilitate smooth automation of tests without the need to manually set up and clean up between runs.

The automated tests in this chapter filled the gaps between the tests at the other levels of the example application. In the next chapter we'll revisit the levels of testing, discuss sizing of tests, and conclude with a few recommendations on how to adapt test-driven development.

CHAPTER 11

Test-Drive Your Apps

The fully functional TO-DO web application is live and healthy. The design and implementation of every single line of code in that application was driven using automated tests. We wrote tests at different levels: the model and the routes on the server side, the client side, and end-to-end integration tests all the way down from the UI. In this chapter we'll revisit the application and review the levels and sizing of tests. With these details, you can begin to gauge the efforts and approach to take for your own applications. We'll also revisit the benefits gained from these efforts and review key practices from the perspective of programmers, architects, and managers.

The Fruits of Our Efforts

Code is written once but is changed several times over the lifetime of any nontrivial application. The membership package, in that popular video-on-demand system, went into production last year. But the company now wants the package to manage multi-month subscriptions and automated renewals. That royalty payment package at the record company needs upgrading to integrate with a new third-party electronic payment system. That tax filing software better handle correctly the last-minute changes to the tax laws. The list goes on.

Relevant and useful applications change constantly. That's one reason why "Embrace Change" is a key principle behind eXtreme Programming (XP). That's also the reason why "Responding to Change" is a core value in the Agile Manifesto.[1]

Sadly, a lot of applications are hard to change. The telltale reasons, the corresponding design smells, and the consequences that we often see are:

1. http://www.agilemanifesto.org

Negative Influences	Design Smells	Consequences
Long functions	Low cohesion, high coupling	Hard to understand, expensive to change, hard to verify/test
A piece of code does many things	Lacks single responsibility	Code is unstable, hard to reuse, hard to verify/test
Code depends on many things	High coupling	Code is brittle, breaks too often
Code directly depends on third-party code	Tight coupling	Not extensible
Code is duplicated	Needless repetition	More time and effort to fix errors
Code has unnecessary complexity	Violates You Aren't Gonna Need It (YAGNI) principle	Hard to change, may contain unused code

Coincidentally, each of these reasons also makes automated testing really hard. For example, the number of tests to verify a function's behavior grows exponentially with the length and complexity of functions. Past a certain small limit, it becomes impractical to write automated tests for poorly designed functions.

When we set out to write test first, the code gets forced toward a better design. The code becomes modular, cohesive, loosely coupled, and minimalistic. It also has far less duplication since repetitive code would lead to repetitive tests.

The examples in Part 2 stand as testimony to how automated tests influence the design of code. Let's revisit the design that emerged. Since the three versions of the client-side code do almost the same thing, but with three different libraries, let's only consider the AngularJS version in this discussion.

The figure on page 317 shows the overall design of the TO-DO application.

The code in both the server side and the client side is highly modular. Each function is cohesive and loosely coupled, and takes on a single responsibility. Also, any logic that's common between the client side and the server side has been designed into a reusable function that's shared by both sides. This keeps the code DRY.

On the server side, the two db-related functions shown at the bottom of the figure manage the connection to the database. The four model functions are

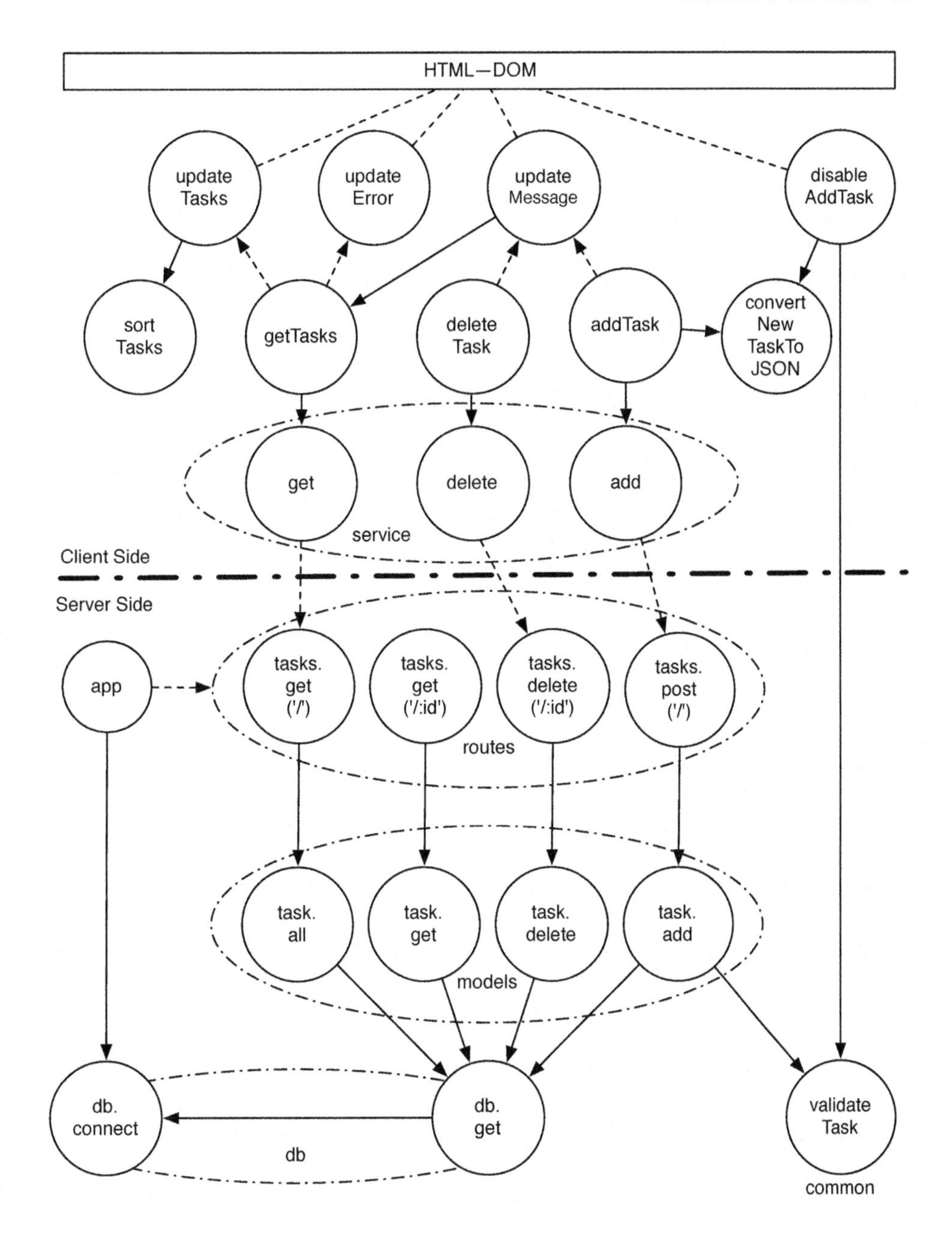

the only functions that directly interact with the persistent data. Each of the model functions focuses on one task-related operation. Furthermore, the add function delegates task validation to a separate reusable function, validateTask, designed in a shared/common library. The router functions each focus on getting data from the request object, invoking the appropriate model function, and pushing the result back to the client through a response object. The get, post, and delete routes are actively used. The get('/:id') is not currently used from the front end. It is, however, readily available to return a single task. The front end may use this to display a single task at a time, if desired.

On the client side, the service and the controller are highly modular. One set of functions interacts with the server while another set of functions manipulates the AngularJS models. When a model changes, AngularJS takes care of updating the DOM and triggering necessary actions.

The validateTask function runs both within Node.js and in the browsers. It first validates tasks on the client side. The same function is also present on the server side. This is necessary in case the data is sent directly to the server, bypassing the browser. Even though this function resides at both sides at runtime, this is not duplication. To the contrary, the code stringently complies with the DRY principle. That's because it's the same exact source code that springs to life on both sides during execution.

The better design that we arrived at offers many benefits:

- First, the code is not unwieldy. It is easy to compose other functions from these cohesive and modular functions.
- Each function is only a few lines long. The longest function is less than 20 lines, while most functions are less than half a dozen lines of code. This means developers can maintain the code without having to endure a great deal of anxiety and effort to understand it. This directly translates to greater productivity, both when changing an existing functionality or when adding a new feature, since the change would affect the least amount of code. In addition, we can benefit from greater reuse and reduced duplication of code.
- Since the code is loosely coupled, any part that's changed can be quickly verified using automated tests without having to fire up the entire application—the server, the browsers, and the database. That's not only rapid but can give us a greater confidence that the changes went well.
- The test coverage has the highest possible value of 100 percent and that's because no code was written without first having a test fail. The key benefit here is not the coverage number but the confidence that every line of code is under the watchful eyes of at least one test.

Automated Tests Thrust Applications Toward a Better Design

While there are multiple ways to arrive at a better design, good automated tests make good design inevitable.

Developers can be vigilant and arrive at a good design through other means besides automated tests. However, when written well, automated tests help to program with intention and are a surefire way to arrive at a better design. In addition to good regression, the efforts lead to the benefits we discussed here and in Chapter 1, *Automation Shall Set You Free*, on page 1.

We've discussed the benefits of automated testing, but not how many tests we should expect to write. We'll discuss that next.

Size and Levels of Testing

Discussing the levels and size of tests is tricky business. Test quotas are not good ideas. In the previous chapters you saw that the number of test lines were roughly three times the number of source lines. That's not a target number. It's merely the result or consequence of writing tests first and then writing the minimum code to make each test pass.

Automated testing is a means to an end. The real goal should be to create highly maintainable and valuable software that can be modified rapidly with confidence.

In the TO-DO application, we wrote unit tests on the server side to verify the behavior of database connection functions, the models for the tasks, the routers to handle URL paths, and the validation logic. That effort resulted in about 40 tests in this level. Likewise, the efforts to verify the behavior of the AngularJS controller and service functions, on the client side, resulted in about 25 tests. Furthermore, to gain confidence that the code functions properly when integrated, we wrote tests at the UI level. However, when writing these tests, we looked for things not covered by previous tests. That effort resulted in 6 tests. The figure on page 320 shows the number of tests and the levels they were written in. Coincidentally, the efforts lead to the figurative test pyramid we discussed in Chapter 1, *Automation Shall Set You Free*, on page 1.

In a typical application, each level would need multiple tests. Then, it's natural to ask the questions:

- How many tests should be there at each level?
- At what level should a test reside?

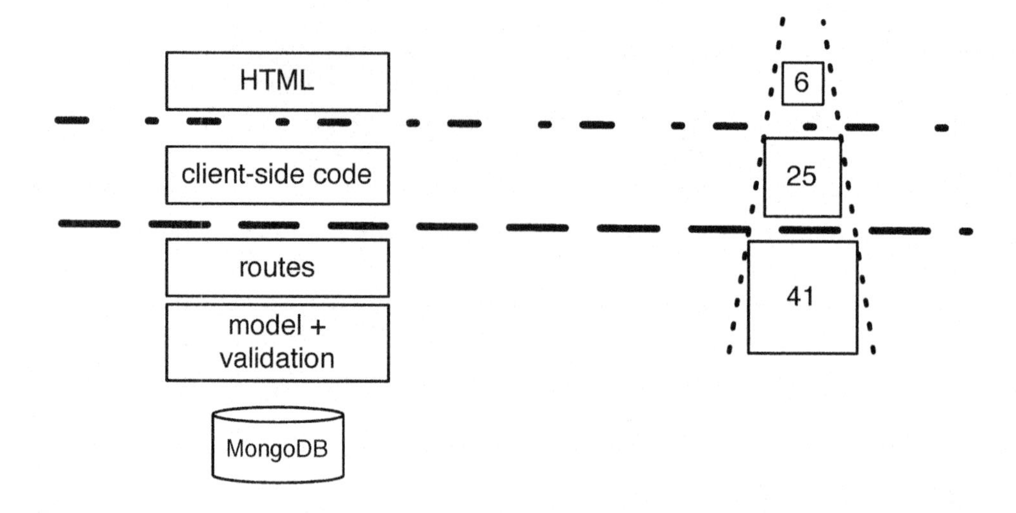

Let's visit the first question about size first. That's hard to answer. It's hard not because it's a tough question—it's hard because it's a wrong question. That question may arise if we're trying to meet a quota or trying to fill in tests after code is written.

In the test-driven approach, right before implementing a part of a function we write a test for it. Then we implement minimum relevant code. If nothing more is needed from a function, no more tests should be written.

Set No Test Quotas

Don't let your team set a test quota or an arbitrary test mandate. Use tests as a tool to create high-quality valuable software. Aim for writing the minimum code with fewer tests and high coverage.

The second question is an important one to ask: what should be the level for a test? The answer: at the lowest level where we can gain rapid, meaningful feedback, with the least amount of effort. Let's discuss this further with some examples from the TO-DO application.

We wanted to design and verify that the application does not permit duplicate tasks. We may be tempted to write this test at the HTML UI level: fill in the form with the same details as an existing task, emulate the `create` button click, and verify the response. But this is not the lowest possible level for this test. Besides, at this level, this test would require the server to be up and running, require the database to be initialized with sample data, and would also need a browser. Let's step back and ask the question: where should the code to check for uniqueness be implemented? The most logical place is in the model—verifying that tasks have to be unique is a concern or responsibility of the

Task model, not of the controllers or views using the Task objects. Well, then, that's the lowest level for this test as well.

On the other hand, to verify that the client-side code is wired properly to the DOM elements, we'd have to write the tests at the UI level. The topmost level is the lowest possible level for this test. At the same time, writing tests at the UI level to check if client-side sorting worked well is not a good idea. The lowest possible level for this would be at the level of client-side code instead of the HTML page level.

Aim for the Right Level for Tests

Tests should be written at the lowest level possible, but not any lower.

A good way to answer the question about level is with another question: Where should the code go? The test to verify a piece of code should be at the same level as that code.

Sometimes the answer to that second question is not clear. For example, we clearly know where the code to check that a task is unique should go. On the other hand, task validation is done at both the server side and the client side. It's easy to get dragged into writing tests to validate tasks at the client-side code level. However, this would result in a violation of the DRY principle. The result of this awareness leads us to validate tests at the common library level. Furthermore, we wrote interaction tests both at the model level and the client-side code level to verify that the appropriate functions invoked the validateTask function. Cumulatively, the tests related to validating tasks are gathered around in three places.

While writing tests, often the questions "what are we doing, why are we doing it, what's the right place, and what principles should we consider in writing this code" lead to the right level of tests and also the resulting better design.

Test Driving: The Programmer's Guide

Many people in organizations can motivate teams to test-drive their development. But no single group other than programmers have a greater ability to influence the outcome of this effort. Let's discuss how test-driving code can give programmers a better leverage to create maintainable code.

When beginning to work on features or a set of features, start with just enough strategic design to get a high-level exposure to the problem and the direction for the solution. Then distill it down to select areas to start the coding efforts.

Write down a test list and pick first the most useful functions to implement. Every step of the way, write a test before writing the minimum code to make the test pass.

While writing a test before writing a piece of code may seem really strange at first, it's a skill that each of us can learn and get better at. Sometimes a concept is quite vague and hard to break into clear steps, and it's hard to start writing tests first. You don't have to fight that battle. Instead, create a rapid spike. Then with the insights gained from the spike, move forward to create the production code, test first.

Often, difficulty in testing a piece of code is a sign of poor design. Low cohesion and high coupling make it hard to write and execute automated tests. Weed out dependencies from code where possible. Where the dependency is intrinsic, use dependency injection to facilitate loose coupling instead of tight coupling.

At times you may get stumped by a problem and simply can't figure out how to test-drive a piece of code. Don't let those moments of confusion or frustration dissuade you. Recall the proverb "When the going gets tough, the tough get going." Engage the method of "Rubber Ducking"[2]: stating a problem out loud often helps find a solution. Once, stuck on writing an automated test for code that did some serious parsing, I called a colleague for help. While waiting for the help to show up, the mere effort of building up words to state the problem at hand helped me to find the solution. If you can't figure out a solution, find a colleague, a fellow programmer, a team lead, or a technical architect, or simply that rubber duck on the monitor, and start describing the problem. You'll be on your way to writing tests in no time.

Testers and business analysts bring in unique perspectives and great value to product development. Recall the discussions in *Testing vs. Verification*, on page 2. Testers and business analysts should never spend time manually verifying application behavior. Instead, they should collaborate in writing automated functional and acceptance tests that programmers help to integrate. While testers convey what they'd like to test, programmers need to figure out the appropriate level to integrate each of those tests.

When testers, business analysts, and programmers collaborate, the tests they create become executable documents or specification by example. Since the test are described in plain-text form, the collection of test names form a ubiquitous language that just about anyone on the team—programmers,

2. http://c2.com/cgi/wiki?RubberDucking

testers, business analysts, architects, domain experts, UI experts—can use to discuss specification details and create tests that illustrate specific scenarios that can be exercised and verified.

Let Testers Author, but Not Execute, Functional Tests

It's a disaster when programmers write functional tests or when they manually run verification tests. Let testers author functional tests and programmers help integrate them for automated run.

The reason to test-drive the design and code is not to attain perfection, but to arrive at a better design and enable fast and reliable regression. The approach does not, however, guarantee zero bugs. When you find a bug or one is reported, write tests that fail due to the presence of the bug. Then fix the code and ensure all tests pass. This small step will prevent the bug from reentering the code at a future date.

Regularly keep an eye on the code coverage. Those who test-drive the design of code often don't have to struggle with the question of what the right coverage number is. Occasionally the coverage report may show that some code is not exercised by any test: unit, functional, or integration. To err is human. Take the bold step to remove that piece of untested code; this is especially easy to do, as soon as you notice it, during development. It's much harder later on for the fear of what may break by removing the untested code. Even if you feel the code is absolutely necessary, first remove it and then implement it test first. This will give you greater confidence that there are tests that verify that piece of code's behavior.

Test Driving: The Team Lead's/Architect's Guide

Since design and architecture heavily impact testability, team leads and architects play a vital role in their team's ability to write automated tests. Furthermore, developers look up to this group for mentorship and guidance on various technical practices. Let's discuss the ways in which technical leads and architects can assist their team in their quest to test-drive development.

Architecture and design decisions involve several key criteria: scalability, reliability, extensibility, security, performance, and the list goes on. Testability should be among the top priority items both when creating and when reviewing architecture and design. For example, if you're creating a service, architect and design a fake service to facilitate easy testing of components that rely on your service. Likewise, if your application relies heavily on third-party services, find out if those services offer fakes. If they don't, then consider routing the calls through an adapter. Then the adapter can easily be faked for easy testing of parts that depend on that external service.

Often teams follow the practice of continuous tactical code reviews. Instead of bringing an entire team into a room for review, these teams encourage programmers to review each other's code on a daily basis. Team leads and architects support the team during this process by periodically reviewing it and also providing guidance when questions arise. Encourage your team to review tests in addition to reviewing the code. During review, teams can examine the tests for quality, consistency, complexity, and clarity. They can also ensure the tests are at the right level and look out for missing tests. For example, they could look to see if tests for some edge cases were missing or if some negative or exception tests need to be included.

Encourage the team to express various assumptions and constraints, functional and nonfunctional requirements, as test cases. These tests will then serve as both documentation and validators of various architectural and design decisions made in the system. For example, the requirement that a receipt for the payment of an invoice should be visible only to the appropriate party should be expressed and verified using a series of tests. Likewise, the requirement that the order processing module should gracefully deal with network failure when talking to the inventory service should be verified using tests. In short, leverage tests to express, document, and verify architectural and design decisions.

Programmers, leads, architects, and various others involved in projects often raise suspicion of how a system handles a particular scenario. A simple, but often overlooked, example is the question "Can a user who just logged out view the receipt of an invoice by hitting the back button?" The solution to the problem may be a short line of code, a before filter, in one of the controllers. The important question to ask, however, is if there are tests to verify this behavior. Instead of arguing or asking for an explanation of how something is handled, write a test for it. The test will confirm beyond doubt if the application works the way it should, avoiding the unnecessary arguments and speculations once and for all. In other words, when in doubt ask for a test.

Test Driving: The Manager's Guide

Teams often look up to their managers for support and guidance. Beyond offering support, managers who are committed to quality and technical excellence can make a bigger difference toward the ability of their teams to succeed. Let's discuss things a manager can do to motivate and facilitate their teams to succeed with automated testing.

Promote Sustainable Agile Development Practices

Most organizations now have adopted or are in the process of embracing agile development. Let's recall a few principles[3] that are behind the Agile Manifesto:

- Welcome changing requirements, even late in development.
- Provide an environment and the support the team needs to succeed.
- Process should promote sustainable development.
- Continuous attention to technical excellence and good design enhances agility.

Agile Calls for Sustainable Pace

Agile development is not about speed. It's not a call to drive projects fast and recklessly into a ditch. Instead, it's a call to adapt technical practices that will facilitate sustainable speed. It's a call to slow down where necessary in order to gain speed where possible.

Managers and organizational leaders in charge of agile adoption have the power to make or break the ability of their organization, and the teams within, to succeed on their software projects. It's part of their responsibility to manage schedules and expectations, and provide an environment for teams to create relevant, maintainable, working software at a reasonable, sustainable pace.

Many organizations put their focus on the short term, the looming deadlines for the current release. In the process, they're not mindful of the technical debt that the team incurs, often due to the perception or the consequences of the pressures and deadlines. This results in short-term gain and a much larger long-term loss—with the "penny wise, pound foolish" outcome.

Gracefully Deal with Legacy Applications

In this book we largely focused on a good test-code rhythm—writing a test that fails before writing the minimum code to make it pass. In reality, projects often deal with legacy applications with little or no tests. Issuing an edict that all existing code will be verified using automated tests is rather detrimental. Writing test for existing code is very difficult—it's not been designed to make that easy or even possible. When programmers try to write a lot of tests in a short amount of time, for existing code, the quality of the tests suffers. These

3. http://www.agilemanifesto.org/principles.html

tests, while not being effective, give a false sense of confidence. There are a few ways to deal with legacy code instead:

- The team should earnestly test-drive any new code they write for the legacy application. Since new code comes in increments, they can take the time to restructure the part of code related to the change. That way they can start writing automated tests. Since they're focusing on a small area, they won't get overwhelmed with the efforts and can create tests with better quality.

- They could write tests before they fix a bug or right after they fix a bug. It's easier to write more meaningful tests when the context of that code is fresh in mind.

- If a part of the code is considered highly business critical or is going through frequent change, then for that part of the application schedule time for the team to investigate the effort to write automated tests. They may have to refactor or restructure the code before they can write automated tests. They have to evaluate the benefit of writing these tests versus the risk of modifying critical code when there are no current tests.

When dealing with legacy applications, encourage the team to set up scripts that will fail the build if test coverage goes below the current level. A client that was suffering from high maintenance cost found that one of their legacy applications had only 26 percent coverage. They set up the build to fail if the coverage dropped below the value from the previous build. Within six months their coverage number was way above that minimum value and they started enjoying the benefits from a greater number of automated tests.

Put an End to New Legacy Applications

Today's new project can turn into tomorrow's legacy. Rather than letting projects run amok, managers and organizational leaders can take several steps to foster an environment that's conducive to create maintainable software. Let's discuss a few of them:

- Learn from current experiences. Measure the time, effort, and cost to fix bugs. Include the time and money it takes to find and fix problems into your development time and costs. This can help us move away from the "let's lower development time" local optimization mind-set. It will help us to move toward the more effective "let's reduce the overall cost to the organization" global optimization mind-set.

- Visibly post test metrics and coverage. When that TV or the monitor in the office break room cycles through the continuous integration dashboards, it conveys that the team is serious about writing test and maintaining high coverage. For projects with a low number of tests or coverage, displaying a trend over time can show that the team is improving and can motivate them to work harder. If the numbers don't look good and there are mounting errors or maintenance issues, it can serve as a reminder the minute anyone walks into the office. As the screen cycles through projects, teams can quickly see projects that are doing better and approach them for advice or guidance.

- Keep a eye out for mixed messages. Teams often complain that they're asked to write automated test but are not given the time, training, or resources to implement. We know that, if a team is new to a technology, they need time to get comfortable and productive with it. Likewise, if a team is new to automation testing, they need time to get productive with it. We don't expect a person with no driving experience to drive just because they were given some keys. Likewise, a person with no experience with test automation can't drive tests just because they were given access to testing tools. They need to take the time to learn and improve their skills. Assess the current skills of the team and devise a plan to get them from where they are to where they will be productive. To get the desired results from the team, invest time and effort for them to learn and build the necessary test-driving skills.

- Give the team the coaching they need. Companies often hire agile coaches to help transition their teams to adopt agile development. Successful teams also hire technical coaches to help their programmers and testers properly adopt sustainable technical practices. Find out if your teams can benefit from mentoring by a technical coach. Another approach that can help is to designate a champion or an automated verification czar. This person, who has adequate technical knowledge, can help to assess and to adopt automated testing.

- Change the definition of done so it's not only about delivering code, but also about delivering valuable features with useful automated tests. When developers are asked to deliver features and at the same time "expected" to create automated tests, those expectations often seem to go by the wayside. Incorporate automated testing into the definition of done to change the way the teams think and operate. They will begin to rethink how they estimate and how much they commit to deliver in each sprint or iteration. In other words, when automated verification is important, include that in the definition of done. This will help to emphasize that for the coding to be considered complete, automated tests have to pass and be reviewed.

Rock On!

You've reached the end of this book. Let this moment serve as the beginning of your efforts to create high-quality, maintainable code with continuously running automated tests.

The following code snippet expresses my sentiment about the results we can achieve with perseverance, hard work, and discipline:

```
expect(success).to.eventually.be.true;
```

Thank you for reading and for your part to raise the bar in this amazing field.

APPENDIX 1

Web Resources

3-As Pattern ______ http://c2.com/cgi/wiki?ArrangeActAssert
A short description of the Arrange-Act-Assert, or 3-As, pattern.

Manifesto for Agile Software Development ______ http://www.agilemanifesto.org
The website for the Agile Manifesto, which espouses some core values and practices for lightweight software development.

Angular ______ https://angularjs.org
The website for the Angular framework.

Book Resources ______ http://www.pragprog.com/titles/vsjavas
Official website for this book, with links to the source code, errata, and forum for discussions.

Chai ______ http://chaijs.com
Website for Chai, a fluent and expressive assertion library.

Express ______ http://expressjs.com
Website for Express, a lightweight web framework for Node.js.

Express Generator ______ http://expressjs.com/en/starter/generator.html
A convenience tool to generate the initial files for Express projects.

Ice-cream cone Anti-pattern ______ http://watirmelon.com/2012/01/31/
A blog that discusses the antipattern.

Istanbul with Mocha ______ https://github.com/gotwarlost/istanbul/issues/44#issuecomment-16093330
Shows how to use Istanbul with Mocha.

jQuery Downloads ——— https://jquery.com/download
Downloads page for different versions of jQuery.

Mocha ——— https://mochajs.org
The website for Mocha, a JavaScript testing framework.

Mocks Aren't Stubs ——— http://martinfowler.com/articles/mocksArentStubs.html
A blog by Martin Fowler where he discusses the key differences between mocks and stubs, and when to use one over the other.

MongoDB Downloads ——— https://www.mongodb.org/downloads
Downloads page for MongoDB, a NoSQL Database.

Node.js ——— https://nodejs.org
Official site for the Node.js server.

npm ——— https://github.com/npm/npm
Site with details about the JavaScript package manager.

Principles behind the Agile Manifeso ——— http://www.agilemanifesto.org/principles.html
Website for the principles that the Agile Manifesto is based on.

Protractor API Documentation ——— https://angular.github.io/protractor/#/api
Presents details of the WebDriver API and the Protractor wrapper functions.

Reflect class ——— http://www.ecma-international.org/ecma-262/6.0/#sec-reflection
A class that provides access to metadata and a way to access annotations and parameters.

Rubber Ducking ——— http://c2.com/cgi/wiki?RubberDucking
A web page that discusses how stating a problem can help find a solution.

Sinon ——— http://sinonjs.org
The website for Sinon, a powerful test doubles library for JavaScript.

Sinon Documentation ——— http://sinonjs.org/docs
Documentation for Sinon test doubles.

Sinon-Chai ______________________ https://github.com/domenic/sinon-chai
Fluent extensions of the powerful Chai assertion library for Sinon-related verifications.

Test Pyramid ______________________ http://martinfowler.com/bliki/TestPyramid.html
Martin Fowler's article about the levels of testing.

The Black Swan Theory __________ https://en.wikipedia.org/wiki/Black_swan_theory
Wikipedia page about the Black Swan theory.

Bibliography

[Coh09] Mike Cohn. *Succeeding with Agile: Software Development Using Scrum.* Addison-Wesley, Boston, MA, 2009.

[Mar02] Robert C. Martin. *Agile Software Development, Principles, Patterns, and Practices.* Prentice Hall, Englewood Cliffs, NJ, 2002.

Index

SYMBOLS

A

B

C

Also by the Author

Catch up on these titles from your favorite author that you may have missed.

Practices of an Agile Developer

Want to be a better developer? This book collects the personal habits, ideas, and approaches of successful agile software developers and presents them in a series of short, easy-to-digest tips.

You'll learn how to improve your software development process, see what real agile practices feel like, avoid the common temptations that kill projects, and keep agile practices in balance.

Venkat Subramaniam and Andy Hunt
(208 pages) ISBN: 9780974514086. $29.95
https://pragprog.com/book/pad

Functional Programming in Java

Get ready to program in a whole new way. *Functional Programming in Java* will help you quickly get on top of the new, essential Java 8 language features and the functional style that will change and improve your code. This short, targeted book will help you make the paradigm shift from the old imperative way to a less error-prone, more elegant, and concise coding style that's also a breeze to parallelize. You'll explore the syntax and semantics of lambda expressions, method and constructor references, and functional interfaces. You'll design and write applications better using the new standards in Java 8 and the JDK.

Venkat Subramaniam
(196 pages) ISBN: 9781937785468. $33
https://pragprog.com/book/vsjava8

Secure JavaScript and Web Testing

Secure your Node applications and see how to really test on the web.

Secure Your Node.js Web Application

Cyber-criminals have your web applications in their crosshairs. They search for and exploit common security mistakes in your web application to steal user data. Learn how you can secure your Node.js applications, database and web server to avoid these security holes. Discover the primary attack vectors against web applications, and implement security best practices and effective countermeasures. Coding securely will make you a stronger web developer and analyst, and you'll protect your users.

Karl Düüna
(230 pages) ISBN: 9781680500851. $36
https://pragprog.com/book/kdnodesec

The Way of the Web Tester

This book is for everyone who needs to test the web. As a tester, you'll automate your tests. As a developer, you'll build more robust solutions. And as a team, you'll gain a vocabulary and a means to coordinate how to write and organize automated tests for the web. Follow the testing pyramid and level up your skills in user interface testing, integration testing, and unit testing. Your new skills will free you up to do other, more important things while letting the computer do the one thing it's really good at: quickly running thousands of repetitive tasks.

Jonathan Rasmusson
(254 pages) ISBN: 9781680501834. $29
https://pragprog.com/book/jrtest

The Modern Web

Get up to speed on the latest HTML, CSS, and JavaScript techniques.

HTML5 and CSS3 (2nd edition)

HTML5 and CSS3 are more than just buzzwords – they're the foundation for today's web applications. This book gets you up to speed on the HTML5 elements and CSS3 features you can use right now in your current projects, with backwards compatible solutions that ensure that you dontt leave users of older browsers behind. This new edition covers even more new features, including CSS animations, IndexedDB, and client-side validations.

Brian P. Hogan
(314 pages) ISBN: 9781937785598. $38
https://pragprog.com/book/bhh52e

Async JavaScript

With the advent of HTML5, front-end MVC, and Node.js, JavaScript is ubiquitous—and still messy. This book will give you a solid foundation for managing async tasks without losing your sanity in a tangle of callbacks. It's a fast-paced guide to the most essential techniques for dealing with async behavior, including PubSub, evented models, and Promises. With these tricks up your sleeve, you'll be better prepared to manage the complexity of large web apps and deliver responsive code.

Trevor Burnham
(104 pages) ISBN: 9781937785277. $17
https://pragprog.com/book/tbajs

Explore Testing and Cucumber

Explore the uncharted waters of exploratory testing and delve deeper into Cucumber.

Explore It!

Uncover surprises, risks, and potentially serious bugs with exploratory testing. Rather than designing all tests in advance, explorers design and execute small, rapid experiments, using what they learned from the last little experiment to inform the next. Learn essential skills of a master explorer, including how to analyze software to discover key points of vulnerability, how to design experiments on the fly, how to hone your observation skills, and how to focus your efforts.

Elisabeth Hendrickson
(186 pages) ISBN: 9781937785024. $29
https://pragprog.com/book/ehxta

The Cucumber Book

Your customers want rock-solid, bug-free software that does exactly what they expect it to do. Yet they can't always articulate their ideas clearly enough for you to turn them into code. *The Cucumber Book* dives straight into the core of the problem: communication between people. Cucumber saves the day; it's a testing, communication, and requirements tool – all rolled into one.

Matt Wynne and Aslak Hellesøy
(336 pages) ISBN: 9781934356807. $30
https://pragprog.com/book/hwcuc

The Pragmatic Bookshelf

The Pragmatic Bookshelf features books written by developers for developers. The titles continue the well-known Pragmatic Programmer style and continue to garner awards and rave reviews. As development gets more and more difficult, the Pragmatic Programmers will be there with more titles and products to help you stay on top of your game.

Visit Us Online

This Book's Home Page

https://pragprog.com/book/vsjavas

Source code from this book, errata, and other resources. Come give us feedback, too!

Register for Updates

https://pragprog.com/updates

Be notified when updates and new books become available.

Join the Community

https://pragprog.com/community

Read our weblogs, join our online discussions, participate in our mailing list, interact with our wiki, and benefit from the experience of other Pragmatic Programmers.

New and Noteworthy

https://pragprog.com/news

Check out the latest pragmatic developments, new titles and other offerings.

Save on the eBook

Save on the eBook versions of this title. Owning the paper version of this book entitles you to purchase the electronic versions at a terrific discount.

PDFs are great for carrying around on your laptop—they are hyperlinked, have color, and are fully searchable. Most titles are also available for the iPhone and iPod touch, Amazon Kindle, and other popular e-book readers.

Buy now at *https://pragprog.com/coupon*

Contact Us

Online Orders:	*https://pragprog.com/catalog*
Customer Service:	*support@pragprog.com*
International Rights:	*translations@pragprog.com*
Academic Use:	*academic@pragprog.com*
Write for Us:	*http://write-for-us.pragprog.com*
Or Call:	+1 800-699-7764